MOURNING AND PANEGYRIC:
The Poetics of Pastoral Ceremony

MOURNING AND PANEGYRIC
The Poetics of Pastoral Ceremony

Celeste Marguerite Schenck

THE PENNSYLVANIA STATE UNIVERSITY PRESS
University Park and London

Library of Congress Cataloging-in-Publication Data

Schenck, Celeste Marguerite.
Mourning and panegyric : the poetics of pastoral ceremony /
Celeste Marguerite Schenck.
p. cm.
Bibliography: p.
Includes index.
ISBN 0-2710-2825-4
1. Pastoral poetry—History and criticism.   2. Elegiac poetry—
—History and criticism.   3. Death in literature.   4. Bereavement in
literature.   I. Title.
PN1421.S34 1988
809.1'9321734—dc19   88-1588
                                                                       CIP

Copyright © 1988 The Pennsylvania State University
All rights reserved
Printed in the United States of America

For
Peter Samuel Schenck
and
Gyneth Stencel Schenck

The stars have grooved our eyes with old persuasions
Of love and hatred, birth,—surcease of nations ...
But who has held the heights more sure than thou,
O Walt!—Ascensions of thee hover in me now
As thou at junctions elegiac, there, of speed
With vast eternity, dost wield the rebound seed!
The competent loam, the probable grass,—travail
Of tides awash the pedestal of Everest, fail
Not less than thou in pure impulse inbred
To answer deepest soundings! O, upward from the dead
Thou bringest tally, and a pact, new bound
Of living brotherhood!

                          Thou, there beyond—
Glacial sierras and the flight of ravens,
Hermetically past condor zones, through zenith havens
Past where the albatross has offered up
His last wing-pulse, and downcast as a cup
That's drained, is shivered back to earth—thy wand
Has beat a song, O Walt,—there and beyond!
And this, thine other hand, upon my heart
Is plummet ushered of those tears that start
What memories of vigils, bloody, by that Cape,—
Ghoul-mound of man's perversity at balk
And fraternal massacre! Thou, pallid there as chalk,
Hast kept of wounds, O Mourner, all that sum
That then from Appomattox stretched to Somme!

Cowslip and shad-blow, flaked like tethered foam
Around bared teeth of stallions, bloomed that spring
When first I read thy lines, rife as the loam
Of prairies, yet like breakers cliffward leaping!
O, early following thee, I searched the hill
Blue-writ and odor-firm with violets, 'til
With June the mountain laurel broke through green
And filled the forest with what clustrous sheen!
Potomac lilies,—then the Pontiac rose,
And Klondike edelweiss of occult snows!
White banks of moonlight came descending valleys—
How speechful on oak-vizored palisades,
As vibrantly I following down Sequoia alleys
Heard thunder's eloquence through green arcades
Set trumpets breathing in each clump and grass tuft—'til
Gold autumn, captured, crowned the trembling hill!

Panis Angelicus! Eyes tranquil with the blaze
Of love's own diametric gaze, of love's amaze!
Not greatest, thou,—not first, nor last,—but near
And onward yielding past my utmost year.
Familiar, thou, as mendicants in public places;
Evasive—too—as dayspring's spreading arc to trace is:—
Our Meistersinger, thou set breath in steel;
And it was thou who on the boldest heel
Stood up and flung the span on even wing
Of that great Bridge, our Myth, whereof I sing!

Years of the Modern! Propulsions toward what capes?
But thou, *Panis Angelicus,* hast thou not seen
And passed the Barrier that none escapes—
But knows it leastwise as death-strife?—O something green,
Beyond all sesames of science was thy choice
Wherewith to bind us throbbing with one voice,
New integers of Roman, Viking, Celt,—
Thou, Vedic Caesar, to the greensward knelt!

And now, as launched in abysmal cupolas of space,
Toward endless terminals, Easters of speeding light—
Vast engines outward veering with seraphic grace
On clarion cylinders pass out of sight
To course that span of consciousness thou'st named
The Open Road—thy vision is reclaimed!
What heritage thou'st signalled to our hands!

And see! the rainbow's arch—how shimmeringly stands
Above the Cape's ghoul-mound, O joyous seer!
Recorders ages hence, yes, they shall hear
In their own veins uncancelled thy sure tread
And read thee by the aureole 'round thy head
Of pasture-shine, *Panis Angelicus!*
                              yes, Walt,
Afoot again, and onward without halt,—
Not soon, nor suddenly,—no, never to let go
    My hand
         in yours,
              Walt Whitman—
                   so—

                              Hart Crane, *The Bridge* (1930)

Contents

	Acknowledgments	xi
	"Every Poem an Epitaph": Introduction	1
1	The Pastoral Scene of Instruction: Plato's *Phaedrus*	19
2	The Funeral Elegy and Careerism: Theocritus, Virgil, Spenser	33
3	"Sacred Ceremonies": Spenser's *Epithalamion* and *Prothalamion*	55
4	"The Marriage Hearse": Anti-Epithalamia of Donne, Crashaw, Blake	73
5	"Unexpressive Nuptial Song": Milton's *Lycidas*	91
6	Failed Elegies: Blake's *The Book of Thel* and Shelley's *Alastor*	107
7	"A Wedding or a Funeral": Wordsworth's Immortality Ode	123
8	Epithalamia Awry: Mallarmé's *Hérodiade* and Hart Crane's "For the Marriage of Faustus and Helen"	137
9	Sea-Changes: The Incarnational Ode and Ceremonial Modes	157
	Mourning and Panegyric: The Poetics of Pastoral Ceremony	175
	Notes	183
	List of Works Cited	207
	Index	219

Acknowledgments

I am grateful first to Eileen Coumont, Alan S. Trueblood, and John Erwin for persuading me in unique ways that pastorals were still the texts with which an initiate might begin a career. Michael Putnam and Albert Cook, generously commenting on early drafts of the manuscript, urged me on to the long georgic task of publishing it. Michel-André Bossy advised me at every stage of this book's preparation, patiently blue-penciling all versions of the manuscript and offering a model for collegial support and exchange for all the years I have known him. Thanks to Philip Winsor at Penn State Press, the manuscript had the good fortune of being read by Heather Dubrow, whose attentive reading and lively editing saved me many errors and excesses.

Barnard College provided me with an Assistant Professor Summer Grant to complete revisions. Seniors in my "Ancients and Moderns" seminar worked through a number of the book's arguments with me. Jill Harris proofread and indexed assiduously, making valuable editorial suggestions along the way. Finally, Gyneth Schenck, providing first the idea and then the actuality of a computer, eased in all the ways she always does the labors I assume.

Acknowledgment is gratefully made as follows for permission to reprint copyrighted material:

Chapters 1, 2, 9, and a version of the Conclusion have been previously published in *Mosaic: A Journal for the Interdisciplinary Study of Literature* (March 1988); *Ariel: A Journal of Interdisciplinary English Literature* 16,1 (1985); and *Classical and Modern Literature: A Quarterly* 6, 2 (1986), and are reprinted by permission of *Mosaic*, *Ariel* (The University of Calgary Press. Copyright © 1985, The Board of Governors, The University of Calgary.), and *CML,* Inc., respectively.

Excerpts from "Little Gidding," "The Dry Salvages," and "East

Coker" in *Four Quartets,* copyright 1943 by T. S. Eliot, renewed 1971 by Esme Valerie Eliot, reprinted by permission of Harcourt Brace Jovanovich, Inc., New York, and Faber and Faber Ltd., London.

Excerpts from "Cape Hatteras," "The Broken Tower," "The Wine Menagerie," "Voyages," and "For the Marriage of Faustus and Helen" reprinted from *The Complete Poems and Selected Letters and Prose of Hart Crane,* edited by Brom Weber, by permission of Liveright Publishing Corporation. Copyright © 1933, 1958, 1966 by Liveright Publishing Corporation.

Excerpts from "The Sad Shepherd" and "The Song of the Happy Shepherd" are from *The Poems of W. B. Yeats: A New Edition,* edited by Richard Finneran (New York: Macmillan, 1983).

Excerpts from "Elegy for a Nature Poet" are from *The Collected Poems of Howard Nemerov.* The University of Chicago Press, 1977. Reprinted by permission of the author.

Translations of Virgil are from the C. Day Lewis translation of Eclogues and Georgics of Virgil. Reprinted by permission of Sterling Lord Literistic, Inc. Copyright © 1964.

© Thomas Kinsella and Wake Forest University Press for lines from "Country Walk."

Lines quoted from Graham Dunstan Martin's translation of Paul Valéry's "Le Cimetière marin" are used by permission of the University Press of Edinburgh.

The excerpt from *The French Lieutenant's Woman* by John Fowles copyright © 1969 by John Fowles Ltd. is used by permission of Little, Brown and Company, Boston.

John Peale Bishop, excerpt from "Speaking of Poetry" from *The Collected Poems of John Peale Bishop* edited by Allen Tate. Copyright 1948 Charles Scribner's Sons; copyright renewed © 1976 Charles Scribner's Sons. Reprinted with the permission of Charles Scribner's Sons, an imprint of Macmillan Publishing Company.

Translations of Mallarmé are from the bilingual edition of *Mallarmé: The Poems,* translated by Keith Bosley (New York: Penguin, 1977). Reprinted by permission of the translator.

"Every Poem an Epitaph":
Introduction

In T. S. Eliot's "Little Gidding," he states explicitly what I will try to suggest throughout this study of lyric ceremonial modes: that in fact "every poem" is an "epitaph" when it marks an initiatory moment, pronounces an elegy upon a past artistic self, and announces rebirth of the artist as a poet.[1] Every poem is an epitaph which celebrates a ritual death—"a step to the block, to the fire, down the sea's throat" to the place "where we start"—and the initiate's consequent restored imaginative power. In fact, every poem in which we suffer a death and live an incarnation is epitaphic, whether it take the form of Neoplatonic allegory of descent or orphic ritual marriage to a death principle, pastoral elegy or modern anti-epithalamium. A prototype of these memorializing dramas of the literary career might be the initiation scenario enacted in the *Phaedrus* and the subsequent imitation of that verbal exchange in the pastoral elegy. But the site of the Scene of Instruction, to borrow Harold Bloom's revisionary term for Freud's primal scene, is as various as the poets: from conventional *locus amoenus* to Hérodiade's tower, from wedding chancel to rooftop jazz club, from the rim of the generated world to the open sea. A pastoral impulse may govern the initiation structure of each poem, but the gesture ceremonial poems make is largely one of protest. Behind the ritual reenactment of significant poetic ceremonies is a consistent "refusal of mortality."[2]

Poetic utterance, then, particularly in vatic or odic registers, might serve as one form of protest against silence, stasis, and that ultimate guarantee of these two, death. In one critic's double sense, vocalizing is a way of satisfying the "incantatory poet's quest for completeness."[3] Another way poets circumvent the issue of mortality is by incorporating structures of transcendence and rebirth in their works. Funeral poems thus ceremonially invoke the power of the dead even as they lay to rest the souls of itinerant forebears. As Eliot writes, "We die with the dying: / See, they depart, and we go with them. / We are born with the dead; / See, they return, and bring us with them." For this reason too marriage poems emphasize passage—often in terms of ritual decease of an earlier, virgin state—and preoccupy themselves with future issue, literary or otherwise. A complex ceremonial ode such as Wordsworth's Immortality Ode rehearses the serial "fallings from us, vanishings"[4] which punctuate a poetic autobiography, and celebrates panegyrically, by means of translated or displaced epithalamic conventions, the compensatory recovery of childish joy in philosophic song. Indeed ceremonial poems, even occasional pieces composed under patronage, often bear a vocational subtext, an obsessive concern with the conditions that occasioned them. These works especially, in rigorously predictable symbolic forms, provide a stage on which the poetic imagination willingly submits to seasoning. During the course of such initiatory dramas, poets pronounce epitaphs on literary apprenticeship and articulate (by means of an epithalamium or birth announcement) successful passage to mature vocation. "Official verse," Mallarmé reminds us, compels the creative artist "in the crisis moments of the soul."[5]

Readings of poems of passage, initiatory scenarios, ceremonial rituals, transformational dramas, continually turn up the emblem and embodiment of those themes, the mythic figure of Orpheus. The orphic task, as understood by the poets, is the search for literary rebirth by means of an initiatory descent. The subsequent recovery (and continuance) of voice is a guarantee of literary immortality. It is enough for our purposes that Orpheus is the very type of the poet, an initiate willing to submit himself to ritual trial. Even more telling is his appearance in many of the poems of this study as both dismembered initiate and potential bridegroom, protagonist of the elegy and the epithalamium respectively. Implicit in either of Orpheus's appearances are the notions of loss and compensation, and the consoling, eternizing possibility of song. Poets from Virgil and Spenser to Stevens, Crane, and Kinsella invoke Orpheus as patron saint of initiation dramas both nuptial and funereal: the "silken skilled transmemberment of song" accomplished by that "floating singer"[6] transcends the loss that these poems record and fills the void with a marriage hymn or nativity ode. The text of the poem, even the mere rehearsal of ceremony in some cases, functions as consolation for the losses sustained.

During the course of these readings, two major initiatory orientations, equally orphic, emerge in the form of two types of poems. At this point the generic or ceremonial classification of the poems becomes less important than thematic considerations. Either poems successfully evolve consolation by means of denial of loss or creation of ample compensation for it—symbolically represented by the singing head spilling forth its spellbinding notes even after decapitation—or else they articulate the impossibility of filling the void by means of a compensatory vision—orphically signaled by the bridegroom's failing voice decrying the loss of the absent, dead, repressed Eurydice.

The aim of this study is threefold. Beginning with classical elegies and Renaissance occasional poems and ending with Romantic and modern ceremonial lyrics, I hope to offer a poetics of pastoral ceremony in both of the thematic categories outlined above, attending particularly to those places where these categories intersect with and problematize the notion of genre. I aim as well to widen the scope of pastoral criticism by including a record of responses to the mode, or survivals, after the so-called demise of pastoral in the eighteenth century and by introducing to the canon a range of poems usually excluded from standard treatments of pastoral tradition by virtue of their puzzling irregularities—an inclusion which bears directly upon, indeed invites critical revaluation of, genre study. As a consequence I offer here not a history of influence, nor by any means a historical account of the development of the elegiac and epithalamic genres, but instead a study of what Hart Crane calls, in the fragment from *The Bridge* prefacing this study, "junctions elegiac." Although Crane is alluding to his own moment of meditation upon Whitman's elegy for Lincoln, I invoke the phrase to suggest as well those points at which genres overlap and conjoin. Genre remains, after all, one of the most interesting avenues of approach to pastoral texts, even when the diagnostics of genre I advocate here call for questioning if not suspension of traditional categories. John Van Sickle's warning to critics of the perils of genre theory, drawing for its central metaphor upon Plato's *Phaedrus,* guides this critical project:

> Generic conceptions, like any other products of literary work, have history. Implied in the work of poets, they are the practical marks of similarity and thus also touchstones of significant difference with respect to other modes of discourse in a period; and through time they measure continuity and change in a tradition. From the actual texts, however, critics abstract conceptions of genre according to the tastes, interests, received and new ideas—intellectual currency of their own time. Abstracted, then, and cast in simple and intelligible form, they begin a tralatitious life in ambivalent, quasi independent relation to their texts of origin. They do provide a ready general view of the material, but by this

very virtue tend to substitute themselves for it. Ersatz, vicarious, they satisfy and misinform the reader, cutting off effective access to the texts. Useful, then, yet pernicious, go betweens that get between, generic conceptions partake of the double nature of critical discourse, procuring insight and blindness, like some *pharmakon,* both good news and bad news.[7]

During the course of these readings of ceremonial poems, I allow the works themselves to give shape to the study: instead of reading them according to the generic categories traditionally assigned to them, I have allowed "mixed kinds and uncanonical forms" to challenge the formal expectations we bring to ceremonial genres.[8] The poems, by failing to "live up or down to generic regulation," call into question the very critical terms used to measure them. But there is danger as well in making strict distinctions between parodic and canonical responses to generic norms. As Heather Dubrow demonstrates in *Genre,* the tension between generic expectation and poem occurs even in what we might call canonical instances of genre as well; even an individual work might profitably be viewed as having a range of attitudes across a spectrum of possibilities toward its predecessor texts.[9] Still, the unavoidable "ideal types" which emerge in any critical discussion of genre—that sameness against which we measure difference during the course of close reading—partake of the duplicity outlined above: "go betweens that get between," these generic categories do facilitate literary analysis, make sense of hybrid forms, indeed make possible critical explanation of specific ceremonial forms, even if the false purity of genre they represent will occasionally threaten to substitute itself for the particular instance at hand. Adena Rosmarin, in a compelling recent defense of an expressly deductive genre criticism, resolves some of the tension implicit in the doubleness of genre (and with it theory's prevailing need to deny the preexistent, invented nature of genre itself) by insisting upon a pragmatic, rhetorical, *ad hoc,* critical generic practice:

> It is, in other words, fully pragmatic and rhetorical, deliberately argued from purpose to premise to particular text. It is also explicitly critical: it places constitutive or constructive power in the genre, and defines the genre neither "historically" nor "theoretically," but in terms of its use in critical explanation. The genre is the critic's heuristic tool, his chosen or defined way of persuading his audience to see the literary text in all its previously inexplicable and "literary" fullness and then to relate this text to those that are similar or, more precisely, to those that may be similarly explained.[10]

Rosmarin's theory of genre, insisting upon the impossibility of perfect repetition—"to repeat is always to differ"—and the certainty that similarity "becomes convincing only when embedded in difference or the particular," extends the critical force of genre in the direction of the cases that interest me here. "The explanatory power [of genre], like affective power, tends to be greatest when the affinities are surprising, when the yokings unite seemingly incongruous matter across seemingly unbridgeable gaps" (25).

"JUNCTIONS ELEGIAC"

The method might be better illustrated than described. A brief reading of Crane's inset elegy for Whitman in the "Cape Hatteras" section of *The Bridge*, quoted in preface above, arrests literary history at a telling junction and assembles the conventions of the poem of passage. Critics do not ordinarily term this "poem" an elegy, yet a highly conventional pattern of imagery informs its structure and clarifies its procedures. These lines are more than tonally or thematically elegiac, so coherently do they reproduce the formal conventions of the classical funeral elegy. At the Cape's "ghoul-mound,"[11] Crane's epitaphic task is to rival his predecessor's poetic stature by alluding to a conventional form of self-seeking address, a pastoral elegy composed over the corpse of a fellow poet. In his invocation to Walt Whitman, Crane thinks of him at "junctions elegiac" when that poet himself, eulogizing Lincoln, looked back upon Milton's elegy for the drowned King; Milton, in turn, looked back at a similar junction upon a healthy pastoral elegiac tradition, which he simultaneously honored and rewrote. Mimesis of highly codified poetic forms occurs with an increasing lack of specificity in literary history, and pastorals, no exception, are soon given local habitations and names. We expect, that is, to find in Milton's poem a dead shepherd, invocation to a muse, appeal to absent nymphs, strewn flowers, and final reversal of the dirge in a hymn of apotheosis against the backdrop of English geography; we are not surprised to find in Whitman's "When Lilacs Last in the Dooryard Bloom'd" a dead president, drooping star, commemorative lilac bush, and bouquets of roses and lilies, cross-country procession with mourners drawn from representative American life, even death carol translating mourning into joy—in short, a literalization of pastoral conventions; but we approach with some confusion Crane's obscure allusion to the pastoral elegiac tradition in a patently unelegiac form and place. In spite of its displacement of the elegiac fiction, and the prior generic claim made upon these lines by the framing epic form, this passage makes most sense if understood as elegy. It has at its core a dead poet whose power the writer of elegy wants to claim—"Ascensions of thee hover in me now / As thou at junctions elegiac." It begins by acknowledging the forebear's superiority and assuming a modest stand at the side of the predecessor's achievement:

> Walt, tell me, Walt Whitman, if infinity
> Be still the same as when you walked the beach
> Near Paumonok—your lone patrol—and heard the wraith
> Through surf, its bird note there a long time falling . . .
> For you, the panoramas, and this breed of towers,
> Of you—the theme that's statured in the cliff.
> O Saunterer on free ways still ahead!
> Not this our empire yet.

But clearly Crane intends to inherit that "empire" of recognition he attributes to Whitman. His own elegy is a deliberate response to the Miltonic convention transformed by Whitman in the Lincoln ode. Thus Crane's version of a flower catalogue begins with Milton's "cowslip" and Whitman's purple flowers—"O, early following thee, I searched the hill / Blue-writ and odor-firm with violets"—but quickly binds a wreath of native American names: "shad-blow," "mountain laurel," "Potomac lilies,—then the Pontiac rose." The placement of the poem in the "green arcades" of an American forest is also freighted with traditional associations, suggesting a site of pastoral seasoning, an American *locus amoenus*. Additionally, Crane as elegist claims no less than deification for the buried ancestor poet now safely laid to rest: Whitman, in a version of pastoral prayer, is termed a *Meistersinger* and hailed three times as *Panis Angelicus* (sic). For such an untraditional elegy, the poem reaches a startlingly recognizable conclusion: the resurrected poet is superimposed upon a rainbow in the sky. He becomes a veritable pastoral guardian angel, recognizable by the "aureole 'round thy head / Of pasture-shine," no less imposing in stature than that genius of the shore, the resuscitated Lycidas. Finally the poem announces the new poet's rising power and celebrates the transfer of title from Whitman to his literary heir: "thy vision is reclaimed! What heritage thou'st signalled to our hands!" Crane's elegy, if I may call it so, dispenses with the Arcadian setting and cast of characters we associate with the funeral obsequy after Moschus's lament for his mentor Bion, but taps directly the source of its characteristic energy: the retrieval of literary recognition from symbolic burial of an ancestor. Crane reading Whitman reading Milton restages a literary initiation ritual.

The same kind of literary junction may be noted in transformations of epithalamic convention. At the close of Milton's *Lycidas,* for example, the swain's sight is trained upon a mystical wedding vision emblematic of Christian admittance to the Kingdom. Evolving his own analogue for Menalcas's panegyric at the end of Virgil's fifth bucolic—the conventional ode to joy which reverses the course of elegy since Virgil—Milton draws, at this junction, upon the allegorical possibilities of marriage symbolism for a vocabulary of restored order and transcendent harmony. The consoling hymn of elegy becomes, at this important junction, readily identifiable with the rising rhythm of epithalamium: "nuptial song," oddly enough, punctuates funeral dirge. Wordsworth's *Ode: Intimations of Immortality,* articulating a private rite of passage in both elegiac and epithalamic ceremonial registers, provides evidence of another junction of this sort: in the pastoral *peripeteia* which crowns the recovery of a mature version of lost primal joy, if not a resurrected dead man, Wordsworth draws for rhythm and vocabulary of celebration upon what we might call a displaced nuptial poetics. Imagery of epithalamic bliss is assimilated to (in a manner which may be idiosyncratic to the Romantic poets) the child's world of Innocence and the garden of Higher, Organized Innocence which it is the work of the mature poetic imagination to regain. Allusions to Spenser's *Epithalamion* and *Prothalamion* thus occur in works not explicitly epithalamic precisely because, I shall hope to demonstrate, these poems echo the careerist strain of his epithalamia; Spenser's wedding poems not only grew out of the consoling hymn at the close of his *Calender* elegy, the "November" elegy for Dido, but they reenact an initiatory scenario as formal and compelling as that of elegy.

Funeral and marriage odes, then, are ceremonial poems which rely for their characteristic imagery and pattern upon the rites of passage of our culture. An elegy is a gesture toward the past, a way of memorializing the "multiple miniature deaths"[12] which compose the poetic life; it often pronounces an epitaph upon apprenticeship and announces literary coming-of-age. Built into the structure of elegy is a confrontation with death, a homeopathic administration of fear, and ultimate transcendence of the crisis which has its origins in the Orphic rituals of archaic Greek religion. An epithalamium, on the other hand, is a gesture toward the future, even though, like an elegy, it commemorates passage from virgin to mature state, valorizing the symbolic death that loss of virginity entails. But the preoccupation of the marriage poem, as insistently careerist in its way as the ceremonial elegy, is with immortality through "issue"— all things permanent which result from the union. Patterned upon the rituals of birth, marriage, and death, the forms of epithalamium and elegy offer a conventional structure for the enactment of initiation dramas and must be understood as literary gestures the significance of which lies in the context of a life.[13]

Certain critics will see in this investigation a kind of "new biographism."[14] In fact I have little to say about the metaphysical crises of individual poets; instead my focus is on comparative careers, the particular response of the creative personality to the ceremonial markers of the literary life. I hope to offer here, through a reading of such poems, a poetics of ceremony, by translating into specifically literary terms what Geoffrey Hartman has called "the vocational crisis that occurs in the poet as poet, in his literary self-consciousness."[15] Evaluating generic and model categories, this method addresses itself to literary, not individual, history.

CEREMONIAL STRUCTURES AND THE PASTORAL MODE

The biographer of such literary rites of passage would do well to begin, as did the poets, with pastoral texts, for since Virgil, the convention of inaugurating a literary career with a collection of pastorals has had the force of sacred text for subsequent practitioners of the mode. Not only the mainstream English poets—Spenser, Milton, Pope, Blake, Wordsworth—but continental poets as well have imitated Virgil's passage from reeds to trumpets, from poetic apprenticeship in the pastoral, through georgic, to the master task of epic. The pattern reproduces in small the evolution of civilization from shepherds to farmers to warriors. It articulates the hierarchy, in generical order, of the three styles: *humilis, mediocris, gravis*. It establishes a gradational plan for poetic initiation: from apprenticeship in crafted Arcadian lyrics to mastery of the collective song of war.[16]

Even at its inception, in the poetry of Theocritus, the youngest of the genres was viewed as a literary proving ground. Virgil's Alexandrian predecessors, poet-critics Callimachus and Theocritus, had assessed the failure of post-Homeric epic as revived by the cyclic poets of the sixth and seventh centuries and elected to write short poems in the Hesiodic tradition rather than retrace the error of imitative epic.[17] In the Alexandrian debate that ensued they proved to be the best judges of what the age would bear. Theocritus's legacy to Virgil, in the form of a corpus of idylls, was an established tradition of announcing one's literary appearance, of sharpening one's literary tools, of signifying one's literary importance, by a ritual donning of shepherd's weeds.

In many ways the Hellenistic world is closer to our own than is the world of the classical Greeks, particularly in its attitude toward literature and the written word. "Literary man as a type," Barber remarks, "is a creation of this age."[18] And the pastoral mode, invented by professional poets, is similarly a creation of this period—an arch-literary genre with issues of art very much on its mind. Like the Corinthian treatment of the architectural capital, for the most part a Hellenistic development, pastoral is an ornate, over-refined mode developed in response to a high-classic standard, indeed partly as a parody of this standard. All pastorals are in this sense works of decadence, mannerist affectations. And pastoral poetry, for all its pretensions to naturalness, has endured as a vital tradition because it comments unceasingly upon the conditions of its own creation. As early as Virgil's rewriting of Theocritus, for example, we are warned of too great dependence upon nature. The triumph of the fifth eclogue is Mopsus's discovery that he must teach nature to sing, and that the reward will be literary recognition. Even in Theocritus, I want to persuade, the literariness of the venture is signalled by the presence in the poem of a singularly literary landscape which the poem makes its own.

As W. J. Bate reminds us, Alexandria was one of the earliest "exemplars of what it can mean to an artist to stand in competition with an admired past."[19] Like the Alexandrian pastoralist, the modern poet looks back upon a tradition with reverence for its proximity to origins and with some misgivings about his own distance from that primal sense. The pastoral phase of a poet's career, literally or metaphorically understood, thus represents a dialogue with whatever he deems traditional or original; as the initiatory genre *par excellence,* pastoral apprenticeship provides the young writer—from the time of Theocritus to the present—with a recognized stage on which to enact his ritual drama of self-presentation.

What, however, remains to be said about the pastoral? Why, if critics have been lamenting with pastoralists that "the nymphs have departed," would anyone want to write again on pastoral, "that merest, most gratuitous of modes"?[20] Clearly we need no more influence studies, catalogues of convention, documentation of borrowings, explications of traditional pastoral poems, chronological summaries.[21] Criticism of the pastoral lacks a sense of how convention functions over time—even when it does not respect generic categories—and beyond that a record of the survival of pastoral patterns and imagery in Romantic and modern poetry. Critics have begun to investigate the pastoral moment in Romantic lyrics, but few have examined the deflection tantamount to rejection of pastoral forms, attitudes, images, in certain nineteenth- and twentieth-century lyrics. The doubt these modern poems raise about pastoral's power to allay the anxiety of mortality, however, exists in the earliest pastoral texts as well, and may be viewed productively as continuing to exploit a rich tension present in the pastoral mode from the outset. To include modern poems and the critical stance they bring to the convention they parody in this history of disjunctions is actually to offer a more cohesive reading of the pastoral ceremonial poem than a traditional generic history of pastoral (with its insistence upon originals and imitations) might provide. And conversely, to insist conservatively upon the presence of conventional motifs in a poem before calling it pastoral is to sacrifice valid indicators of literary history. Arcadia is, as has been said many times, not a place on the map of the world, but a country of the mind.

ELEGY AND EPITHALAMIUM

"Pastoral," as Heather Dubrow notes in her book on genre, "has a predilection for binary oppositions so fundamental that one suspects that if the genre did not exist the structuralists would have invented it."[22] One of the most fertile avenues of pastoral criticism remains, in fact, the attempt to account for pastoral reciprocities like the ancient binary opposition of amoebean dialogue, the traditional contrast of country and city, even the generic interpenetration of elegy and epithalamium. It will fall within the scope of this study to allude to a host of ceremonial forms—epitaphs, nativity odes, etc.—but to focus principally upon two. The pairing of elegy and epithalamium, poetic treatments of ritually opposite ceremonies, was suggested to me by Peter Marinelli's fairly fundamental recognition that love and death are intimately related in the pastoral world:

> The only combats it [Arcadia] knows are those of the shepherd *conflictus* in hours of idleness, a poetic rivalry whose theme is the superiority of one shepherdess to another, and which is motivated by a hope of gain aiming at nothing more precious than a beachen bowl, a lamb, a pipe. When, as happens frequently, Arcadia darkens with recollections of an external world of hard reality, that leisure becomes monotony, the poetry turns into complaint and elegy, and love, thwarted of all ambition, becomes desire for death.[23]

Helpful too was Renato Poggioli's assertion that "to most pastoral poets Eros and Thanatos appear to be twins: or, in Freudian terms, they seem to know that the pleasure principle is related to the death principle."[24] It is no accident that Poggioli's chapter on the funeral elegy follows his exposition of pastoral love or, for that matter, that the subject's death in the first funeral elegy, Theocritus's first idyll, was a consequence of excess of love. I have also drawn upon David Wagenknecht's study of the idea of pastoral in William Blake: a nucleus of pastoral vocabulary, attitude, and ideational content which Blake derived from Spenser's *Epithalamion* and Milton's *Lycidas*, the two greatest pastoral achievements in the English tradition.[25] As Wagenknecht notes, the "collision of eros and thanatos" in pastoral literature dates from the earliest and most central of pastoral myths: the story of Venus and Adonis. In Theocritus's fifteenth idyll, "The Women at the Adonis-Festival," the epithalamium chanted at the palace flows into a dirge; Tomorrow "wi' the dew," Adonis is to be carried "where plashing wave the shore doth lave" for symbolic burial.[26] Similarly Bion's "Lament for Adonis" is a funeral elegy that looks back upon the wedding song.[27] In Apuleius's *The Golden Ass,* love and death collide violently in the story of Psyche and Amor:

> The hour came when a procession formed up for Psyche's dreadful wedding. The torches chosen were ones that burned low with a sooty, spluttering flame; instead of the happy wedding-march the flutes played a querulous Lydian lament; the marriage-chant ended with funereal howls, and the poor bride wiped the tears from her eyes with the corner of her flame-colored veil.[28]

In the interplay of elegiac and epithalamic strains, the conventions of the one are exchanged for those of the opposite ritual: the procession of the wedding march, for example, finds its complement in the cortège.

By looking comparatively at two miniature genres—synecdoches for pastoral itself—it is possible to imitate the very function of pastoral art, to reproduce in small concerns wider than the ostensible compass of the poetry: the issue of succession that writing within a tradition raises, the interplay of dramatic and lyric forms, the interpenetration of elegiac and epithalamic conventions within a single work, the transcendence to which both genres aspire in spite of their seeming opposition. Bearing toward one another what Claudio Guillén would call a relationship of genre and counter-genre,[29] these two forms, so opposite in what genre theorists have called subject matter or occasion, evidence important, if unexpected, similarities. Each, for example, attempts to circumvent mortality by effecting transcendence to a higher state. Elegy reverses the course of loss by ensuring the corpse's resuscitation: apotheosis and stellification are the most characteristic forms this retrieval takes. The most conventional of epithalamia end with insemination of the bride and imagined future of her issue. Beneath both of these strategies, inscribed at the level of convention, is a ceremonial poetic economy designed to defer closure by ritually marking passage *from* one state *to* another. Looked at this way, the elegy and the epithalamium are companion genres, invested *in* similar ways of managing loss and guaranteeing continuity. Invested *with* a host of complementary conventions, they serve, as Paul Van Tieghem understands the function of genre, a similar human psychological need.[30] Many of the poems addressed in this study will thus refer to both forms, often intertwining them in ways that make traditional generic criticism, the establishment of limits and borders, impossible. But the most interesting work being done in the field of genre theory—Guillén's effort to construct "literature as system," Fowler's attempt to account for "modal admixtures" and "generic modulations," "counterstatement" and "inclusion,"[31] Dubrow's concern with seeing responses to canonical form along a spectrum, Rosmarin's work on the relationship between the dramatic monologue and the mask lyric—rather than policing generic purity, calls for close attention to the specific instance, radical attention to the relationships between literary genres kept distinct by a generic practice of exclusivity. As Paul Hernadi reminds us in *Beyond Genre*, "the finest generic classifications of our time make us look beyond their immediate concern and focus on the order of literature, not on the borders between literary genres."[32]

My own interest in canonical funeral and marriage poems thus extends to an array of variant poems—hybrids, mutants, crossbreeds. Even Spenser's *Epithalamion* and Milton's *Lycidas,* critically acclaimed as the apex of each minor genre's development in the English tradition, are more idiosyncratic than exemplary, and demand a rethinking of generic definitions. Spenser's marriage poem, for example, borrows elegiac structures during the course of ritual self-presentation of a new "I" voice. Spenser also claims to reunite Orpheus and Eurydice in his marriage poem, redeeming their separation and death by an epithalamium—a marriage song which the mythic Orpheus himself, we recall, was unable to effect. Milton's *Lycidas,* by its self-conscious erasure of references to marriage, draws attention to its deeper purpose: Milton ends his funeral elegy with a nuptial chorus, superimposing upon elegy's traditional apotheosis an emblematic heavenly wedding procession. Stéphane Mallarmé and Hart Crane have each written odd epithalamia, very much aware of the conventions of the marriage poem but ending with images of decapitation and death. These poems ultimately interest me more than the epithalamium's hyper-civilized appearance as an occasional poem—Ronsard's "Chant pastoral sur Les Noces De Monseigneur Charles Duc de Lorraine & Madame Claude Fille II du Roy" or A. E. Housman's "Epithalamium," more recently Betjeman's poem of state for the marriage of Prince Charles and Princess Diana, Ted Hughes's lyric in honor of Prince Andrew's marriage. Similarly Shelley's *Adonais* and Arnold's *Thyrsis* and all the mortuary melancholia which preceded them are less interesting than a range of poems which respond less directly, less imitatively, some would say less successfully, to Milton's *Lycidas*. Blake and Shelley write elegies without consolations, truncated poems eschewing conventional endings in favor of dramatizing the difficulty of transcendence. Whitman and

Crane enact seaside initiation dramas wholly devoid of recognizable pastoral props—no corpse to mourn, no bier to strew, no formal dirge to pronounce—but more successfully epitaphic (in the sense we have been exploring) than elegies critically deemed canonical.

Throughout the course of this study, elegy and epithalamium are used not only as generic classifications, where these can be confidently ascribed, but also as "modal terms" allowing for "enormous flexibility of reference."[33] Elegy and epithalamium manifest themselves *both* ways in this study: I therefore intentionally interuse, but do not mean to confuse, genre and mode as descriptive terms. In his *Kinds of Literature,* Alastair Fowler suggests that genre is substantive and mode adjectival, but in general he is more tentative than prescriptive about the relationship between genre and mode: since "mode's relationship to kind is particularly unclear," "in principle any kind might be extended as a mode" (not all are or should be, but some are and might profitably be). Mode seems to imply for Fowler an orientation, an amalgam of conventions without a "complete external form," which is precisely why I underscore the modal presence of elegy and epithalamium in poems we might classify (generically) otherwise (106, 108). Additionally, the symbolic reciprocity of these seemingly distinct forms will be emphasized as much as their individual representations for what this collision tells us about initiatory patterns in particular, poetic structures in general. The chiasmus of elegiac and epithalamic aims, to which I shall return after marking conventional distinctions between the two genres, points to an identity beneath all poems of ceremony.

The classical epithalamium was traditionally a song sung outside (*epi*) the nuptial chamber (*thalamos*) upon the consummation of the union.[34] By the time of Catullus, however, any kind of wedding song was termed an epithalamium; not long after, any work dealing even metaphorically with marriage received the title. The set of conventions that determines the lyric epithalamium is fairly predictable in classical and Renaissance poetry: the ceremony runs the length of the day during the late spring or summer season; the poem describes marriage preparations and participants; it features a bride describable in natural metaphors and virtually definable by her virginity; it projects a fiction of erotic union, sensual integrity, and fulfillment, a veritable golden age of harmony with the natural world. It also projects a communal ritual or dramatic ceremony which, beginning with Spenser, the poet orchestrates and controls. The epithalamium is a literary rite of aggregation. As our greatest champions of eros—Plato, Dante, Freud—knew very well, eros is the force that draws us out of ourselves into a resplendent vision of community. The marriage ritual eternally symbolizes in a series of concentric relations the wedding of man to woman, harmony between the sexes, adequacy between the human psyche and the natural world, aspiration of human to godly life. For Spenser and the mystic poets, the marriage ceremony was a ritual drama by means of which the soul ascended toward its celestial home, an allegorical journey often bound to the parallel voyage of the literary imagination in its effort to incarnate. For Blake and Wordsworth, nuptial imagery and related conventions, surprisingly, convey the blissful, undifferentiated state of the child at ignorant play or, more pointedly in the poetry of Wordsworth, the wedding of mind and nature in exquisitely matched spousal bliss. In short, the entire movement of the epithalamium as genre is toward conservative resolution and transcendence. It is to this achievement of cosmic harmony that Richard Cody refers when he writes that all pastoral aspires to the condition of epithalamium.[35]

If epithalamium is modeled on a communal ritual, elegy rehearses a rite of separation. Its attendant imagery is generally the reverse of that of the wedding poem. Marriage necessitates witnesses, the projection of a testimonial surround, whereas elegy—whose "closest association and most necessary formal kinship . . . is with the literature of self"[36]—increasingly becomes the mode of the reflective mind. Even as early as Theocritus's eighteenth idyll, wedding functioned as a metaphor for social harmony. The landscape of elegy, on the other hand, is barren—all nature mourns—or deserted—an unpopulated garden, like that of Marvell's nymph complaining. Elegy is appropriately, since Sannazaro and Milton, a night or evening song. Whitman's "When Lilacs Last . . ." is a later poem than Milton's *Lycidas,* as its appropriation of imagery suggests: the earlier work, already belated, ends at sunset, but Whitman's poem takes place so late at night that the moon lags drunkenly on the water. Similarly the "autumnal mood" of the mellowing year in Milton's elegy for King sets the tone for elegiac meditation. Elegy is also a song of disjunction with nature: *Lycidas* begins with a rape of natural order; Whitman's poem turns on the breaking of a branch. The singer of elegy is alienated by the unalterable fact of death, from nature's cyclic rhythm by his own mortal one, from the tradition by his place in literary history, and from communal celebration by the increasingly lyric and personal nature of his utterance.[37]

The contrast I have been sketching must be clear at this point. Epithalamium survives as a lyric genre only as long as the poet remains central—poetically and politically—to his world. Because the epithalamium generally reaffirms social hierarchy, it may have found its truest home in the extroverted dramatic mode of comedy:[38] from the pastoral romance of Longus, *Daphnis and Chlöe,* to Shakespearean forest comedies, from the wedding celebrations at the close of Aristophanic comedies to the projected marriages which circumscribe Jane Austen's novels, marriage as metaphor speaks for the restoration of human community as much as it figures the union of true minds. Even Virginia Tufte's examples of epithalamia in her history of the genre are chosen from the drama of the periods—Aristophanes, Euripides, Seneca—after brief mention of Sappho and Catullus. Aside from the strictly imitative occasional poem, such as a commissioned poem of state, lyric epithalamia after the Renaissance do not seem to work, as if the formulation were oxymoronic: a single lyric voice attempting unsuccessfully to produce the illusion of ceremony, the effect of choral response. While epithalamia continue to be sung in dramatic works, after Spenser a certain kind of wedding poem tends more and more to reflect lack of confidence in what the epithalamium traditionally celebrates. For Paul Miller, who has charted "The Decline of the English Epithalamium," the mode dies out without exception in the late Renaissance.[39] And after this time, the best responses to the tradition, a leap Miller does not make, are those works which use the conventional epithalamium as a negative model. Thus Pope's *The Rape of the Lock* is as much a mock-epithalamium as it is a mock-epic, and may profitably be read as a parody of Spenser's poem.[40] And Blake's *The Marriage of Heaven and Hell,* in the words of yet another critic, is "Romanticism's best answer to Spenser's *Epithalamion.*"[41]

Elegy is the form in which pastoral endures the longest, perhaps because it offers greatest scope, within prescribed limits, for innovation, probably because it exploits increasingly—once Milton chooses to imitate in his monody the lyric form of Virgil's tenth bucolic rather than the dialogue structure of the fifth—the subjectivism of lyric. I see no reason to limit elegy to Ellen Lambert's exclusive definition as "pastoral dirge" or "*epicedium*" and to restrict its field of influence to classical, neo-Latin, and medieval texts. Abbie Findlay Potts's expanded view of elegy, as a speculative literary genre with its own identifiable themes and devices and with a characteristic *anagnorisis* or discovery, allows for more inventive readings of poems and attempts to discover literary processes beneath vaster groups of texts. Even S. T. Coleridge, in *Table Talk,* October 23, 1833, was content to call elegy that "form of poetry natural to the reflective mind. It *may* treat of any subject, but it must treat of no subject *for itself,* but always and exclusively with reference to the poet himself." To these open-ended conceptions, I add my own qualification: an elegy need be no more than a lyric meditation proceeding from the thought of death which signals the readiness of the pastoral apprentice for transcendence of the mode. Crane's "elegy" for Whitman, embedded in his American epic, accordingly, cannot be excluded from a study of pastoral initiatory scenarios. The writing of an elegy, even in the absence of a corpse, is a literary gesture signifying admittance of the poet-initiate to the sacred company.

As interesting as the separate fortunes of epithalamium and elegy is the varied and rich commerce between them: this collision ultimately forms the basis for a poetics of ceremony. Both forms strive to render poetically the same transcendent vision of restored harmony. Both record a death and celebration passage to the fresh woods and pastures new enjoyed by Milton's swain. Since Virgil, and perhaps even beginning with Plato's notion of transcendence by means of devoted, reasonable pursuit of Eros, the dirge is followed by consolation, a poetic victory not unlike that accomplished by the epithalamium over the disjunction between this-worldliness and other-worldliness. The imagery attendant on passage in both forms of the ceremonial poem is remarkably similar, offering interpretive problems to the diagnostician of genre. For these reasons, study of conventional and easily categorizable examples of elegy and epithalamium should include "imperfect" forms as well: laments *manqués,* marriage poems that suddenly become dirges, elegies that fail to assuage or that lack a proper dead man, epithalamia in which the bridal veil metamorphoses into a shroud—in short, a range of poems excluded from the pastoral canon by their failure to conform to traditional patterns.

"EVERY POEM AN EPITAPH"

The reader will not find a history of convention here unless literary history may be construed as a history of those "junctions" at which poems dialogue across the gap of time. The first chapter, "The Pastoral Scene of Instruction: Plato's *Phaedrus,*" investigates the classical siting of the pastoral initiation scene in the *locus amoenus* chosen by Socrates and Phaedrus for their oratorical debate, ultimately considering the *Phaedrus,* for its elegiac imagery and tone, an important early pre-text of the pastoral elegy. The representative poems of Theocritus's first idyll, Virgil's fifth bucolic, and Spenser's "November" eclogue are explored in Chapter 2, "The Funeral Elegy and Careerism." Underscoring the importance of subsequent restagings of the initiation drama, this chapter shows the writing of elegies to be inextricably bound to an appropriate setting, a need for memorializing past forms and voicing the new songs that will succeed them. From the first, an elegy is an expression of careerism: Theocritus uses it as a frontispiece, an overture to his revolutionary poetic corpus; Virgil places it at critical points—middle, end—of his own *Bucolics* and is the first to make elegy into an epitaph upon a former self, a virtual farewell to the mode. Spenser balances it with the blazon to Elizabeth, a proto-epithalamium, in his *Shepheardes Calender* and shows it to be the marriage poem's opposite, both in imagery and intent. In the last poem of the second chapter, the resolution of elegy calls for an epithalamic vocabulary: Spenser's desire to write a pastoral dirge is outstripped by his consuming interest in the marriage poem. Both elegy and epithalamium provide for orphic transcendence of nature within the scheme of the *Calender,* but Spenser makes more innovative use of the nuptial convention.

The remaining chapters read individual poems against the generic models proposed in chapters one and two. The third chapter, " 'Sacred Ceremonies,' " explores Spenser's marriage poems, locating an initiation ceremony in the literary orphism of the *Epithalamion* and, oddly enough, an elegiac pronouncement on the poet's subsequent decline at court beneath the nuptial form of his betrothal poem, the *Prothalamion.* The fourth chapter, " 'The Marriage Hearse,' " takes up three parodies of Spenser's *Epithalamion* which amount to critical revaluations of that canonical poem: Donne, Crashaw, and Blake borrow the imagery of the funeral poem to subvert the symbolism of marriage in their respective antiepithalamia; all three poems, however, offer an alternative, if inverted, rite of passage by means of direct parody of Spenser. A reading of Milton's *Lycidas* against representative elegies of Marvell and Rilke forms the core of " 'Unexpressive Nuptial Song.' " But instead of seeing Milton's poem for King as the fulfillment of the elegy as genre in English, I read it as covert epithalamium: Milton wants, on his literary appearance, all of the publicity of the marriage ceremony. His poem is as dramatic a celebration of the imagination's emergence from obscurity as Spenser's *Epithalamion,* the nuptial conventions of which Milton alludes to in a range of revealing ways. "Failed Elegies" considers Blake's *The Book of Thel* and Shelley's *Alastor* as responses to Milton's poem and measures the distance between those Romantic elegies ending in solitude and death and the transcendent vision of Milton's swain. " 'A Wedding or a Funeral' " considers the rich profusion of ceremonial languages and imagery in Wordsworth's Great Ode. A comprehensive ode celebrating the double birth of man and poet, the poem borrows elegiac conventions as well in order to mourn and memorialize a lost faculty of the soul. "Epithalamia Awry" considers poems which ostensibly borrow the fiction of the wedding poem, but do not achieve its final synthesis: ending rather with imagery of death and violence, Mallarmé's *Hérodiade* celebrates a strange marriage of remote princess and decapitated saint; Hart Crane's "For the Marriage of Faustus and Helen" also dramatizes the difficult wedding of opposite principles. Finally, in "Sea-Changes: The Incarnational Ode and Ceremonial Modes," several modern piscatorials are viewed next to *Lycidas* as equally literary self-pronouncements, initiations however idiosyncratic. In Whitman's "Out of the Cradle Endlessly Rocking" and Crane's "Voyages," pastoral imagery and *dramatis personae* are conspicuously missing, but the elegiac effect of both poems is a dramatization of each poet's orphic ritual descent in search of poetic voice and literary identity. Consolation in these incarnational odes takes predictably epithalamic form.

To return to the T. S. Eliot lines with which I began this introduction, "every poem" might be termed an "epitaph" to the extent that epitaphs, classically understood, are graven evidence of a life now ended as well as invitations to passing and potential readers to reflect upon that life.[42] All poems are genuinely epitaphic in their attempt to record verbally and lastingly the death (and implied rebirth) of the poet *as poet* each time he lifts his pen to begin a new poem. By way of conclusion, in "Mourning and Panegyric: The Poetics of Pastoral Ceremony," I consider several modern poems of passage from the vantage point of lyric processes in general. The ceremonial poems of Nemerov and Kinsella elect each of the thematic directions outlined above: Kinsella affirms the possibility of vision and renewed orphic song, whereas Nemerov declares that the reunion with Eurydice is no longer possible. Seemingly what survives the demise of pastoral conventions, characters, symbols, is pastoral's initiatory function as a mode in which the young careerist demonstrates his fitness for the literary life. Either he invokes a ceremonial frame for his self-presenting utterance, or else, by means of sophisticated parody, he refuses the conventional symbols of poetic immortality and exposes the celebratory tone of such pastorals as hollow. Poetic ceremonies—the orphic protagonist faces two ways—either decry a loss or voice a consolation.

1
The Pastoral Scene of Instruction: Plato's *Phaedrus*

I

Our investigation of the pastoral elegy as an initiatory scenario in a defining landscape begins, perhaps, in an unlikely place. The end of this chapter may seem equally incongruous, focusing as it does upon a passage from John Fowles's *The French Lieutenant's Woman*. Yet, Plato's *Phaedrus* may be read as both an important pretext and a context for the elegies of Theocritus, Virgil, and Spenser, and for subsequent translations of the *locus amoenus* in English and continental literature. I do not mean to suggest that the *Phaedrus* stands in unique originary relation to the bucolics of Theocritus, or that Plato as pastoralist in this dialogue might not write out of the collateral ancient traditions of pastoral convention to which Theocritus also had access.[1] Yet, pastoral poetry in general is more indebted to Plato's *Phaedrus* (for both a thematics of initiation as well as conventions and motifs) than scholarship has acknowledged.[2] I focus necessarily here on the Dialogue's form as a verbal initiation ceremony—outlining first its relationship to the pastoral in that regard, and finally its function as elegy—and on its importance as perhaps our earliest exposition (by means of indictment) of that dynamic which lends resilience and longevity to literary forms. Whereas the pastoral elegies of Theocritus and Virgil, and Spenser's "August" eclogue, formally mimic the initiation of Phaedrus at the hands of Socrates, placing the ceremony in the ritual landscape of the Dialogue or explicitly choosing another, they all—in a final irony—fall into the category of bad writing outlined in the *Phaedrus:* in their successive parody of the initiation scene, these elegies show representatively just how subversive, in Plato's sense, a pastoral text can be.

As urbane a city philosopher as Plato might have been, he plainly made the Eleusinian Mysteries his allies in the service of philosophy: the *Phaedrus* records the gradual enlightenment of the initiate—Socrates calls him youth, child, and one of the young ones—by his spiritual father to a transcendent vision of the Forms. Mircea Eliade underscores the relationship between the imagery of the Mysteries and the ritual symbolism of archaic initiation ceremonies, pointing to the influence of ritual language upon philosophical and theological literature:

> Homologizing philosophy to initiation had been a common motif even from the beginnings of Pythagoreanism and Platonism. But the hermeneutic procedure (from the root maia, "midwife") by which Socrates sought to "deliver" a new man had its prototype in archaic societies, in the work of the masters of initiation; they too delivered neophytes, that is, helped them to be born to spiritual life.[3]

In archaic rites, in the *Phaedrus,* in funeral elegies, even in modern lyrics of poetic incarnation, initiation scenarios are "the expression of a psychodrama that answers a deep need in the human being."[4] The message of the Mysteries, assimilated to writing, secularized, has been transformed: "though preserving its primitive agricultural structure, the Mystery no longer referred to the fertility of the soil and the prosperity of the community [here the reader thinks of pastoral's Adonis festivals] but to the spiritual destiny of each individual *mystes.*"[5]

The crucial link between pastoralism and Platonism, and between Arcadian and modern forms of initiatory pastoral, is Orphism, a pre-Socratic theology which syncretized around the figure of the mythic Orpheus—poet-singer whose musical subduing of the beasts, whose ritual dismemberment, whose singing head floating on the Hebros guaranteeing transcendence of death, were legendary.[6] David Wagenknecht dethrones Adonis as mythic representative of the pastoral in favor of Orpheus, possessor of "the erotic power, *par excellence,*"[7] and Richard Cody signals as "orphic" that Renaissance pastoral "celebration of poetry's old power as a ritual language of the mysteries,"[8] but both are indebted to W. K. C. Guthrie for a masterful scholarly demonstration of Orphism's collision—in the minds of Pico and Ficino among other Renaissance commentators—with Platonism in the visual art of the period. Guthrie calls Orphism the "most hotly disputed area" in the "field of Greek religion," and sketches in this theology deriving from a belief in the "latent divinity and immortality of the human soul," in the "body as prison or tomb of the soul," in the rebirth or transmigration of souls into union with the divine, and in the salvation by "mystical initiation" in the *teletai* at Eleusis.[9] For Edgar Wind, "philosophy itself was a mystical initiation of another kind," one which required a deliberate feint: a self-conscious, riddling obscurity protective of the unnameable mystery at the core. According to Wind, this Orphic countenance masking its true purpose was read onto Socrates by the commentators, but was justified by Plato's appropriation of the language and imagery of the Mysteries for his own philosophic scene of instruction. Wind quotes Pico: "Orpheus interwove the mysteries of his doctrine with the texture of fables and covered them with a poetic veil, in order that anyone reading his hymns would think them to contain nothing but the sheerest tales and trifles."[10]

Like Orpheus, Socrates hides his true mission—articulation, singing. He is poor and pretends a bumbling naïveté, an attitude we recognize as peculiarly pastoral. No wonder then that in the *Symposium* Alcibiades offers as tribute a cryptic image of Socrates as a satyr figure; finding Socrates like the "busts of Silenus, which are set up in the statuaries' shops, holding pipes and flutes in their mouths," he tells the company that these toys are rude and unassuming only on the outside: "When they are made to open in the middle, [they] have images of gods inside them."[11]

> His [Socrates'] words are like the images of Silenus which open; they are ridiculous when you first hear them; he clothes himself in language that is like the skin of the wanton satyr—for his talk is of pack-asses and smiths and cobblers and curriers, and he is always repeating the same things in the same words, so that any ignorant or inexperienced person might feel disposed to laugh at him; but he who opens the bust and sees what is within will find that they are only words which have a meaning in them, and also the most divine, abounding in fair images of virtue, and of the widest comprehension, or rather extending to the whole duty of a good and honourable man. (*Symp.* 221–22)

The satyric pose concealing serious purpose suggested by the image of the rough bust is Orphic in origin. Such was the sacred message of philosophy that Socrates went to great lengths to disguise it: his affected modesty ("But, my sweet Phaedrus, how ridiculous it would be of me to compete with Lysias in an extempore speech! He is a master in his art and I am an untaught man," 236), his invention of a new literary form and language in which to couch it, his extensive use of cryptic symbolisms and myths. Such was the sacred mystery of poetry that pastoral poets resorted to complex symbolisms intelligible only to the initiate, duplicitous tones, shepherds' weeds over the robes of academia. "The deepest things," Wind reminds us, "are spoken in a tone of irony."[12]

This Orphic-Platonic *serio ludens,* or "sacred play," lies beneath both the masquelike impenetrability of the pastoral eclogue and the calculated obscurity of certain modern poems founded upon it. In his study of the play element in culture, *Homo Ludens,* J. Huizinga locates the very source of poetry in play, calling pastoral life one of the two "golden ages of play."[13] Modern poetry shares with Arcadian pastoral the ritual secrecy surrounding the mystery and the initiatory pattern enacted by poetic celebration which assures the neophyte an initiated audience.

> Modern schools of lyric which move and have their being in realms not generally accessible and are fond of wrapping the sense in an enigmatic word are thus remaining true to the essence of their art. With their restricted circle of readers who understand or are at least acquainted with their special language, they are a closed cult group of very ancient descent. It is questionable, however, whether the civilization that surrounds them is capable of appreciating their purpose sufficiently to nurture an art whose raison d'etre is yet the fulfillment of a vital function. (135)

It is to this "special language" of pastoral which we now turn in our investigation of the literary form of the *Phaedrus:* its cast of characters, patron deities, times and places, verbal structures, and lyric inspiration.

II

The birth of Alexandrian singing contests from the spirit of Socratic play is implicit from the first in the fiction of the *Phaedrus.* Like the *Symposium* it is an ironic speech contest. At Plato's banquet, the speech of each intoxicated speaker is intended to inspire the next; boasting, wagering, and animated repartee obscure the serious content of the speeches and intensify the impact of this most dramatic of the Socratic Dialogues.[14] To the student of pastoral, the staging of the *Phaedrus,* a colloquial exchange on the banks of the cooling Ilissus at midday, partakes of a familiar constellation of images. Socrates is, of course, here and elsewhere, an urbane city philosopher with the proper government of the polis foremost in mind. As he reminds Phaedrus, "I am a lover of knowledge and the men who dwell in the city are my teachers and not the trees of the country" (220). I agree with Adam Parry that Socrates means the opposite of what he says here;[15] in fact the countryside and the trees have a good deal to teach him. In spite of Socrates' protestations, rather remarkably in this important Dialogue, the country setting and the rhetorical message are inextricably bound.

Socrates is sensitive to the charms of the Ilissus even as he protests that the natural setting has nothing to teach him. Most of the Platonic Dialogues do take place within city walls, but this one does not. Here images of closure accompany Phaedrus's description of the city. In fact the pretense for leaving the "walls" of the city is that "it is much more refreshing to walk in the open air than to be shut up in a cloister" (227). The pastoral setting of this exchange is no wise accidental. "To withdraw from the city" is not, I think, as Michael Putnam believes, "an act of whimsy."[16] Phaedrus's initiation is a rite of separation; it demands to take place in a specified locale at a remove from the city community. He *returns* to the city enlightened from the pastoral scene of initiation. Beginning with Virgil, for whom pastoral is a place one leaves after poetic seasoning has taken place, the return becomes as important a motif as the sequestering in a pastoral landscape. For example, Spenser's eclogues in the *Shepheardes Calender* end with a return from the "greene cabinet." Pastoral, it seems, as both symbolic setting and a phase of a poet's career, was from the outset a temporary stopping place: a landscape to which one retires, for natural inspiration and challenging fellowship, but from which one returns citybound at dusk.

In the *Phaedrus,* the exchange shared by the two contestants is pastorally sited. Once in the country, Socrates and Phaedrus embark on an oratorical contest, a kind of dialectical exchange that works, through incremental repetition and gradual refinement, toward naming a winner. Like the Sicilian singing contest which is the pretense for pastoral song, this exchange is a framed dialogue. The colloquial conversation of the opening and closing sections embraces the three speeches on love, Lysias's first speech read by Phaedrus and Socrates' two orations. The contest opens with a challenge, sets up a prize for the winner, and begins, subject to mutual approval of the appropriate natural setting. A pastoral wager results: if Socrates can make "another and better oration, equal in length and equally new on the same subject," Phaedrus promises to "set up a golden image at Delphi, not only of [him]self, but of [Socrates] and as large as life" (235). An invocation to "come, O ye Muses" in true pastoral style inaugurates the proceedings (237). The prize, according to Phaedrus, goes to the one who says the same thing in a different way, in other words, to the best rhetorician. When the heat abates, they return to the city. As in Virgil's first bucolic, the epiphanic moment in the Dialogue is the close of day, at which time they cease speaking, offer a prayer to Pan—which Werner Jaeger calls the "only prayer in the whole of Plato"[17]—to invoke that unity and integrity of all things to which Socrates aspires, and turn homeward. Even in this earliest pastoral text, or "prose idyll," to use Cody's intriguing phrase,[18] pastoral is a place to visit, a ritual to which one submits for initiation, but from which one inevitably returns to the city enlightened.

Both the timing and the placement of Phaedrus's initiation are prescribed. From this Dialogue pastoralists derived not only a succinct portrait of the *locus amoenus,* the pastoral scene of instruction, but sanction for the importance of the noon hour as a time for self-discovery and verbal interchange. Only in the open air, under the influence of nature and nymphs, "local deities," can this speech contest take place. The right place, prior to singing, is sought by the two contestants: looking to locate "some quiet spot" (229), they turn away from the road and follow a river. The place they choose—composed of the familiar grouping of tree, spring, grassy knoll[19]—becomes a self-consciously literary landscape, prototype of Spenser's "greene cabinet" and Marvell's "green place in a green shade."

> By Here, a fair resting-place, full of summer sounds and scents. Here is this lofty and spreading plane-tree, and the agnus castus high and clustering, in the fullest blossom and the greatest fragrance; and the stream which flows beneath the plane-tree is deliciously cold to the feet. Judging from the ornaments and images, this must be a spot sacred to Achelous and the Nymphs. How delightful is the breeze;—so very sweet; and there is a sound in the air shrill and summerlike which makes answer to the chorus of the cicadae. But the greatest charm of all is the grass, like a pillow gently sloping to the head. (230)

As Paul Friedländer reminds us, "the setting of the *Phaedrus* is always keenly felt."[20] The stock motifs—plane-tree, cooling stream, grove consecrated to the Nymphs—are balanced by a direct appeal to the five senses. As in Theocritus's landscapes, sights, sounds, scents, bring a literary landscape alive. Note as well the presence of cicadae in the *locus*: the deafening chant of the cicadae throbs as well in pastoral idylls, but here they are invoked for their symbolic value, for what they can teach us about the proper use of *otium*. Either one can be lulled to sleep "like sheep lie asleep at noon before the well" (259), or one can be roused to increased creativity by these singing sirens. The cicadae, located in the trees above our heads, have the power to draw us upward; their intermediary position between Muses and mortals, and their role in "reporting to the Muses of those that do them honour" (259), link them to the sources of poetry and the arts.[21] The reference to the cicadae here reveals the proper use of the noon hour for inspired self-betterment and insists upon arbitration by the watchful cicadae over the activities of noontime orators. In fact, Plato's *Phaedrus* offers the earliest evidence of the noon hour as a time for "exaltation and creative communication," a tradition preserved by Alexandrian poets.[22] The pastoral hour of *otium*, the noontime retreat from blazing sunlight into the coolness and shelter of landscape, first finds expression here. "Spare time" (227) is deemed important enough by Socrates and Phaedrus to be well spent in mutual enlightenment and enjoyment. Finally, for pastoral poets, the conventionality of the *Phaedrus*'s timing and placement cannot be underestimated: Thyrsis is initiated by the unnamed goatherd in Theocritus's elegy for Daphnis, Virgil's Mopsus receives instruction at the hands of the patient Menalcas, in the same literary landscape, against the same ritual backdrop, and at the same prescribed moment as Phaedrus, who, by verbal means, is initiated into the proper use of *otium:* how properly to sing or use language.

III

The first half of this necessarily long exposition explored the relationship between the *Phaedrus* and pastoral's function as a literary apprenticeship in the uses of language. It remains to read the *Phaedrus* as elegy: a dirge upon the demise of oral culture (with its emphasis on the presence of speaker and listener, the performance of speech, the resilience of memory) and initiation into the abstract thinking and philosophical introspection that determine written culture and the very form of the Dialogue.[23] In fact the Dialogue is full of regret for the passing of a golden age of Original Meaning. In his allegory of the soul, for example, Plato describes a decisive fall from a state of grace, the very precondition of pastoral poetry. In the struggling pair of horses he images the contradictory call of two worlds: one is the privileged spiritual Arcadia of philosophy, the other an abased mortal ensnarement in worldly matters. Having fallen from a state of visionary apprehension of the Forms into this world of vague appearances, we look longingly over our shoulders and "linger over the memory of scenes which have passed away" (250). It is precisely this note of nostalgia for a previous existence—Wordsworth's "whither is fled the visionary gleam?"—that is sounded repeatedly in pastoral poetry from Theocritus's loving transformation of his native Sicilian landscapes to Robert Frost's latter-day evocation of New England countryside. The myth of the golden age, equally compelling in its pagan and Christian forms, is imaged "in a figure" (246) in Plato's Dialogue, becoming in the poetry of Virgil pastoral's central informing metaphor.

What is lost, for Plato, is a proximity to a state of innocence in language which is left behind in the descent into written language's duplicity. But for all his regret for this earlier mode of apprehension and transmission of cultural values, for all Plato's nostalgia for Homeric (or, for that matter, Socratic) immediacy and presence, the Dialogue in its very form as a written document betrays itself. And in fact Plato's conspicuous refusal to acknowledge the act of writing—what pretends to be a transparent speech contest is really a philosopher seated before a tablet—shows just how aware he is of the conventions of writing. His silence at this crucial moment evidences conflict over the supremacy of oral culture upon Greek thought. Reconciled to the prison-house of language, Plato tries to make a strength of it by distinguishing between good and bad forms of writing and devoting himself to pursuit of philosophical truth in written form. After all, when Phaedrus proposes to recount Lysias's speech from memory, it is Socrates who persuades him to read the speech hidden in the folds of his coat. In fact the Dialogue offers itself as successor to the oral culture whose passing it so eloquently mourns: its fiction is an exchange of speeches dramatized as if presently occurring, but its form is written. Plato, however, insists upon a distinction between writing used rightly and writing abused, and this is where poetry and philosophy part ways.

In the end Plato places the imitative poet on probation for having seen truth only in the sixth degree, only a degree or so better than the sophist. "The mind of the philosopher alone has wings," he writes:

> and this is just, for he is always, according to the measure of his abilities, clinging in recollection to those things in which God abides, and in beholding which He is what He is. And he who employs aright these mysteries is ever being initiated into perfect mysteries and alone becomes truly perfect. (249)

Plato's quarrel with contemporary rhetoricians, whose unseriousness and indifference to truth he deplored, may well have provided the impetus for the Dialogue, but the indictment extends as well to poets, whose use of language he deems irresponsible. As Jacques Derrida has convincingly shown, the whole Dialogue revolves around the myth of origins of language, for which eros, sexuality, is merely a metaphor, a manner of speaking. Derrida's *La Pharmacie de Platon* is an entertaining, yet serious, critical examination of Plato's *Phaedrus,* a philosophical inquiry as dramatic in its own way as the *Symposium,* and as duplicitous as the Dialogue it exposes.[24] By means of an elaborate word game, Derrida teases out the meanings of a range of motifs in the Dialogue—*pharmakon,* remedy/poison, liquidity, sperm, drug, Phaedrus's spell over Socrates—arising from the myth of Boreas and Orithyia and the story of the god of writing. For Derrida, Plato is the creator in Western culture of that "metaphysics of presence" which depends upon a myth of origins, a paternal speaker of the Logos (Plato's cherished Socrates, whose life's work it was to give the word and leave no written record of it), and longs for a "truth behind every sign: a moment of original plenitude when form and meaning were simultaneously present to consciousness and not to be distinguished."[25] Derrida deconstructs the text, setting it free from both origin and end, giving it over to the play of language, by locating the moment at which the text reveals itself, in the double-edged word *pharmakon* and the absence of the word *pharmakos*.[26]

Critics have long debated the importance of the coda on writing appended to Socrates' second speech and its role in contributing to a structural imbalance in the Dialogue. In fact the two ostensible subjects of the Dialogue, love and rhetoric, are one and the same. Socrates' concern here is to instruct Phaedrus how best to use the noon hour: to love properly—by passionately devoting himself to a philosophical pursuit of Beauty—and to write rightly—by harnessing language to the service of a single philosophical truth. Earthly love and rhetoric, the province of pastoralists, have the same unfortunate result for Plato: both excite, but neither raises the soul to a vision of the absolute. They stimulate the philosopher's divine possession and erotically motivated desire for the truth, but they arrest the attention of the initiate and focus his efforts in a wasteful, worldly, unrewarding manner. In fact the whole second speech of Socrates, using the language and symbolism of the Mysteries, is a gradual enlightenment of the initiate: at the outset, the aspiring poet is called incomplete, or unfinished; by the close, right activity of the soul makes him blessed.[27] The lover whose wings carry him heavenward and the rhetorician whose garden is sown in earnest are admitted to the sacred company.

Pastoralism is a secularization of the Mysteries at Eleusis, a fallen version of that literature which aims, through mature erotic activity, to envision a world of essences "visible only to mind, the pilot of the soul" (247) and hence heavenward from its present state to the ideal state of the soul. The kind of writing outlined in the coda remains for him a direct and sustained threat to the dialectical enterprise. Plato condemns and Derrida celebrates its fundamental unseriousness as opposed to the important business (*spoudei*) of philosophy. He calls writing a "mere routine and a trick" (260), recognizes only its limited importance as the "art of enchanting the soul" (271), and fears its power to please. "Amusement and pastime" (276) are reason enough for its existence. Moreover, any writer who seeks to enchant the soul "not with any view to criticism or instruction" (278) is fueled by a lower order of erotic motivation. In both the *Symposium* and the *Phaedrus,* Plato insists upon philosophy's independence from ambition. The second type of lover in the *Symposium* is propelled by "love of an immortality of fame" to content himself with the "lesser mysteries of love" (208, 209–10). In the *Phaedrus*, similarly, the "lower life of ambition" (256) takes erotic form:

> If, on the other hand, they leave philosophy and lead the lower life of ambition, then probably after wine or in some other careless hour, the two wanton animals take the two souls when off their guard and bring them together, and they accomplish that desire of their hearts which to the many is bliss; and this having once enjoyed, they continue to enjoy, yet rarely because they have not the approval of the whole soul. (256)

Pastoral poetry too knows this convergence of eros and ambition, for erotic conflict (lament, contest, serenade), general unseriousness (games, singing duels, wagering), and literary ambition are mainstays of the pastoral mode. The pastoralist has always known himself to be no less than a player with words: from the outset the pastoral fiction rested upon the notion of pastime. The irony, of course, is that Alexandrian poets would perfect a literary art that was just the sort of writing Plato feared and condemned. They viewed themselves as literary professionals, reveled in the freedom of their art from the classical injunction to instruct, and indulged the tendency of literary language to ape, to distort, to parody itself by direct contest with rival forms.

Plato would term "fallen" that literature which inverts the chaste quest for universal Beauty by means of an erotic and human epithalamium, however symbolically its significance was meant to be felt. The elegist, too, secularizes the sacred *teletai,* the ritual means by which the Orphic initiate—having been "purged of his fear of death and admitted into the company of initiates"[28]—is empowered to sing. Nothing less than Orphic success in literary terms—immortality or fame—inspires that range of poets from Theocritus to Milton to make the literary gesture that is the writing of an elegy. Plato gives us in the *Phaedrus*, then, more than stock pastoral motifs, a *locus amoenus,* pastoral attitude. He provides the model for an initiatory scenario: a younger aspirant by an older seduced, a place and time in literary terms prescribed, initiation by means of amoebean argument ritually established.

IV

In *Poetry and Repression,* Harold Bloom writes that a "poem both takes its origin in a Scene of Instruction and finds its necessary aim or purpose

THE PASTORAL SCENE OF INSTRUCTION   29

there as well."²⁹ Quoting Thomas Frosch's summary of his own concept, Bloom calls the Primal Scene of Instruction "a model for the unavoidable imposition of influence," a "complete play or process." Bloom does not stress, however, that the Scene is not only a confrontation between new poet and precursor but is also a *place* with its own distinctive literary topography. Landscape functions symbolically in pastoral poetry, as the earliest practitioners of the mode knew very well: either poetic geography responds to and embodies the imaginative vision imposed upon it (the essence of the pathetic fallacy), or else it functions as a ritual location for the fiction of the pastoral singing contest, a literary formula transformed and repossessed eternally by the beholder's eye.³⁰ The pastoral initiation scene becomes practically formulaic in subsequent imitations of Plato's *locus amoenus*, as Theocritus's, Virgil's, and Spenser's revisions of the scene will attest. Even John Fowles's contemporary, yet equally representative, *locus* evidences the prevailingly intact features of the pastoral initiation scene.

> It was this place, an English Garden of Eden on such a day as March 29, 1867, that Charles had entered when he had climbed the path from the shore at Pinhay Bay . . .
> When Charles had quenched his thirst and cooled his brow with his wetted handkerchief he began to look seriously around him. Or at least he tried to look seriously around him; but the little slope on which he found himself, the prospect before him, the sounds, the scents, the unalloyed wildness of growth and burgeoning fertility, forced him into anti-science. The ground around him was studded gold and pale yellow with celandines and primroses and banked by the bridal white of densely blossoming sloe; where jubilantly green-tipped elders shaded the mossy banks of the little brook he had drunk from were clusters of moschatel and woodsorrel, most delicate of English spring flowers. Higher up the slope he saw the white heads of anemones, and beyond them deep green drifts of bluebell leaves. A distant woodpecker drummed in the branches of some high tree, and bullfinches whistled quietly over his head; newly arrived chiffchaffs and willow warblers sang in every bush and treetop. When he turned he saw the blue sea, now washing far below; and the whole extent of Lyme Bay reaching round, diminishing cliffs that dropped into the endless yellow saber of the Chesil Bank, whose remote tip touched that strange English Gibraltar, Portland Bill, a thin gray shadow wedged between the azures.
> Only one art has caught such scenes—that of the Renaissance, it

is the ground that Botticelli's figures walk on, the air that includes Ronsard's songs. It does not matter what that cultural revolution's conscious aims and purposes, its cruelties and failures were; in essence the Renaissance was simply the green end of one of civilization's hardest winters. It was an end to chains, bounds, frontiers. Its device was the only device: What is, is good. It was all, in short, that Charles's age was not; but do not think that as he stood there he did not know this. It is true that to explain his obscure feeling of malaise, of inappropriateness, of limitation, he went back closer home—to Rousseau, and the childish myths of a Golden Age and the Noble Savage. That is, he tried to dismiss the inadequacies of his own time's approach to nature by supposing that one cannot reenter a legend. He told himself he was too pampered, too spoiled by civilization, ever to inhabit nature again; and that made him sad, in a not unpleasant bittersweet sort of way. After all, he was a Victorian. We could not expect him to see what we are only just beginning—and with so much more knowledge and existentialist philosophy at our disposal—to realize ourselves: that the desire to hold and the desire to enjoy are mutually destructive. His statement to himself should have been, "I possess this now, therefore I am happy," instead of what it so Victorianly was: "I cannot possess this forever, and therefore am sad."[31]

This English Garden of Eden, visited by the hero of *The French Lieutenant's Woman* on a spring day in 1867, is far more than a picturesque description of a garden overlooking Lyme Bay, a starting-off place for novelistic character development. It is a potent literary-historical indicator, an evocation of landscape so codified, so pastorally sited, so replete with canonical imagery of the *locus,* that it demands comparison with the cool spot near Plato's Ilissus. Even in an unpastoral context, the rather extravagant description of this English garden contains all the components which the *Phaedrus* has taught us to look for in pastoral texts: 1) a restorative natural setting outside and beyond city walls; the oasis, in this case, "quenched his thirst and cooled his brow"; 2) the triadic composition of "slope," "little brook," and "some high tree," which remains remarkably consistent even in Romantic and modern versions (Wordsworth's "meadow, grove and stream," for example, still figures as a shorthand *locus* at the head of his Immortality Ode); 3) the appeal to the various senses; 4) the sound of birdsong; 5) the flower catalogue, which becomes in Spenser and Milton the curious trademark of the aspiring careerist, elegiac or epithalamic.

The actual place, with its distinctly literary feel, also encourages, in a second movement of this extended description, meditation on the scene's significant and typical—that is, conventional and therefore illustrative for our purposes—pastoral attitudes. First and most important, we gain a double perspective by means of the clash Charles imagines between his own "obscure feeling of malaise, of inappropriateness, of limitation" (not far, I suspect, from Milton's sense of his own "belatednesse") and what he deems pure and original. Where earlier pastoralists might measure their own song against a predecessor's blazing orphic presence, the idealizing vision here falls upon a whole period, "the art of the Renaissance," that "green end of one of civilization's hardest winters," assigning to that earlier period the pastoral symbolism of bower or green place. Even Charles, however, is aware that to invest the scene with traditional Edenic associations is to have recourse to primitivism—a "childish myth." But all pastoral, and not only that of Charles's Victorian sensibility, turns upon exclusion from whatever a poet deems canonical and original—"he tried to dismiss the inadequacies of his own time's approach to nature by supposing that one cannot reenter a legend"—and generally mourns loss of that immediacy in one of two ways: either it voices compensation for what has been lost by substituting a replacement poetics, by the act of vocalizing itself, or else it records the impossibility of transcendence by singing a dirge for the forever-lost presence which the orphic poet names Eurydice.[32]

2

The Funeral Elegy and Careerism: Theocritus, Virgil, Spenser

I

When William Empson calls death "the trigger of the literary man's biggest gun"[1] and smartly catalogs those attitudes toward it which "tell you what else to love," or substitute for it "any conceived calm," he cuts through centuries of cultural hypocrisy in the treatment of death which pervades even the most recent criticism of the funeral elegy. Beneath both Empson's blankness in face of the existential fact of death and Milton's baroque, blatantly excessive lament for King lies the recognition that the "sad occasion dear" provides the impetus for the finest of literary performances. Neither, I think, confuses art with life in the way that Ellen Lambert does in her *Placing Sorrow*.[2] Lambert's meticulous scholarship is crippled by the central premise of her book: she burdens elegy with the task of "placing sorrow" in a "concrete, palpable world, a world in which the elegist can place diffuse, intangible feelings and thereby win his release from suffering" (xiii). And "everything in these laments," she continues, "from the opening lines of the frame to the herdsman's final exchange, bears upon the healing process, works to console us" (xv). Likening "literary conventions" to "behavioral conventions," she obscures the very nature of literary *mimesis:* the peculiarly literary feel of inherited landscapes, the ritual submission to a ritualized literary form, the initiation of the individual talent at the hands of tradition. We do not read *Lycidas* to be consoled, any more than Milton wrote it to "win his release from suffering" (xvii). As Northrop Frye reminds us, Milton had in fact been "practising since adolescence on every fresh corpse in sight, from the university beadle to the fair infant dying of a cough."[3] Just as Bion's dirge gives Moschus his first chance to seize those pipes which are his first inheritance of song, so King's elegy is but a pretense for Milton's first great literary "appearance."[4]

If the writing of pastorals constitutes since Virgil a literary apprenticeship for poets, the funeral elegy is the most formal expression of aspiring careerism. Of all pastoral forms it has come down to us most intact. It remains the most rigidly codified, the most elevated—indeed vatic—in tone as pastoral can muster. Treating, after Theocritus, of the death of a friend-forebear, it guarantees, under the guise of singing a dirge, a kind of literary immortality to the singer. It offers him a chance to confront the tradition poetically on a sanctioned literary stage. It promises him an audience of initiates who can be depended upon to interpret its relation to the canon, to measure its departures from the norm. Whereas for Theocritus the elegy was a frontispiece, announcing his literary program, already in Virgil it has become a poet's way of bidding farewell to the pastoral mode, of singing an elegy for a phase of his own life. It is to this significance of elegy that Virginia Woolf appeals when she labels her *To the Lighthouse* an "elegy."[5] The act of writing the novel was a "necessary act" which laid familial and artistic ghosts to rest. I wish to argue here that we read as elegy in just this sense both Plato's "prose idyll," the *Phaedrus*,[6] and the first idyll of Theocritus: these texts stage a scenario of ritual competition which parallels, in its drama of succession, the very "narrative" or "plot" of elegy itself.[7] By ritually celebrating the death of a fellow poet or master, a new poet separates himself from the forebear and simultaneously offers himself as a successor at singing.[8] After Virgil, the most important convention of elegy becomes the deification of the dead one in a process that lifts him out of nature, out of the poem, and, conveniently, out of the inheritor's way. This scene of succession at the heart of elegy uniquely suits the genre, more than other "programmatic" poetic forms such as satire or love elegy, to an enactment of ceremonial initiation.

To study the elegy as a kind of literary initiation ritual is to examine—with the help of Van Gennep, Eliade, and other historians of rites of passage—the symbolic language which has attended upon its celebration since Plato, and to record and evaluate translations of that imagery in the work of successive poets widely separated in time. To that end I have assembled a series of "key texts"—Theocritus's first idyll, Virgil's fifth eclogue, and Spenser's "November," and brief mention of Calpurnius's and Nemesianus's elegies in conclusion—which manifest in their juxtaposition the development of elegy as genre. Although my linear scheme may invite interpretation as a reading of direct and unmediated influence, I am less interested in establishing pastoral continuities generally in the line of texts I marshal than in marking the point at which pastoral setting and initiatory moment collide in the poetic scenario of the funeral elegy. My aim is to compile not a history of influence but a comparison of pastoral initiations-by-elegy, a profile of the pastorally launched career.

II

What most commentators on Theocritus forget, canonizing him as the "originator" of pastoral poetry, is that he received, like any other poet, a vast and encompassing literary legacy. The curious immediacy of Theocritus's first idyll—the vital presence of the subject at his own funeral ritual, bucolic song contest energetically and spontaneously portrayed—has led critics to assume that the poem "makes no reference to anything outside itself" (Lambert, 22–23), as if any literary product could spring full-blown from the forehead of its creator. The first idyll, so far as we can ascertain, does not look backward upon a tradition of pastoral elegy proper against which it must define itself, but it does declare its independence from, celebrate the symbolic death of, other prevailing literary traditions: notably, heroic and tragic high-classical forms, confessional lyric, contemporary criticism, perhaps even Platonic philosophy. No doubt Theocritus felt as strongly as any Alexandrian "what the old epigram once said of Plato: that in whatever direction you happened to set out, you met him on his way back."[9]

The time is long past for seeing Theocritus as the "romantic" poet of Sicily, conveying a nostalgic picture of rustic life. As John Van Sickle reminds us: "Alexandrian poetry, made by poets conscious of their craft and its traditions, acts as a form of criticism, offering judgments implicit but intelligible to careful readers."[10] The reading of the first idyll I wish to offer here—as a staging, a dialogue, in which a younger singer is initiated into the proper use of *otium* and bucolic song by an older one—results in a view of Theocritus as possessor of a very different literary ethos from that normally attributed to him. He is a deliberate transformer of poetic convention, very much aware of the generic and philosophic traditions against which he strained. The eleventh idyll, for example, opens and closes with the identification of poetry as *pharmakon*, at once remedy and poison. Plato's *Phaedrus,* of course, turns on the same double possibility for writing: discourse can be good or bad, a medicine for the soul which guarantees transcendent vision and devotion to philosophical life, or it can be the bad news, the falsifying, deceitful kind of writing that Phaedrus clutches under his cloak. Theocritus puts the same word into Polyphemus's mouth, signifying his understanding of this double nature of language.[11] The first idyll, similarly, offers two possibilities for singing and sets them against each other—both formally, in the very structure of the poem's division between frame and inset songs, and metaphorically, in the contrast between the central symbols of the two songs; finally, it celebrates the awarding of the bowl to the younger singer, not to acknowledge his superiority over the goatherd, as many critics have believed, but to symbolize the transference of the unnamed goatherd's values, his conception of pastoral poetry, to the young initiate.[12] It is into the literary, as against the philosophic or even the bucolic, life that Thyrsis is initiated.

The frame of the first idyll, which introduces and ultimately contains the "woes of Daphnis,"[13] becomes intelligible as a ritual literary gesture when placed next to the opening of the *Phaedrus*. Like the Dialogue, it begins with a series of metaphoric contrasts and a homely challenge. The two pastoral participants engage in sophisticated repartee and exchange attitudes couched in terms of shepherds' absolutes. As a prologue, their spare, stylized conversation is not unlike that preliminary philosophical discussion in mythic terms that announces Socrates' stance against the rationalists. In Theocritus's idyll, Thyrsis promises the lesser of two gifts to Pan to the goatherd in exchange for his "sweet ... piping" (5); the latter, a superior dialectician—and in his disclaimers very Socratic—answers Thyrsis part for part. In exchange for singing his "sweeter" song, Thyrsis will receive whatever the Nymphs do not choose, even if they pick the lesser gift. Deferring to his opponent by improving upon his challenge, he honors his adversary and dynamically continues the song. Theocritus lifts motifs from the Dialogue in order to find a place for them in the new kind of poetry he announces, and transforms them in the process: formulaic landscape, noon hour, cicadae, even Platonic longing for transcendence, receive revisionary treatment in the pastoralist's hands. But he remains loyal to one thing: the initiation ritual which takes place in the *locus,* in the country, by water, beneath a cooling tree.

A second symbolic gesture preceding the pastoral dirge is the selection of an appropriate landscape in which to sing. Lambert undermines its importance as a literary symbol when she writes that "we feel as if we were in a world whose objects we could reach out and grasp" (5). I do not mean to imply that the landscape chosen is wooden, lacking in sensuous appeal, but its literary antecedents are obvious: Thyrsis's offer to sit on a slope and mind the other's goats is topped by the goatherd's rejoinder—he rejects the real Sicilian shepherds' landscape in favor of a literary one like that chosen by Socrates in the *Phaedrus:*

> Come hither then, and let us sit beneath the elm,
> facing Priapus and the springs, where is yon shepherds' seat
> and the oaks. (5–7)

The choice of a sacred, recognizable literary landscape as the *locus* of this pastoral song is telling, alerting us to the difference between this poem and real scenes of shepherds sitting on a "sloping knoll" among the "tamarisks." But the goatherd's addition to the familiar three-part composition—grove, spring, comforting slope—may be intended to defamiliarize our expectations here, even though the presence of Priapus in a Platonic grove bespeaks tensions latent in pastoral even before Theocritus.

Three times the unnamed goatherd is victor over Thyrsis. By declining to pipe at noon "for fear of Pan" who "is resting wearied from the chase," he succeeds in getting Thyrsis to "sing the woes of Daphnis." Thyrsis is induced to sing much as Phaedrus is seduced into reading Lysias's speech, by means of flattery—you "art come to mastery in pastoral song"—and the promise of rewards. The noon hour is redefined in pastoral terms: by their use of it, each of the singers characterizes himself. In his rhetorical refusal to sing then in deference to Pan, the goatherd signifies not real fear of Pan but wary respect for the special charge, as T. G. Rosenmeyer puts it, of the noon hour.[14] Thyrsis, whose song of Daphnis's woes is a confessional lyric of self-indulgence in love, is content to be its representative singer; in his enthusiasm to show off, he seems unaware of the ritual demands of the time of day. In fact Thyrsis's improper use of *otium* is the central issue of the idyll. But before turning to the goatherd's challenge of Thyrsis's stance, we must examine in more detail Thyrsis's "pastoral song" itself.

Paradoxically, Thyrsis's song, containing Daphnis's dirge, manifests all the structural and metaphoric conventions to be repeatedly and at times ludicrously imitated by later pastoralists, who missed, perhaps, the verve of the unnamed goatherd's ironies. His song includes the invocation to the Muses, reproach of the nymphs for their absence, appeal to a mythic landscape, use of the pathetic fallacy, description of a cortège of visitors to the deceased, diatribe against nature for her role in the untimely death of the subject, the ritual appeal to Pan and the Nymphs. The song falls into three parts, roughly analogous to the three scenes on the cup described in the goatherd's song, and punctuated by changes in the refrain. "Begin, dear Muses, begin the pastoral song" introduces the section exploring the nature of Daphnis's sickness unto death and recording the responses of two visitors, Hermes and Priapus. "Begin, dear Muses, begin again the pastoral song" sounds repeatedly through the section in which Daphnis confronts Aphrodite's version of Priapus's advice. The final section—marked by "Cease, Muses, come cease the pastoral song"—concludes with a prayer to Pan, as in the *Phaedrus,* a farewell to the pleasant place from the lips of the dying Daphnis and a farewell to the nymphs. Thyrsis receives for his pains the promised carved cup.

Yet, and this remains our problem, Thyrsis's song is undermined repeatedly in the poem, not only by its placement, its containment between the gibes of the goatherd, but also by his implicit criticism of its very content. Critics of the poem have long been troubled by Daphnis's larger-than-life stature in the poem, but most attribute it, wrongly I feel, to his actual physical presence at his own funeral. Rosenmeyer worries about *otium*'s equilibrium "when the heroic herdsman occupies the center of the stage," but is content to call him "pastoral man writ large."[15] In fact Daphnis is the opposite of "pastoral man" in this poem: he is a tragic actor, a "second Hippolytus,"[16] resolutely defending his tragic choice with a vigor that even Rosenmeyer views as "bordering on *hubris.*"[17] He is a parody of a Platonic lover in pastoral guise, refusing the earthly pleasures that Aphrodite offers in favor of the passionate, otherworldly claim of eros; he is an inward-turned singer of lyric self-absorbedly enjoying his excess of suffering. In short, Daphnis has to die within the idyll: he is the representative of poetic forms dead and deadening to Theocritus. Epic, tragedy, lyric, all need transvaluing in his new Alexandrian poetics. The pipes go back to Pan at the end of Thyrsis's song because Daphnis's song exceeds them—his is not "pastoral song," however much Thrysis would like it to be.[18]

What is properly pastoral in the poem—and clearly this idyll, placed first in the collection, is intended as an *ars poetica*—is all that is offered in contrast to the "woes of Daphnis." Even within the song of Thyrsis, the three visitors challenge Daphnis's stance, providing a standard of judgment against which we can measure Daphnis's excess. Hermes, who comes first, is protector of flocks and herds, an ancient fertility god and true guardian of the pastoral *locus;* he seems willing to call Daphnis "friend" but finds his torment as perplexing as do Priapus and Aphrodite, advocates of a warm, unserious eroticism instead of enslavement to love. Aphrodite is spokesman here for that "nexus of activity including joy, sexual pleasure, perceptual awareness, song, in sum, with the 'sweetness' of life,"[19] that dominant tone of the herdsmen's encounter established in the opening lines of the poem. The growing concord between the pastoral singers' attitudes aligns with her stance and not Daphnis's: they too would counsel an affair over melodramatic self-denial. Rosenmeyer himself notices that Priapus and Aphrodite "are good Epicureans"—predisposition for which philosophical orientation he wishes to attribute to Theocritus—but he wonders inconclusively that "not Daphnis, but Priapus and Aphrodite . . . are the spokesmen for this attitude in Idyll I."[20]

The strongest pressure on the self-termed "pastoral song" of Thyrsis is, of course, the presence of the unnamed goatherd, secret hero of the poem. He excels at dialectics; he locates and personalizes the literary landscape lifted from Plato; and he refuses to misuse the noon hour; finally, his words embrace and place in perspective the song of Thyrsis. His ecphrastic description of the cup, with its vivid *tableaux vivants,* is both a preface to Thrysis's song and implicit criticism of it. Critics from

Rapin to the present have wrongly lamented the lack of unity in the first idyll, the poem's division between two "centers of interest" and "two different tones."[21] Few view as deliberate the effect of the meticulously rendered cup, which is more than extended description of the proffered bait. It does, in fact, "delay the action, and it sets up a different mood from that of Daphnis' song":[22] the reader is asked to consider the exaggerated contrast between the two sorts of poetry. The goatherd's evocation is practical, anti-romantic; his description of the cup begins with praise of its usefulness. On every front he undermines Thyrsis's song to come. He demonstrates a dry, suggestive, symbolic poetry corresponding to the program of the Alexandrians, a poetics directly opposed to the sentimentality of lyric, the trite repetition of post-Homeric epic, the otherworldliness of Platonic philosophy.

By means of static pictorial description the goatherd manages to convey complex, even ambivalent, images of *otium* used wrongly, examples which bear directly on the story of Daphnis's "woes" to follow. The first of these is an image of wasted passion in which "two men with long fair locks" gaze with longing at a fair maiden who plays them off against each other. In the second, human cunning interferes with nature: an "old fisherman" "gathers up a great net for a cast." In the last vignette, a "little boy" becomes so involved in weaving a basket to entrap cicadae (perhaps an image, within the text itself, of Thyrsis's own artistic product) that he loses the fruit of his harvest when two foxes carry off the grapes from his vineyard and his breakfast as well. All three scenes warn of the dangers of self-absorption. In fact the goatherd here champions a relaxed, perceptive, creative, but pragmatic, use of *otium*. Plato, of course, distrusts *otium* except when its use is philosophical. How the pastoral goatherd secularizes that sacred time of day—he merely wishes Thyrsis might take himself less seriously!

The goatherd's final function in the poem is best illustrated by the last words of his song, and the final lines of the idyll. Twice, literally and figuratively, he has the last word over Thrysis, whose song so compellingly dominates the poem. At the end of his description of the cup, he caps the message of his song:

> come, sir, for of a surety
> thou canst not carry thy singing to Hades that brings
> forgetfulness of all things. (8–9)

The *carpe diem* note was never perhaps sounded so simply, so practically, so good-heartedly. And its bias is strongly anti-Platonic, even Epicurean as Rosenmeyer would have it. It is the goatherd's subtly masked irony and not Thyrsis's youthful confidence in his singing prowess that lies at the heart of the Theocritean pastoral attitude. In the final lines of the poem the goatherd becomes the "dominant character, or winner of the contest"—which Rosenmeyer is unwilling to concede to him here—"who achieves the humorous breakthrough designed to subvert the threat of overrefinement."[23]

> Come hither, Cissaetha; and do thou milk her.
> And you she-goats be not so friskly lest the he-goat
> rouse himself. (15)

This line not only throws a wrench into the serious, inflated machinery of Daphnis's funeral, but it harks back to the comic ironies of Priapus, leaving his warning with the listener in the last line of the poem. Equally ironic is the goatherd's good-natured praise of Thyrsis's singing as better than the cicadae. In the *Phaedrus,* cicadae were halfway creatures, the proper imitation of which promised most creative use of the noon hour. To call Thyrsis's obvious misuse of it here better than their sacred duty is too extravagant not to be ironic. The overall effect of the ending of the poem, however, is friendly and restorative. As Harriet Edquist puts it, "an all-consuming destructive *eros*" is supplanted by a "more fruitful and productive *philia*."

If indeed this poem is to be viewed as a poetic manifesto, Daphnis cannot remain its protagonist, even within the sealed-off song of Thyrsis; his rebirth cannot be celebrated. The critical debate over the manner of his death, centering upon the precise translation for the "waters" that close over him or the symbolic weight to accord his death by drowning, goes too far when it insists upon Orphic immortality for a resuscitated Daphnis.[25] The passing reference to resurrection—Aphrodite "would have raised him up again," signifying her readiness to compromise—which becomes in later pastoral elegies a convention (apotheosis of the dead), is quickly countered by the words: "but all the thread the Fates assigned was run, and Daphnis went to the stream." The deliberate vagueness about the location and symbolism of these waters is designed, I feel, to counteract the suggestion that anything awaits Daphnis besides drowning. The impulse to panegyric and transcendence here is roundly denied, antithetical in fact to the Epicurean bias of Theocritean pastoral. When Ellen Lambert writes that "Daphnis too must make his song heard even in Hades. More is involved here than a playful challenge, for, in the end, everything depends upon how far our songs can carry," she puts more pressure on the poem than it can bear (8). For Theocritus, Daphnis's desire for transcendence, his longing to see his passion absorbed in a higher order, circumvents *otium*. If anyone is to sing a "better song," as the idyll tells us in the second singer's words, it is Thyrsis, who, by means of an initiatory pastoral exchange with the unnamed goatherd, has learned to spend the noon hour more wisely.

III

Virgil honors the centrality of Theocritus's first idyll by imitating it twice in his *Bucolics,* and both times at strategic locations. Virgil actually doubles Theocritus twice: he doubles the dirge of Daphnis by assigning it to two singers, and he doubles the elegy itself by writing two, the fifth and tenth eclogues. The fifth poem, which closes the first half of the book, is a bold restaging of the initiatory scenario: wholly transformed here are the shamanistic induction of a young initiate by a wise elder, the deliberate, careful choice of landscape, the symbolic *agon* of the singing-contest fiction, and, finally, the telling exchange of gifts. Finding a new way to present the familiar scene functions as an initiation ritual for the poet himself: this poem is, for the bucolic corpus of Virgil, as much a statement of program as it was for Theocritus. But the fact that it closes, rather than opens, the first half of the collection points to an important change in the idea of pastoral as an apprenticeship, a revaluation that begins with Virgil. When, in the last eclogue, he rewrites not only Idyll I but also his own fifth bucolic, the literary function of pastoral elegy becomes clear: by celebrating in ritual fashion the death of a fellow poet—Mopsus is specifically rewarded for poetically mourning his "master's" passing—a poet announces his own literary aspirations. In the tenth eclogue he is free to go beyond the formula, to sing himself out of the pastoral world and to mourn the passing of an entire phase of his own life.

From the first lines of the fifth eclogue, the reader is aware of a certain staginess in its enactment: the poem is so stylized in its symmetries, the elements in the opening dialogue are so willfully manipulated, that the reader's attention to the poem's artistry is guaranteed. Even the pastoral participants seem to know why they are here. Since a rewriting of the initiatory scenario amounts to mastery of it, Virgil's Mopsus is a very different sort of *mystes* from Theocritus's Thyrsis. He acts as director of the scene, subtly manipulating the apparently acquiescent Menalcas. In this poem the younger poet determines the conditions of the scene of instruction; he becomes a maker of ritual.

The fifth bucolic is a dialogue with Virgil's literary predecessor. Like the first idyll it begins with a proposed singing contest, but the stage directions of the former poem are systematically inverted. The master goatherd of Idyll I who finds the *locus* and determines which song Thyrsis will sing is irreverently parodied here by a very self-confident young herdsman who assumes the authority to make those choices himself. He rejects outright Menalcas's proposal for a traditional site for singing (and with it the landscapes of Plato and Theocritus) even as he pretends to defer to his counsel:

> Tu maior; tibi me est aequum parere, Menalca,
> siue sub incertas Zephyris motantibus umbras
> siue antro potius succedimus. aspice, ut antrum
> siluestris raris sparsit labrusca racemis.[26]

> You are the elder, Menalcas: it's for me to fall in with your wishes.
> Shall we go under the trees, where light airs stir the shadows,
> Or would you prefer a cave?—look, there is one, its opening
> Festooned with hanging swags of wild vine, over there.[27]

The cave—a new location for a new song—is rightly associated symbolically with poetry-making;[28] it evokes as well the darkness of epic *descensus,* that rite of passage which suggests poetic initiation at its most symbolic.

Twice more Mopsus rewrites the rules. He undercuts Menalcas's age and stature by bristling at his elder's comparison of him with Amyntas and responding ironically to the intended praise. In a third matching of wits, the younger proves himself once again preeminent. Unlike Theocritus's Thyrsis, who gladly took the goatherd's flattering suggestion, Mopsus elects to sing a song which does not number among the three typical pastoral subjects Menalcas suggests. His proposal to sing a new song recently written on green bark is a signal of sorts: we are to look here for a new kind of pastoral poetry. In the last lines of the frame, the wager and establishing of prizes is noteworthy by its absence: the outcome of this encounter is prearranged. Mopsus's rather perfunctory graduation to poetic stature, his accession to the title of his master, will be symbolized by an *exchange* of gifts at the end of the poem.

In several important ways, Virgil's poem is a "later" one, to make a statement about literary history, than Theocritus's. In the first instance it marks a shift from victim to survivor: "Exstinctum . . . Daphnin" is the precondition of the poem.[29] Whereas Daphnis was a marginal inhabitant of the pastoral world of Theocritus, Virgil makes room for him within the pastoral here, where he stands, lifted bodily from the predecessor's poem, for the predecessor himself. Second, the poem warns against too great reliance on nature or naturalness for inspiration, emphasizing instead the shaping power of imagination upon nature. Menalcas underscores the dependence of this poem on art itself when he concedes, praising Mopsus, that the willow and valerian are inferior to the cultivated olive and rose. Then, too, Theocritus's and Plato's initiation scenes were strongly father-based: the elder in each case bestows vision upon a younger man. In Virgil we mark the beginning of a shift toward greater equality in their exchange; this initiation is a cooperative venture. Finally, the pose of spontaneity in the first idyll is replaced here with the whole historical apparatus of writing, recording, engraving. Thyrsis's song, like that of a rhapsode, was on the tip of his tongue and could be rendered orally upon demand. Mopsus's song, on the other hand, has been first written down and now will be sung from memory. We think here of that shift in cultural transmission marked by the *Phaedrus*—the change from oral to written culture, the nostalgia that it evokes and the opportunity it provides for the creation of essentially new cultural artifacts, parodies of the old. Virgil's poem stands in a derivative relation to Theocritus's: no wonder, then, that Daphnis's song at his own passing figures in the fifth bucolic in a powerful image, that of an epitaph engraved upon a tombstone. A literary tradition, seemingly, has been created in the interim.

The surprise of this son-dominated poem, however, is the worthiness of the two opponents: Mopsus's initiation includes recognition of the older singer's wisdom. Cooperation between them will be needed to lay Daphnis properly to rest, for in Virgil's poem the dirge will require fulfillment by a panegyric. When Paul Alpers writes that Virgil is the "speaker of all his characters' speeches,"[30] he gets at the real significance of the doubling: it takes two speakers here to engrave Daphnis's tombstone, to honor Theocritus as forebear, but also to correct the vision of poetry and of the poetic life offered in the first idyll. Mopsus's song fulfilled by Menalcas's, the dirge paired with and completed by consolation, represents a revision of Theocritus's poem.

Menalcas's panegyric cannot be seen as the definitive statement of the poem. In fact the two songs taken together constitute the real strength of Virgil's response to the predecessor poem: structurally, the second song echoes the first, but echoes between songs are established as well. Mopsus's song begins where Theocritus's leaves off and records the impact of Daphnis's death upon the pastoral world. He concretizes and condenses the first idyll, echoing many of its motifs, but he also subtly alters Thyrsis's portrait of Daphnis as an exiled wanderer. In Theocritus, Daphnis was content to call himself a neatherd—"I am Daphnis that herded here his cows, and watered here his bulls and calves" (13). Within Mopsus's song, however, he articulates his desire for a fame known even to the stars by speaking his own epitaph:

> 'Daphnis ego in siluis, hinc usque ad sidera notus,
> formosi pecoris custos, formosior ipse.' (ll. 44–45)
>
> 'I lived in woods, my fame lives in the stars:
> lovely my flock was, lovelier I.' (39)

It is Mopsus who makes Daphnis a *custos* of the land and who gives Menalcas the dominant image for his song: Daphnis enstarred.

The real force of Mopsus's song, however, is to give us a portrait of nature operating threateningly apart from human intervention.[31] Nature is bereft after Daphnis's death of that shaping consciousness whose singing voice answers it Orpheus-like part for part.[32] The failure of imagination that Mopsus experiences after Daphnis's death, the fear that he will be unable to match the singing fame of his master in pastoral song, is read onto the landscape by means of the pathetic fallacy: stars appear cruelly distant; animals display uncharacteristic behavior; nature reverses her courses. In Theocritus's poem the "sweet" collusion between man and nature gives way to disjunction only when Daphnis rather vengefully wishes havoc on the pastoral world from which he is excluded. In Virgil's poem, nature's upheaval, her threatening *adynata,* is a response to the vacuum left by a very human singer, an orphic poet who must manage nature's rhythms. Order, fertility, song, can only be restored by a successor to Daphnis, a possibility not even tendered in the first idyll.

Menalcas's panegyric, which celebrates just this occurrence, is not independent of Mopsus's dirge; from the first song he takes an image of Daphnis as *genius loci* of the pastoral world. Menalcas too echoes Mopsus's definition of him as he who led the revellers in a kind of Bacchic ritual, a fertility celebration which guaranteed the continued protection of Ceres, harvest goddess, and Apollo, lord of song. What the second song does add to the first, however, is the promise that Daphnis's power over the lands—like the orphic power of song—can be repossessed, indeed inherited. Nature can be restored by imaginative means. The "rites" offered to Daphnis are not funerary but initiatory: offerings of oil, milk, and wine flow as in Bacchic rituals; the festivities take on the lineaments of an Orphic celebration; singing, dancing, and general merriment punctuate the experience.

The reference to a fertility ritual in both songs has been variously explained,[33] but the allusions to celebration of the Mysteries, I think, are not at all out of place in this initiation poem. In *De Legibus,* Cicero associates the deification of Bacchus with mystic rituals which enable us to transform our fear of death into imaginative strength:

> nam mihi cum multa
> eximia divinaque videntur Athenae tuae peperisse
> atque in vitam hominum attulisse, tum nihil melius
> illis mysteriis, quibus ex agresti immanique vita
> exculti ad humanitatem et mitigati sumus, initiaque
> ut appellantur, ita re vera principia vitae cognovimus;
> neque solum cum laetitia vivendi rationem accepimus,
> sed etiam cum spe meliore moriendi.
>
> For among the many
> excellent and indeed divine institutions which
> your Athens has brought forth and contributed to
> human life, none, in my opinion, is better than
> those mysteries. For by their means we have been
> brought out of our barbarous and savage mode of life
> and educated and refined to a state of civilization;
> and as the rites are called "initiations," so in very
> truth we have learned from them the beginnings of
> life, and have gained the power not only to live
> happily, but also to die with a better hope.[34]

Michael Putnam too uses the language of the Mysteries when he explains the awarding of the reed pipe to the younger singer by the elder: the "acknowledgement [of "nature's more violent side"] is enough for Menalcas to initiate his young colleague further into the mysteries of song."[35] Although the traditional view of the fifth eclogue holds that "Mopsus has been indoctrinated into a new aspect of poetry which broke with tradition,"[36] the induction, I think, has not been so one-sided as we have thought. In fact the fifth bucolic celebrates the mutual enlightenment of the two singers. Menalcas gladly hails Mopsus as *diuina poeta* and commends him as a worthy successor to his master. He also rewards his accession with a pastoral reed pipe: the very act of handing on the reed on which Menalcas learned to sing pastoral song implies transfer of poetic power. The exchange has been utterly civilized, for Menalcas's song too has depended upon Mopsus's for its inspiration. The upstart who so took charge of his own initiation ceremony, once he achieves the imaginative mastery to teach nature to sing—that is, orphic power—is entitled to hand the crook to Menalcas. A symbol of friendship, of shepherding, both literal and otherwise, it effectively registers age as well.

The problem with the fifth eclogue, in Poggioli's words, is "whether we identify the funeral elegy it contains with one of its two songs or with both of them."[37] For it is the consolation and not the lament which becomes the dominant motif of the elegy; particularly among Christian imitators of the form, it becomes inseparable from the dirge. Virgil saw something psychologically true (and perhaps politically profitable) in Daphnis's longing for transcendence in the first idyll, in spite of the gods' and Theocritus's own determination to reconcile him to the modulated pleasures of *hayschia*. The panegyric, hailed as "Virgil's most important contribution to elegy,"[38] clearly accomplishes two things for the poet. On the one hand it allows him, within the elegy's initiatory structure, to praise his boyhood political hero. Virgil's pastorals, as Putnam most notably has pointed out, know the cost and rewards of politics: he comments elsewhere in the eclogues on the relation between politics and poetry. And a hymn of praise to a ruler, a paean to a patron of sorts, is hardly out of place in the elegy, a symbolic statement of the poet's literary aspirations. In the second place—and here we return to Virgil's view of the poet as a teacher of nature—the panegyric effectively reverses nature's courses and celebrates the singer's dominion over natural processes. To deify is to lift out of nature, to conquer nature by imposing a timeless structure upon her cycles. Man's mortality is classically viewed in pastoral elegy as inferior to nature's eternal continuity, but apotheosis is preferable even to her seasonal round. The pastoral Adonis here begins to undergo the transformation charted by Renaissance scholars like Richard Cody and David Wagenknecht: the hero of elegy, freed of the yearly repetition of funeral and wedding rites, becomes an Orpheus—an Orpheus who, singing, controls his world, not an Adonis who yearly must submit to it.

After a song of death—"exstinctum"—through which one sublimates one's own threatened mortality, there comes a song of celebration—"candidus." The language and imagery of elegy reverse in the consolation. The initiate's exultation at his mastery of death causes mourning to spill over into its opposite: spring follows on the heels of winter; the sequestered ones seek reintegration with the community; literary appearance suddenly calls for an appropriate audience of witnesses. Later poets were to recognize in the rites Menalcas wanted for Daphnis the lineaments of a wedding feast. Spenser, as we shall presently see, will be compelled to balance the dirge explicitly with a wedding song within the natural scheme of his own apprenticeship sequence, the *Shepheardes Calender*. In fact Spenser's Platonism will find ultimate expression in epithalamium rather than elegy. Milton too echoes the *hieros gamos*,[39] that ritual culmination of the Mystery festivals, in the "inexpressive nuptial song" of his *Lycidas*, the consoling "immortal nuptials" of his *Epitaphium Damonis*.

IV

Edmund Spenser's pastoral poetry offers us one of the Renaissance's most complex "poetic mingling[s] of the languages of love and death or pain and pleasure."[40] In fact the range of imagery and overt careerism shared by the wedding poem and funeral dirge becomes explicit here. Two of Spenser's poems demand to be read next to Virgil's fifth bucolic: where Virgil doubled Theocritus's poem by assigning it to two singers, in the *Calender* Spenser writes two poems to Virgil's one, answering part for part the two songs of the Daphnis poem. As early as the *Shepheardes Calender* we have a precedent for hiding the face of ambition behind a pastoral mask,[41] as well as evidence for the convergence of two genres eminently suited to articulating career issues, elegy and epithalamium. In fact the almost chiastic relationship between "Aprill" and "November" here anticipates the interpenetration of elegiac and epithalamic modes in Spenser's marriage poems, the later *Epithalamion* and *Prothalamion*. Metrically related, authored by Colin, resonant with Elizabethan political mythology,[42] linked by possible references to Elizabeth in "November,"[43] organized around the bipolar opposition of marriage and death, these two eclogues are resting places in the *Calender* and both tender the possibility of orphic success: both "Aprill" and "November" combine a vision of this world and the *champs élysées;* both hint that Colin prefigures Spenser's own transition from *poeta* to *vates;* both aim at lifting the bridal subject out of nature's round into transcendent realms; finally, both point to a way out of Colin's labyrinth of love by means of poetically sublimated eroticism. An important connection exists between the female subject of Spenser's mourning in "November" and apotheosis in "Aprill" and his nuptial odes, the future conversion of epithalamium into a poetry of ambition. Consolation far outshadows mourning here: not only are career aspirations, for Spenser, best articulated in the wedding song, but the nuptial mode offers greater range to the orphic voice than elegy's more traditional procedures of apotheosis. The elegy's record of failure here and the epithalamium's successful counterpressure call for a reconsideration of the relationship between these twin genres. Before treating the "November" eclogue, Spenser's *Calender* version of the elegy, and its companion piece, the "Aprill" blazon to Elisa, we turn first briefly to the "August" eclogue, in which Spenser playfully rewrites the opening scenario of the pastoral contest.

That the pastoral initiation of Spenser's *Calender* was virtually a *fait accompli* can be seen in the confidence with which he alters inherited patterns. Early on in the sequence he inverts the conventional pastoral respect of youth for age by awarding the palm to the younger. In

"Februarie," Cuddie is all but deferential to the hoary Thenot; E.K.'s notes insist that "olde men are muche more enclined to such fond fooleries, then younger heades" ("Februarie," Embleme, 28). The August poem too is a healthy impertinence: Spenser casts Cuddie as the arbiter of two pastoral songs. Instead of judging the contest, Cuddie offers a song of his own, a lay so intricate, so calculated in its effects, that it overshadows the others. The pastoral exchange between Perigot and Willye—stichic, stylized, and utterly perfunctory—is a fine foil for Cuddie's song, an elaborate Petrarchan sestina. Both performers nominally get a prize; but Cuddie, shadowing Colin, is here "ycrouned . . . / In Colins stede" (ll. 145–46). Casting his predecessors in a parody of amoebean song, Spenser offers in contrast one of the most self-consciously literary songs in the *Calender,* as if Spenser's own pastoral predecessors were being both parodied and superseded by the sestina Cuddie sings. In fact references to singing as a specifically literary activity are so numerous here as to invite comparison with Virgil's fifth bucolic: as in Virgil's poem, *carmina* are proof of human mastery of nature, Orphic mastery of her unmanageability.

The *Calender* in fact investigates, as Colin tells us in the first eclogue, what happens when "barrein ground, whome winters wrath hath wasted, / Art made a myrrhour, to behold my plight" ("Januarye," ll. 19–20), when human emotions submit to the natural cycle and are in turn mirrored and absorbed by it—in short, when the poetic voice cannot orphically announce its triumph over nature and escape her seasonal cycles. Cuddie's song in "August," drawing on Colin's vocabulary and sung in his absence, betrays an attitude toward the singer in nature upon which the "November" and "Aprill" poems comment more fully. Cuddie's "trickling teares" do not "augment" nature's "streames" here, nor does he succeed in getting the "wild woodes" his "sorrowes to resound" ("August," ll. 156, 166). Though he calls upon "wastefull woodes" and "banefull byrds" to "helpe me," he hears only the "hollow Echo of my carefull cryes" (ll. 151, 173, 160). Although he hints that the "returne" of she "whose voyces siluer sound / To cheerefull songs can chaunge my chereless cryes" might reverse his hopeless dependence upon nature, he fails to achieve poetic mastery here (ll. 180–81). As Isabel MacCaffrey would have it, "submission to the seasonal round" leads only to the death of "December"; it records the "failure of man to realize his *own* nature."[44]

Most critics stress the successes of "November" as against those of the Elisa poem, but to my ear it is the "Aprill" lay—epithalamic in tone and imagery, orphic in pitch and intent—that dominates the *Calender,* in spite of Spenser's attempt to offer the compliment of deification more traditionally in the "November" elegy. "November" and "Aprill" are companion poems, but they are far from the "pure expressions of celebration and grief" that conclusively, for Nancy Jo Hoffman, "humanize nature."[45] Indeed the generic statement each poem makes is far from pure. The elegy, paradoxically, begins with a request for "songs of some iouisaunce" (l. 2); the epithalamium begins with a recognition that things are awry—"is thy Bagpype broke, that soundes so sweete?" (l. 3). In the "November" eclogue the pressure to write pastoral elegy discourages even Colin, who would rather "merimake" than tune the "mournefull Muse" (ll. 9, 19)—he is patently out of harmony with the seasonal demands. Having to submit to the season's call for a sad song is here viewed as repression; Colin's muse would rather sing a spring song:

> But if sadde winters wrathe and season chill,
> Accorde not with thy Muses merriment:
> To sadder times thou mayst attune thy quill,
> And sing of sorrowe and deathes dreeriment.
> (ll. 33–36)

"November" is also dependent upon "Aprill," not only for the nuptial metaphors of its conclusion, but as context against which to define itself. The funeral procedures of the Dido elegy first unmake the bridal preparations of "Aprill" and then remake them at its close: the elegy here begins with an anti-epithalamic gesture. Surprisingly, more effort is spent in this elegy on undoing the wedding song—which becomes very much present by so much dwelling on its absence—and on reinstating the "ioyfull verse" in the *peripeteia* than on mourning proper. First, too much is made of finer weather and "myrth" not to recall the setting of the April poem. Next, the laying out and decking of Dido's bier superimpose funeral rites on the marriage preparations and blazon. The "sonne," which was emblematic of Elisa in the spring poem, is "dimme and dark" here. Additionally the three Graces of the wedding poem—to which Elisa would make a fourth—have become "fatall sisters" and "fyrie furies" here. In another transposition of imagery, flower catalogues lifted from previous pastoral elegies, specifically Marot's lament for Loyse, become the property of epithalamium in the *Calender*.[46] In the funeral poem, wilted wedding garlands replace the traditional flower-bedecked bier. The bridal bouquet offered to Elisa in "Aprill" reappears, faded and sere, in "November."

> The gaudie girlonds deck her graue,
> The faded flowres her corse embraue.
> (ll. 108–9)

But Spenser had learned from Virgil, Ronsard, and Marot to lift a hymn of joy after the dirge, conceiving of consolation in explicitly epithalamic terms, as the similarities between the epithalamic hymn to Elizabeth in "Aprill" and the consolation of "November" attest. Colin seems only too happy to find cause for panegyric: "careful verse" is so willingly exchanged for the "ioyfull verse" of the closing measures that the transition from dirge to apotheosis seems more than a pat imitation of the conventional "turn." Spenser's consummate *Calender* elegy, like Milton's *Lycidas*, runs ahead to epithalamic resolution. As elegy, "November" succeeds in its imitation of precursor poems, but it fails to achieve the confident tone of those allegories of aspiring careerism. In fact all of the ambivalence of the "November" poem, its division between two ceremonial registers, is caught up in the final oxymoronic formulation of the poem: Thenot, at the end of Colin's song, professes not to know "Whether reioyce or weepe for great constrainte," finding his lay mingled with "doolful pleasaunce" (ll. 205, 204).

The epithalamic imagery of "Aprill," by contrast, supports less ambivalently a specifically literary rite of passage, celebrating, however temporarily, Colin's achievement of orphic success.[47] For all the apprehension in the frame of the "Aprill" song that Colin's wasteful love, submission to nature, will prevent recognition of his poetic achievement, he comes closest to orphic power here: "trickling tears" begin by being adequate to "April shoure"; at the outset his song is "tuned . . . unto the Waters fall" (ll. 7, 36). But the poet soon surpasses nature in his symbol-making power, creating a rival nature in his portrait of Elisa: Phoebus dares not "his brightnesse compare / With hers" (ll. 80–81); Cynthia too is "abasht" in her presence (l. 83). Elisa is lifted *out* of nature at the end of the panegyric where she will "reigne with the rest [of the Graces] in heaven" in that "fourth place" Spenser designates as hers. Only in the turn of the "November" poem will an equivalent tone of imaginative strength be mustered. In fact the celebration of Dido's ascension in the winter elegy so far exceeds the requirements of elegiac consolation, so exceeds its models, that elegy is unseated by epithalamium here. Harrison suggests that the elegy might have been originally slated for the February slot in the *Calender,* by which strategic placement it would be followed by the more authoritative April poem.[48] The vatic tone Spenser achieves in the April blazon—result of an orphic marriage of his imaginative and heroic roles as "new poete"—looks forward to his epic celebration of Elizabeth and the orphic marriage of the *Epithalamion* and, like Virgil's tenth bucolic, puts us beyond pastoral apprenticeship here.

V

The pastoral funeral elegy, it has been my intent to demonstrate, has been from the outset a statement of careerism.[49] In fact transforming the initiation scene becomes, for Theocritus, Virgil, Spenser, and their imitators, a way of proving imaginative adequacy, fitness for the literary life. In the sequence of elegies traced above, the *agon* of form contesting earlier versions of the form is enacted in the fiction of the singing contest itself: Theocritus's first idyll effectively buries outmoded literary conventions and evolves a new poetics in the course of an amoebean exchange in much the way that Socrates exposes the conventions of oral culture and introduces those of written language within the fiction of an oratorical debate. A history can be traced in subsequent variations of the theme. In Plato and Theocritus, the scenario is strongly father-based: an obvious greenhorn receives tutelage at the knees of an elder. This arrangement of participants—youth initiated by age—is what one might expect to find at the outset of a tradition before too many poetic fathers clutter the stage. But Theocritus's version of the primal literary scene is itself a parody of the Platonic one; in his first idyll a mock-Socratic, unnamed goatherd champions just the sort of relaxed attitude toward *otium* which Plato so fervently distrusts. Virgil's fifth eclogue, a direct response to the first idyll, falls midway through the bucolic sequence and subtly rewrites the scenario. It preserves the fiction of a youth inducted by an older singer, but it accords new regard to the younger, a neophyte one notices for his energetic contributions to the disposition of the scene.

Between Virgil and Spenser are the late-Latin elegies of Calpurnius and Nemesianus, elegies equally preoccupied with revision of the primal pastoral scene. The careerist strain we have detected in Theocritus and Virgil becomes as insistent as the distractingly loud "prattling waters" and "garrulous" pine that mark the eclogues of their later Roman imitators, and this shift is once again signaled by a rewriting of the inherited *locus amoenus*. In his fourth eclogue, Calpurnius gives elegiac ambition new meaning, seeming as he does to rival Virgil and Theocritus in his anticipatory elegy for Nero. Not only does he prefer the "watery bank" to the "unwonted place, beneath this plane-tree at whose roots brawl the prattling waters," not only does he supplant the Virgilian poetics of inspiring "woodland ring" with a nationalist and post-pastoral poetics "fit to celebrate the golden age," not only does he identify with Virgil's younger singer, reinforcing Mopsus's strength by doubling him into a pair of brothers, he also remains skeptical throughout this literary exercise that pastoral will be adequate to *his* task: "the divinities of mighty Rome are not to be extolled in the same style as the sheepfold of Menalcas."[50] In Nemesianus's version, the elder begins by remembering when he was young and a possessor of pastoral power, but he concedes in the first exchange of the poem the younger man's accession to power and celebrates *his* victory over Mopsus, Virgil's young poet. Additionally this contest is staged deliberately at an alternate time of day—not during the noon hour, but in the early morning "while the country-side is free from the harsh-toned grasshoppers"[51]—and his pastoral singers find the Theocritean pine tree too noisy to provide shelter, seeking out instead a grove of "elms and beeches." Comparison of these representative pastoral works yields a clear illustration of generic development: subsequent rewording and restaging of the pastoral contest have preserved the vitality of the pastoral elegy.

The placement of elegies in the corpus of representative poets is also a significant indicator of literary history. Theocritus's elegy provides a preface to a collection of revolutionary works. Virgil attempts the elegy twice: the first time to demonstrate his mastery of the Theocritean dialogue form, the second time to phrase his farewell to the mode itself before attempting the somewhat higher strains of georgic and epic. The tenth eclogue, which concludes the *Bucolics,* imitates the content of the first idyll—Gallus, like Daphnis, is sick with love—but invents a new form for the pastoral elegy and widens its field of reference significantly. When the singing contest no longer yields sufficient opportunity for transformation, elegy flows into a lyric meditation. Milton, for example, borrows the form of the tenth eclogue in his *Lycidas,* condensing Virgil's two elegies into a single lyric work which is at once an announcement of poetic program and a transcendence of the pastoral mode. Virgil's tenth bucolic too substitutes the shadows of dusk for the Theocritean noon hour. Beginning with the last bucolic of Virgil, the elegiac moment is a sunset epiphany; as twilight deepens, pastoral singers turn homeward, *away* from Arcadia.

Spenser's pastoral contribution similarly rewrites convention. The last Virgilian eclogue concludes at sunset, but it still unfolds in the pastoral spring. Spenser's elegy for Dido, on the other hand, already conscious of its belatedness, is sung in the "sollein season" of the winter months. For this poet, "sad winters wrathe and season chill" are fitter analogues for the subject matter of elegy and for the emotional state which precipitates the writing of elegy: fear of imaginative loss of vitality and need to assert imaginative control, orphic mastery, during the panegyrical close. Spenser conceives of elegiac consolation in terms of a wedding feast, as the chiasmus between "November" and "Aprill" attests. In *Daphnaïda,* an elegy written some fifteen years after the *Calender,* the symbolic language of Christian consolation becomes explicitly epithalamic:

> I, since the messenger is come for mee,
> That summons soules unto the bridale feast
> Of his great Lord, must needes depart from thee,
> And straight obay his soueraine beheast:[52]

A successor to Spenser, Milton too brings *Lycidas* to a close with a nuptial hymn sung by blessed troops—emblematic of the soul's admittance to the Kingdom of Heaven—supplying a nuptial conclusion to a traditional dirge.

As the Christian elegy tends more and more to end with a demonstration of nuptial testimony, an epithalamic allusion marked by that genre's structure of transcendence, language of orphic expansion and control, imagery of reconciliation and celebration, the wedding poem comes into its own as symbolic enactment of an initiation drama. Falling between baptism and burial, the marriage ceremony too celebrates passage and calls for witness of graduation to stature by a community of initiates. It is no wonder that the climax of the Orphic ritual ceremony was a "sacred marriage" or that the moment of Christian assumption to the Kingdom is rendered symbolically as "immortal nuptials." In Spenser's *Epithalamion*, for example, as I shall hope to show in the following chapter, marriage symbolism supports specifically literary rites of passage: in the portrait of the poet as Orpheus singing an epithalamium for his own bride, we get a celebration of the incarnate artist demonstrating his centrality to both literary and political worlds.

3
"Sacred Ceremonies": Spenser's *Epithalamion* and *Prothalamion*

I

Spenser always comes home, Richard Helgerson tells us, "to the pastoral, the personal, and the amorous,"[1] and I would add that this nexus of drives and genres serves particularly in Spenser as a context for and site of poetic ambition. *The Faerie Queene* included, a double emphasis on literary ambition and erotic desire (on the politics of careerism *as* erotic pursuit) frames Spenser's entire poetic corpus from the *Shepheardes Calender* to the *Prothalamion*. But if we look to Spenser's erotic poems for a record of his creative strategies, a certain strain of Spenser's pastoralism achieves consummate expression in the "sacred ceremonies" of the *Epithalamion* and *Prothalamion*.[2] If indeed the central function of Elizabethan pastoral was the "symbolic mediation" of power relationships, a mode of addressing conflicting claims in an ambitious and competitive society,[3] then the deliberate confluence of lovemaking and career-making in Spenser's marriage poems serves a dual purpose: it allows him to air anxieties about the poet-patron relationship in terms of a twin and parallel relation of dependency, that of the nuptial couple, and it provides a ceremonial structure for the symbolic enactment of career and imaginative scenarios.[4] Accommodating the inherited conventions of the wedding poem—a minor genre invented by Sappho, satirized by Aristophanes, developed lyrically and dramatically by Catullus, rendered rhetorical and allegorical by medieval poets, classified critically by Scaliger and Puttenham[5]—to pastoral vocabulary and imagery, and a decided interest in careerism, Spenser exploits the nuptial mode both to demonstrate his own graduation to literary stature in the *Epithalamion* and, when this sense of himself goes unrewarded, to register the full extent of his disillusionment and withdrawal in the *Prothalamion*. I want to suggest, in this context, that we rethink the generic underpinnings of the marriage poems: Why does Spenser co-opt conventions of another genre obsessed with poetic achievement, if not to invoke elegy's power to celebrate a poet's orphic command of center and circumference, self and audience? And why is the tone of his betrothal poem so dominantly elegiac, if not to comment ironically on the poet's displacement from center to periphery of a ceremony his brides anticipate all too innocently? Finally, what do the self-seeking registers of the pastoral elegy have in common with the epithalamium, as Spenser knew and shaped it? Since an occasional poem often bears a subtext of ambition, a concern with the conditions that called for it, we might say of *Epithalamion* and *Prothalamion* that taken together they suggest preoccupation with poetic ambition in an erotic context, a pairing prefigured by the similarities between "Aprill" and "November" in the *Calender*. Related in ways I will explore to the pastoral elegy, epithalamium becomes, in Spenser's hands, an effective genre *in* which and *against* which to register thoughts about poetry, potency, power, love, and loss.

Theoreticians of the Renaissance epithalamium argue that the genre's importance during the period results from its allegorical possibilities and sociological significance. Thomas Greene demonstrates convincingly that the epithalamium is evidence of a distinct social phenomenon, the bourgeois idealization of marriage.[6] For Leonard Forster, the Renaissance nuptial ode acts as a "safety valve," offering sexual consummation quite acceptably under the canopy of the marriage bed.[7] To this approach must be added a theory of what the marriage poem accomplishes for the creative artist. From the poets of the Pléiade and Marot, Spenser had learned to write a special kind of wedding poem—one that spoke directly to the poet-patron relationship, recognized the issue of literary dependence at court, and offered the poet a chance to distinguish himself as a literary man upon that limited stage. In fact Spenser had been rehearsing epithalamia since the *Calender* blazon of 1579,[8] finding in the panegyric greater opportunity for patronage and a more extended language for self-celebration than the traditional elegy afforded. As the consolation of the "November" elegy in his *Shepheardes Calender* attests, Spenser looked to the metaphors attendant upon the marriage ceremony for symbolism of transcendence and a vocabulary of literary initiation.

Additionally Spenser saw the consolation of Virgil's fifth eclogue, like the much-allegorized Pollio eclogue, through the Neoplatonic lens of the commentators. Daphnis's assumption imaged for him heavenly nuptials: sign and symbol of that sacred marriage at which the *mystes* is inducted into the secret society of initiates, that marriage feast at which the Christian soul is greeted by Blessed Troops. The tradition of spiritual allegory of Song of Songs also provided Spenser with a nuptial vocabulary for the progress of the Christian soul. As early as Origen, Canticles was thought to dramatize mystic incarnation: the wedding of Christ to the Church, human soul to the Logos, flesh to the spirit.[9] To the extent, then, that allegory allows the artist to overcome the dualism between this world and the next, Canticle commentary supported the pastoral attempt to mediate between conflicting claims. Allegories to the soul, as Spenser's marriage odes richly demonstrate, in some cases also record the effort of the poetic imagination to reconcile the literary and political call of this world with the spiritual claim of the transcendent realm.

Spenser's innovations in this regard are bolder, I believe, than critics have acknowledged.[10] Beyond his numerous contributions to the conventions of the epithalamium, and more important to interpretation of the poem itself, however, is Spenser's blatant orphism. Drawing upon medieval and Renaissance portraits of Orpheus as the perfect lover and finest orator, Spenser virtually calls himself another Orpheus and casts himself as singer-bridegroom at the center of his poem. The utter confidence with which Spenser epithalamically celebrates the marriage of poet and receptive court, indeed orphic dominion over his literary world—he was in fact England's only literary man[11]—is never achieved again in English poetry. Within a few years Spenser has to invent a new term, prothalamion, for a poem which radically reexamines the fiction of the earlier poem. This occasion piece, inverting the promise and sanctity of nuptial imagery in what amounts to an inversion of genre, becomes a record of his very earthly dissatisfactions, both political and literary. Before turning to the poems, I wish to explore in more depth Spenser's inheritance of literary orphism. The mythic figure of Orpheus plays the double role of both dismembered initiate and potential bridegroom and presides over funeral and marriage poems alike. In fact the accommodation of the myth to both epithalamic and elegiac structures begins in the Renaissance and recurs in the context of literary initiation in late-Renaissance, Romantic, and modern forms.[12]

II

The visage of Orpheus is manifold: as Spenser received it, in the intellectualized and Christian version, it looks outward in a range of directions.[13] In the first instance we have Orpheus's association with Dionysian mystery cults dating as far back as the sixth century. The parentage of this native of Thrace remains obscure—his mother was reportedly a Muse (Calliope in the accounts of Ovid and others), and his father either a local king or Apollo himself—and his historicity has never been proved. Specialists in the field are divided as to the proper weight to accord Orphism in Greek religious culture.[14] But from the first he is associated with the cult worship of Dionysus and the Mystery Initiations. As a kind of "shaman figure, he possessed magic powers and prophetic vision; his special attribute was that of a lyrist of such magnificent seductive force that all nature, animate and inanimate, was subdued by and followed him."[15] This role of medicine man/initiator is the pose Socrates adopts (and to some degree fears), for the express purpose of seducing Phaedrus to philosophic vision in Plato's Dialogue of the same name; it is in turn the intellectual model modified by Renaissance commentators like Pico and Ficino, who made of those early agricultural mysteries—via the *Symposium* and the *Phaedrus*—"mystéres littéraires."[16] From Plato they derived "an adoption of ritual terminology to assist and incite the exercise of intelligence."[17] The initiatory pattern Spenser inherited was thus a transvaluation of the pagan rites of purification, initiation, and sacred marriage. The debt of Renaissance verbal and visual art to this complex of ideology, imagery, and mysticism has been copiously documented by Edgar Wind in his *Pagan Mysteries in the Renaissance*.

The second mask Orpheus wears is that of the consummate artist, the archetypal bard—*sacer interpresque deorum*—of Horace's *Art of Poetry* and Virgil's fourth georgic. In these accounts, Orpheus becomes a kind of literary patron saint: poetic immortality was guaranteed him when, after his dismemberment at the hands of Bacchic maidens, his severed head continued to sing as it floated down the Hebros toward the Lesbian shore. When the head reached its destination, a shrine was erected and Orpheus's lyre ascended into the heavens and became a constellation. The dismemberment, like the flaying of Marsyas, is an Orphic initiatory motif, a rite of purification and mortification preliminary to spiritual rebirth. Wind reminds us of the conflation in Alcibiades' *Symposium* speech of the names of Socrates, Silenus (a Bacchic follower), and Marsyas: Orphic initiation is founded upon tearing apart to make whole; laying bare the rough exterior, one reveals the rich inner man.[18]

By his religious association with the dying god, Orpheus becomes a brother of the pastoral Adonis.[19] In Moschus's "Lament for Bion," the eulogist explicitly calls Bion a Dorian Orpheus and claims for him a filial relationship to Calliope. In the closing lines of the poem, the singer hopes to make Orpheus's power his own by singing so sweetly that he is granted the chance to raise Bion with his own voice:

> Even as once she granted Orpheus his Eurydice's
> return because he harped so sweetly, so likewise
> she shall give my Bion back unto the hills;
> and had but this my pipe the power of that his harp,
> I had played for this in the house of Pluteus myself.[20]

It is this version of Orpheus's story, his watery death and subsequent rebirth, that Milton claims for pastoral elegy in his own pastoral initiation poem, *Lycidas*. Late in *Paradise Lost* as well, Milton returns to the same image to claim it personally, this time to record the myth's emptiness in the face of worldly disappointments. "Both harp and voice" are drowned by the "savage clamor" (*Paradise Lost,* VII. 36–37).

Spenser invokes Orpheus in his third manifestation—as the disappointed bridegroom of Eurydice. This version of the myth attributes to him a *katábasis,* a descent to Hades by which means he hopes to resurrect his beloved wife taken from him lately by untimely death. Orpheus's unsuccessful attempt to raise her is, in Ovid's lonely version of the story, an anti-bridal ritual. The metamorphosis Ovid records in his tenth book is an inversion of the marriage feast: Hymen refuses to answer Orpheus's call; auspicious words, joyful faces, lucky omens, are all conspicuously absent; the marriage torch sputters. Eurydice's double death turns Orpheus to stone. For three years he remains silent, shuns the company of women (earning him the medieval satiric label of homosexual), and wanders ceaselessly. As Virgil puts it, "nulla Venus, non ulli animum flexere hymenaei" ("No love, no marriage could turn his mind away from grief").[21]

Invoking Orpheus's power at the outset of a marriage poem, Spenser symbolically unites the pair:

> So Orpheus did for his owne bride,
> So I vnto my selfe alone will sing,
> The woods shall to me answer and my Eccho ring.
> (*Epithalamion,* ll. 16–18)

Lest Spenser's claims seem unprecedented here, it is necessary to retrieve a medieval portrait of Orpheus as well. For Spenser's sense of the myth's literary significance is filtered as well through medieval interpretations of Orpheus's allegorical weight.[22] Earliest medieval views of Orpheus saw him as a prophet, a pupil of Moses who had been initiated into the mystery of monotheism: utterly un-Hellenic, this version explains Orpheus's interest for centuries of Jewish and Christian commentators. A second interpretation makes the identification of Orpheus and Christ, seeing in the pagan psychopomp—conductor of souls to immortality—a type of the Good Shepherd. Christianity, Neoplatonism, and the syncretistic thought of magic and theurgy all contributed to this image of Orpheus. Finally, and most important for Spenser, a third tradition focused on the relationship between Orpheus and Eurydice, either for purposes of moral allegory or, increasingly, for secular entertainment. In the case of the former, the story of husband and wife was infinitely elaborated as a Neoplatonic drama of the soul: the struggle between judgment and vice, mind and passion, immortal and temporal concerns, was figured in their union. The latter portrait depicted Orpheus as a model lover and a courteous knight. This treatment so superseded that of the commentators that it became a commonplace to feature a happy ending to the separation of Orpheus and Eurydice.

Two identifications of Orpheus had particular resonance for Spenser. The first was the allegorical view of Orpheus as the Solomon of Canticles. In Pierre Bersuire's mythographic treatise on Ovid, the whole of human history can be seen in the story of Orpheus and his bride: Orpheus's song for Eurydice becomes the New Song of Christianity, the invitation of Christ to the Church to join him in marriage. Not surprisingly, Orpheus descends to retrieve Eurydice with the words of Solomon: "Rise up, my love, my fair one, and come away."[23] The second is the late-secular view of Orpheus as minstrel and consummate artist: by Carolingian times it was a convention to boast of oneself as "another Orpheus."[24] Clearly Spenser draws upon both of these traditions in his figure of the courtier-bridegroom of *Epithalamion*. As anxious to see poetry and the Muses accorded a proper place at court as French poets of the fourteenth and fifteenth centuries and the sixteenth-century members of the Pléiade, Spenser wanted to see his literary role as that of a musical conductor commanding political stature by the excellence of his art. The song he directs in this poem for his own marriage is in the fullest sense "sacred": it honors the sacrament of holy matrimony with its cosmic and allegorical implications; it apes the sacred marriage of the Orphic ritual, climax of the Neoplatonic initiation ceremonies; and it exults in the power of poetry to put the earthly singer beyond nature's endless wheel. The orphic courtier-bridegroom of the *Epithalamion,* fulfillment of that organizing epithalamic voice in the "Aprill" eclogue, is a Renaissance portrait of the artist: a poet-singer self-conceived as so central to his civilization that he can command echoes from every corner of his world.

III

The *Epithalamion*—a "ritualistic public statement" implying a "social context"[25]—issues directly from the Elisa blazon in the *Shepheardes Calender,* a fact confirmed by a reading of the *Englands Helicon* version of the "Aprill" eclogue.[26] In this miscellany, the frame of the piece is missing, and Colin's song stands alone, dominated by the first-person voice of the epithalamist directing the action.[27] Like the *Epithalamion,* the blazon calls upon choruses of nymphs, virgins, Muses, Graces, and townspeople; it plays coyly with the red and white imagery of Song of Songs; it appropriates the pastoral flower catalogue and flower symbolism; it prepares dramatically, in the mode of the biblical Songs, for the bride's entrance. But where the Elisa poem is panegyric on the verge of epithalamium, Spenser's marriage poem expands that complex of imagery into a fully realized poetic statement. In the *Calender,* "Aprill" represented a temporary and renewable imaginative achievement, but the scope of the poems seems to deny Colin permanent orphic stature. In the *Epithalamion,* Spenser himself speaks—without a pastoral mask—to announce through the symbolisms of marriage the full extent of his orphic success.[28] For Greene, Spenser's uneasiness over the "comparative social obscurity of his own marriage"—the true occasion of the poem—accounts for his radical "reversal of the traditional relationship" between poet-celebrator and patron-bridal pair. Here, claims Greene, Spenser sings his own nuptial hymn, assigning both bridegroom and master-of-ceremonies roles to the "I" voice.[29] I would argue that if the poem betrays some social insecurity it fairly exults in its author's very earthly contentment with his ability to command echoes from an attentive audience. Published with *Amoretti*—and these sonnets are prefaced by W.P. and offered to Sir Robert Needham Knight as the product of "that weldeseruing gentleman, maister Edmond Spenser: whose name sufficiently warranting the worthinesse of the work"[30]—the *Epithalamion* is noteworthy for its absence of dedication.

Epithalamion is, from invocation to envoy, a poem beyond patronage. The first lines of the poem call upon the Muses, by now old friends, with whom he has shared a profitable literary relationship:

> Ye learned sisters which haue oftentimes
> Beene to me ayding, others to adorne:
> (*Epithalamion,* ll. 1–2)

The Muses who in the past had helped Spenser write works worthy of patronage—and here Spenser alludes briefly to success in those terms: "That euen the greatest did not scorne / To heare theyr names sung in your simple layes, / But ioyed in theyr prayse" (*Epithalamion,* ll. 4–6)—are now confidently enjoined to "Help me mine own loues prayses to resound" (*Epithalamion,* l. 14). The invocation reaches a crescendo when the unmasked "I" voice declares its intention, seemingly forgetting his bride for the moment—"So I unto my selfe alone will sing"—and posits triumphantly nature's cooperation with the orphic singing voice. The poet of *Epithalamion* can depend upon the antiphonal response of nature in a way that Colin of the *Calender* could not: where the poet's earlier literary persona found his emotional states often at odds with the seasonal requirements of nature and unable to control her rhythms, here pathetic fallacy reigns supreme until the moment when the poet commands the woods to cease its response. The invocation concludes with the first variation of the famous orphic refrain: "The woods shall to me answer and my Eccho ring" (*Epithalamion*, l. 18).

The strongest support for the view that Spenser is talking about poetry as much as marriage in the *Epithalamion*, indeed using in very Platonic manner an erotic metaphor for worldly success, is his explicit use of elegiac motifs and conventions in his nuptial hymn. In several important ways, Spenser converts elegy—for classical and Renaissance poets a ritual hymn of literary appearance at the bier of a forebear or patron which signals consecration of the initiate to the literary life—into epithalamium. Spenser's orphism, as outlined above, is the first of such indicators, linking his poetic project with that frequenter of both funeral and nuptial ceremonies. Invoking the archetypal bard at the outset of a marriage poem, Spenser claims competitively that he will accomplish what Orpheus failed to do: he will reverse that poet's unsuccess.[31]

The second convention Spenser lifts from elegy is the continuous orphic refrain which becomes the poem's most insistent feature. Bearing more resemblance to the refrain of previous pastoral elegies than it does to those of previous epithalamia, Spenser's "The woods shall to me answer and my Eccho ring" is closer to Virgil's line in the tenth bucolic—"Non canimus surdis, respondent omnia siluae" ("Not to deaf ears I sing, for the woods echo my singing")[32]—than it is to the standard refrain of the epithalamium since Theocritus and Catullus. Spenser knew very well the "Sing Hey for the Wedding, sing Ho for the Wedder," of the eighteenth idyll, or its equivalent in Catullus 61,[33] and he assigns it in his poem to the running boys: "Hymen io hymen they do shout" (*Epithalamion*, l. 140). By contrast, the refrain of the classical elegy, "the most common formal element in the pastoral dirge," works as a controlling device: it functions to "stop movement in its tracks, to stabilize the flux, and exhaust the reservoir of significant moment charged with feeling."[34] The refrain of the elegy is often incrementally varied to emphasize its ritual function—to mark the alternate response of nature to man, the compactual relationship between singing voice and surround, the concentric widening of the impact of the song—and Spenser uses it precisely to that effect in *Epithalamion*.

The third convention Spenser lifts from elegy, notably Virgil's fifth bucolic, is the composition of the rites themselves. When Spenser's marriage poem is placed next to the consolation of Virgil's fifth eclogue, funeral and marriage rites complement one another. In Virgil, Daphnis's assumption—and presumably Mopsus's poetic initiation—culminates in

Bacchic celebration: feasting and dancing of the faunlike Alphesiboeus accompany the ritual pouring of oils, milk, and wine. Here too woods carry the song of celebration to the heavens. The whole is conducted before the ritual witness of nymphs. Beneath the lively wedding feast in Spenser's poems, the lineaments, not only of Elizabethan seasonal festivals, but also of ancient Orphic ritual celebration, come into focus:

> Poure out the wine without restraint or stay,
> Poure not by cups, but by the belly full,
> Poure out to all that wull,
> And sprinkle all the postes and wals with wine,
> That they may sweat, and drunken be withall.
> Crown ye God Bacchus with a coronall,
> And Hymen also crowne with wreathes of vine,
> And let the Graces daunce unto the rest;
>   (*Epithalamion*, ll. 250–57)

Spenser's fourth borrowing from the imagery store of elegy is the appropriation of the pastoral flower catalogue. In fact a double tradition of flower-strewing existed—elegiac and epithalamic—as Shakespeare was to demonstrate a few years after Spenser in *The Winter's Tale*. But even though flowers had their place in the epithalamia of Catullus, Statius, and Claudian, and before that in the Song of Songs, Spenser seems to draw in the extended catalogue of the *Calender* blazon and in the proliferation of "bridale poses," "gay girlands" in the *Epithalamion,* not only upon brief mention of strewing leaves in Virgil V but even more importantly upon the detailed floral encomium in Marot's elegy for Loyse. The English epithalamic flower catalogue is thus a transformation of elaborate bier-strewing rituals, received by Spenser as a feature of elegy, which he appropriates for the erotic purpose of decking a very lifelike lady. And when Milton draws in turn upon Spenser's epithalamic flower passages in his *Lycidas,* the presence of the flower passage in elegy and epithalamium marks both genres as a poetry of ambition.[35]

For all of Spenser's use of elegy—and his incorporation of elegiac motifs in his epithalamium is, I believe, signal of similar ambition—his poem is the opposite of elegy. Spenser's poem is anything but monodic, the mode of Virgil's tenth bucolic and Milton's elegy for King. Concerned with poetry's public status, Spenser exploits the full dramatic resonance of epithalamium in his nuptial ode, drawing upon the narrative structure of Catullan poems, the tradition of masque, even the dramatic structure of Song of Songs. This poem is high pastoral drama in Milton's sense of Canticles.[36] And it is not far from the dramatic treatment of marriage in

Shakespeare's *The Tempest*: although at the close Ferdinand would "live here ever" in this "Paradise," Prospero knows the nuptials must be "solemnizèd" at Naples in an encompassing social and political surround (*The Tempest*, IV.i.122–24; V.i.309). Spenser's achievement here is doubly significant: he supplies a social context for a private ceremony, all within the confines of a lyric poem, and he provides it by means of his commanding poetic voice alone. For Richard Neuse, the movement from convention outward to natural and social circles is enforced by the "poetic principle" of the echo: "The echo is thus truly incremental: in response to the (initially) single voice there is created a regular polyphony of voices which, interpenetrating, form an expanding context for the rite to be enacted."[37] Spenser's confidence in his authorial power is reflected in the *Epithalamion* in the control he marshalls over the other participants in the ceremony. Who, in fact, is there to echo his song? Muses, Hymen, nymphs, Rosy Morne, Phoebus, Graces, and Holy Priest appear in person. Additionally the poem projects veritable choruses of "fresh boyes" (l. 112), "many a bachelor" (l. 28), "Minstrels" (l. 129), "damzels" (l. 96), "virgins" (l. 111), "choristers" (l. 221), "Angels" (l. 229), "mayds and yongmen" (l. 332), "merchants daughters" (l. 167), and "blessed saints" (l. 423). Most important, a general unspecific audience witnesses these "sacred rites" (l. 393): "So many gazers," Spenser calls them at one point (l. 160); earlier, their applause is the very emblem of approval:

> To which the people standing all about,
> As in approuance doe thereto applaud.
>   (ll. 143–44)

Similarly all aspects of the natural world respond to the English Orpheus's song. In fact the last stanzas of the poem, marking the advent of night and circumscribing (within the larger structure of the celebratory nuptial hymn) the threats to imaginative vitality night brings with it, demonstrate Spenser's power to exclude even nature from the intimacy of consummation. The final variations on the refrain, couched in the negative, are no less commanding: "Ne let the woods us answere, nor our Eccho Ring" (l. 333).

Finally, Spenser plays upon a pair of metaphors for "issue" in the last stanzas of the poem—a chiasmus which suggests further commerce between elegiac and epithalamic modes. Even as the *Epithalamion* mounts the Platonic ladder upward toward a transcendent future—"haughty pallaces," "heavenly tabernacles"—Spenser's mind is on a very "large posterity," and not merely that of children (ll. 420, 422, 417). Spenser's marriage poem provides an analogue for the immortality symbolically conferred upon Daphnis at the end of the fifth eclogue. Epithalamium thus evolves its own version of elegiac immortality: but whereas in elegy the transfer of literary power and the guarantee of lasting fame help the neophyte to transcend fear of imaginative death, in epithalamium immortality no less literary is achieved by symbolic reference to issue. In Diotima's reported speech in the *Symposium,* we recall, babies and books are seen as offspring of man's desire to conquer death, although each results from erotic stimulation of differently inclined souls.[38] Spenser clearly plays on the collision of these metaphors for issue in his preoccupation with "generation" and "progeny" in the last stanzas of the poem.[39] But genesis of the *poem* seems to be foremost in mind, since what I read as three parallel endings of the *Epithalamion*—the first confirming the "lawes of" earthly "wedlock," the second the "religion of the faith," and the third the power of poetry to create eternal monuments—enforce that the last is far from least. The stay against short time which the poem represents, and human children complement, is the eternizing "song" itself.

No student of Spenser can fail to acknowledge that this marriage symbolizes all marriage, but where others have illuminated the political and cosmological marriages reinforced by the elaborate numerological structure,[40] I want to lay stress on one particular marriage: that of orphic poet and listening surround. It is unlikely that Edmund Spenser, careerist, will proceed to philosophical contemplation of the Beautiful; Spenser's professionalism, I agree with David Wagenknecht, "tends to overwhelm both the lover and the Christian" here.[41] The poem's envoy, or *tornata,* Spenser's address to his own work, underscores beyond repair the artifactual nature of the work:[42]

> Song made in lieu of many ornaments,
> With which my loue should duly haue been dect,
> Which cutting off through hasty accidents,
> Ye would not stay your dew time to expect,
> But promist both to recompens,
> Be unto her a goodly ornament,
> And for short time an endlesse moniment.
> (ll. 427–33)

Spenser, I think, is not speaking about marriage at all in this very self-conscious coda, except to liken its difficult dependency to problems of poetic indebtedness. What attracts Spenser to the nuptial configuration is, in my view, precisely that it represents a relation of dependency (healthily productive in the *Epithalamion* or disappointingly barren in *Prothalamion*): marriage as operative metaphor, in conventional terms, bespeaks a hierarchical relationship, whether of man and woman, Christ and Church, or even patron and poet. In fact Spenser was very much aware of the earthly limits of marriage and love. "Hasty accidents" (l. 429) sum up the range of hints in the poem at stresses in the romantic relationship—"paynes and sorrowes past" (l. 32), "cares" (l. 317), "feare of perrill and foule horror" (l. 321), "false treason" (l. 322), and "dread disquiet" (l. 323)—now happily overcome. Although far from elegiac in *tone,* the *Epithalamion* is a drama of self-presentation relying upon a language of orphic expansion and control, in which the poet identifies with the bride's initiatory journey and her ideal dependence upon a protector: like a good marriage, the poet-patron partnership should be fruitful and issue fruit. Spenser could hardly envision a poetic career outside the patronage system, even if the *Epithalamion* sounds at times like a wishful declaration of independence: the fully supported poet, as *Epithalamion* figures it, would stand at the center of a circle of listeners in a configuration reminiscent of Elizabeth's positioning vis-à-vis her subjects in the woodblock heading the "Aprill" blazon.

The *Epithalamion,* then, as "song made" in the wake of Spenser's literary coming-of-age—he had just published the first three books of *The Faerie Queene*—is more than a "goodly ornament" to Spenser's bride; the "endlesse moniment" it claims itself in its last line is also a literary-historical marker, harking backward to Daphnis's tombstone in the fifth eclogue as guarantee of literary fame and succession as resonantly as upon earlier wedding songs. Additionally, it also looks forward to another timeless statue, that of Marvell's nymph complaining eternally that elegy has utterly lost its power to assuage. Placing Spenser's wedding poem between these two elegies sharpens the significance of both ritual poems: Spenser's Neoplatonist sensibility found in the transcendent consolation of Virgil's elegy for Daphnis fitter form for literary self-celebration; Marvell, looking backward upon pastoral's epithalamic promise, inverts nuptial imagery systematically in his elegy for pastoral itself.[43]

IV

The *Prothalamion* is an enigmatic poem, but indispensable to a full account of Spenser's poetic career.[44] If the *Epithalamion* strikes the reader as an expression of ebullient, successful orphism, the later poem is obsessed with the issue of literary patronage and far less confident in tone. The full title of the poem, stressing its occasion, appears as follows in the Variorium edition:

> Prothalamion
> Or
> A Spousall Verse made by
> Edm. Spenser.
> IN HONOVR OF THE DOU-
> ble mariage of the two Honourable & vertuous
> ladies, the Ladie Elizabeth and the Ladie Katherine
> Somerset, Daughters to the Right Honourable the
> Earle of Worcester and espoused to the two worthie
> Gentlemen M. Henry Gilford, and
> M. William Peter Esquyers.
>
> (*Prothalamion*, p. 25)

In point of fact, critics have generally agreed that this perhaps last written of Spenser's poems is problematic: a ten-stanza nuptial song in which two verses are devoted to the poet's "sullein care" (l. 5) and another to some "patron-seeking praise of Essex" is indeed divided in its allegiances.[45] But I do not agree with Jay Halio that Spenser "overlooked what was happening to the poem as a unified work of art."[46] The poem's division between the aloof poet's "olde woes" and the "ioyes" of the bridal day is in my view wholly intentional (l. 142). Where epithalamium had been for Spenser a mode in which to celebrate his own achieved stature as orphic *vates*, prothalamion—and here the coinage alerts us to a difference between the two poems—becomes for Spenser a mode in which to articulate career and imaginative disappointments, but once again, tellingly, under nuptial guise. Like Virgil's tenth eclogue, which constitutes a backward glance upon the precinct of Arcadia, Spenser's *Prothalamion*, too, senses the inadequacy of its metaphors. Incorporating anti-epithalamic conventions, fully elegiac in tone, the poem is, in Sidney Lee's words, "Spenser's fit farewell to his muse."[47]

Prothalamion is not only a possible bid for patronage,[48] but erotic and creative themes are quite separate in this poem, as if the fusion were no longer possible. Halio suggests that since Spenser was in London supervising the printing of several books of *The Faerie Queene* he may have tried to win some favor at court by dedicating the spousal verse to Elizabeth's favorite, Edward Somerset. The weddings were to take place at Essex House: this allowed Spenser, by the implied comparison of Essex with his former patron Leicester to offer the stanzas of praise to Essex himself—clearly in hopes of royal endorsement.[49] Nuptial celebration and panegyric of praise tend to separate like oil and water in this poem: the former is reproduced in miniature and assigned to an attendant nymph; the latter receives embarrassingly direct treatment in a pair of stanzas framing and sealing off the epithalamium. Hinting broadly at Essex's future need of poetic trumpeting, Spenser offers his literary services:

> Yet therein now doth lodge a noble Peer,
> Great *Englands* glory and the Worlds wide wonder,
> Whose dreadful name, late through all *Spaine* did thunder,
> And *Hercules* two pillors standing neere,
> Did make to quake and feare:
> Faire branch of Honor, flower of Cheualrie,
> That fillest *England* with thy triumphes fame,
> Ioy haue thou of thy noble victorie,
> And endlesse happinesse of thine owne name
> That promiseth the same:
> That through thy prowesse and victorious armes,
> The country may be freed from forraine harmes,
> And great *Elisaes* glorious name may ring
> Through al the world, fil'd with thy wide Alarmes,
> Which some brave muse may sing
> To ages following.
>
> (ll. 145–60)

Yet after such brazen self-sale, the recognition follows that earlier ambitions have been denied. At the same time as it admits dependence upon patronage, the poem evidences deep discouragement over previous poet-patron relationships, denies the solace afforded by previous pastoral landscapes, and in effect reverses the sacramentalism of Spenser's earlier wedding poem. Far from an "endlesse moniment" to the imagination, we have in *Prothalamion* a brief record of decaying hopes played out against a wedding ceremony from which the poet pointedly distances himself.

Since in the *Epithalamion* the marriage celebration (and its attendant symbols) was appropriated for rendering the literary and cultural recognition of the poet, and in the *Prothalamion* marriage symbolism is invoked to dramatize the decline of that glorious sense, it comes as no surprise that *Prothalamion*—in title a nuptial ode—manifests elegiac conventions. Spenser's sympathy for his brides on the brink of marriage is now that of one somewhat wiser to its ways. While I agree with Harry Berger's suggestion that we "view the narration about *others* at least partly as an aspect of what happens to the *self*," I do not read the brides as a gloss upon the poet's imaginative state.[50] The poet's distance from the nuptial celebration gives us a curious dual perception of events. The opening stanza of the poem, for example, sets the disappointed poet against the floral excess of the "Brydale day" (l. 17). Throughout the poem, the poet's "olde woes" sound a bass note, setting off the anticipatory trebles of the brides' expectations. Not only does the poem set up narrator at a distance from blushing brides, it also differs from *Epithalamion* in mode of presentation of the brides, in the nature and resonance of the refrain, in its management of the conventional nuptial mechanism, in its final—elegiac—treatment of the theme.

The brides in this poem do not receive in homage a Canticles catalogue of their attributes, nor are they offered the special tribute Spenser's own bride receives in the earlier poem. Symbolization of the brides deprives them of a certain humanity and holds them at a desired distance: they metamorphose into "two Swannes of goodly hewe" (l. 37) whose course down the river the poet controls. Additionally, as many critics have noted, there is an inappropriateness about the metaphor. Marriage in this poem cannot escape association with rape for the poet (the mention of dirtied swans prompts a vision of Leda, raped rather than wedded by Jove in that disguise, along with other complementary myths of sexual capture): it takes on an anti-bridal cast in which a relation of dependency brings death—to the virgin, to the creative imagination, to the "expectation vayne" of both.[51]

A further indication of the distance between this poem and *Epithalamion* is the contrast in use of the refrain. The ending of each stanza, orphic in pitch in the wedding poem, is ambiguous and poignant here: "Sweet *Themmes*" is exhorted to "runne softly" only "till I end my song" (l. 17). The poem's brief achievement as an occasion piece, and a doubtful one at that, is thereby acknowledged, as is the poet's present curtailed power over the natural and political worlds. Even more problematic is the repeated phrase "Against their Brydale day, which is not long" (l. 71). Depending upon intonation, the line cuts two ways: "against" can imply friction, withdrawal from, as easily as it can connote a shoring up or leaning toward. Both happen here: the brides lean expectantly, innocently, toward; Spenser knowingly resists. Similarly the phrase "which was not long" suggests two interpretations. Either the bridal day is not long off or its very shortness is proof of its ephemerality. The word choice is too deliberate to yield to simple paraphrase: the poet of *Prothalamion* resists absorption into the watery procession and all that it represents even as he yearns to participate once more in its symbolisms. The ambiguity of the refrain catches up the resonance of that ambivalence.[52]

Nor is *Prothalamion* the echo chamber that *Epithalamion* was. Within *Prothalamion* itself, Spenser gives us an epithalamium in small: the intent in the second stanza is to give a miniature portrait of the nuptial preparations of the "Daughters of the Flood" against which can be measured the bridal preparations of the present ladies. The flower catalogue, with its erotic suggestion and freighted literary allusion, comes within this tiny rehearsal and not at all in the context of the ladies' marriage. A poetic miniature, the epithalamium is by now a set-piece for the poet, effectively supplying in this poem a contrast to this "Brydale day." *Prothalamion* taken as a whole similarly seals off the poet's prior achievements, setting against it a parody of the earlier poem. Spenser even assigns the role of benediction-pronouncer to another—"Whil'st one did sing this Lay, / Prepar'd against that Day" (ll. 87–88)—a nymph who, in yet another set-piece, offers the customary blessing, request for favor from the gods and hope for "fruitfull issue" (l. 104). Echoes in this poem take place between the nymph and others who resound back her song; the poet, displaced from center to periphery, does not participate in the prenuptial ceremony.

> So ended she; and all the rest around
> To her redoubled that her undersong,
> Which said, their bridale daye should not be long.
> And gentle eccho from the neighbor ground,
> Their accents did resound.
> (ll. 109–13)

The absence of the first-person pronoun in these two stanzas celebrating the marriage (VI and VII) suggests that if anyone is enjoying orphic dominion in this poem it is not the speaker. With the return of the "I" voice and its meditations on "aunciet fame" in the eighth stanza, the tone of the poem shifts to a register we might call elegiac. Placed for contrast next to *Epithalamion*, *Prothalamion* may be read as an elegiac articulation of loss: of a previous sense of literary adequacy, confidence in the literary life, reverence for the marriage ritual as symbolic expression of orphic control. The day's briefness here contrasts with the "longest day in all the yeare" of the *Epithalamion* (l. 271), just as the latter poem runs exactly half the length of the former. Since both weddings take place during the summer, the irony cannot be missed. The poet's wintry state of mind (in the *Calender* sense) in the *Prothalamion* is counterposed to the epithalamic conventions its title invokes. A marriage day with its expectations of protection and support, Spenser seems to want to warn his brides, is all too brief. Stanzas VIII and IX, digressing to cover the historical decline of "Templer Knights" into "studious Lawyers" "decayd through pride" (ll. 135, 134, 136) and the succession of Essex at Leicester's previous residence, freight the poem with elegy's charge that things are not as they were. When, halfway through the final stanza, the poet remembers his brides in time to hand them over hastily to the waiting gentlemen, it is too late to recover a sacramental tone. I doubt that the marriages ceremonialized in the last lines of the poem signify on the poet's part "the self opened to greater organisation in the life-repairing communion of love."[53] The poem's deliberate lack of resolution is more honest, if less satisfying, than the critic's generically biased interpretation. If the tone of the *Epithalamion* was utterly sincere, its use of nuptial metaphors almost sacramental, the *Prothalamion* works against the epithalamic mode a sober reminder of the burdens and anxieties of the patronage system and an elegiac lament for the poet's "long fruitlesse stay / In Princes court." The sharpest difference between these two marriage poems comes to the fore in a comparison of their refrains: whereas Spenser projects an encompassing surround of right witnesses in his management of the *Epithalamion*'s orphic refrain, the poet of *Prothalamion* is lucky, and he knows it, to have the Themmes's cooperation even for the duration of this wistful and diminished song.

If Spenser seems somewhat out of breath by the end of the *Prothalamion*, it is because the orphic voice fails him here. He has had to work hard at conjuring a spousal verse and seems aware that this desperate bid for recognition is incommensurate with his sense of the state of his career. Like Mallarmé's faune—and Spenser's elegiac song for his two brides does find a distant cousin in this modern eclogue—the speaker of *Prothalamion* happens on two ladies, traces their metamorphosis before his eyes, strains at the distance between his own diminished self and them. Both poems are written after the pastoral noon hour, in the wake of classical prescriptions, and each acknowledges that lateness by means of counter-generic protest. Both poems hover between epithalamium and elegy: eroticism and consummation are desired in each case, but failure to connect is recorded instead. From its opening projection of desire—"Ces nymphes, je les veux perpétuer"—to its closing recognition that they have escaped—"Couple, adieu; je vais voir l'ombre que tu devins"[54]—Mallarmé's poem turns, as does Spenser's, on that complex pastoral analogy between erotic success and careerism, between lovemaking and poetry-making. The literary ambitions of the speaker are at stake in both poems, as is the poet's power to involve himself in the erotic fortunes of two girls. I do not mean to belittle the differences between Spenser's so-called betrothal poem and the "comic fiasco" of Mallarmé's afternoon eclogue,[55] but the confluence of pastoral concerns in poems as widely separated in time as these illustrates the resilience of pastoral epithalamium as a genre in which to couch literary ambitions in erotic terms.

4
"The Marriage Hearse": Anti-Epithalamia of Donne, Crashaw, Blake

I

Historians of the epithalamium trace its development from the classical period—Sapphic fragments, Aristophanes' bridal choruses, Theocritus's Idyll XVIII, Catullus's three *carmina*—to the Latin panegyrics of Statius and Claudian, from medieval hymns written in imitation of the biblical Canticles and 44th Psalm to the profusion of Renaissance, neo-Latin, and vernacular poems of the fifteenth and sixteenth centuries. The mode, it is generally acknowledged, reaches its apex in Spenser's *Epithalamion*, then declines gracefully but irremediably over the next forty years.[1] Epithalamia written after that date tend to find their place in the masque, where panegyric is still called for dramatically. Lyric epithalamia after Spenser almost always receive critical censure: servile, localized imitations, they achieve little of his public, and publicizing, tone.

To view the development of the epithalamium in this way, as an organic flowering and fading, is to deny the satiric epithalamium or anti-epithalamium its own vital and perhaps more enduring history. Virginia Tufte coins the term in *The Poetry of Marriage* to identify "works in which epithalamic imagery and conventions are used to dramatize situations and emotions of a directly opposite kind."[2] She notes a conspicuous absence of ritual in these works, reverse function of epithalamic imagery, inversion of atmosphere and imagery, and tragic or ironic tone. I borrow her term, and her mention of Bion's "Lament for Adonis" in this context, and extend it beyond the classical period. In fact Tufte's examples are largely dramatic—Euripides' *Trojan Women* and *Phaethon*, Seneca's *Medea*, the tale of Tereus and Procne in Ovid—and classical only. The anti-epithalamium is, however, as old as our association of love and death and issues from the chiasmus of epithalamium and elegy in the earliest of pastoral texts. Bion's "Lament for Adonis," eluding most critics of elegy, is perhaps our first lyric anti-epithalamium. Bridal couch is exchanged for a bier in this poem, and the hymeneal hymn becomes a dirge:

> The Wedding-God hath put out every torch before
> the door, and scattered the bridal garland upon
> the ground; the burden of his song is no more
> "Ho for the Wedding"; there's more of "Woe" and
> "Adonis" to it than there ever was of the wedding-cry.³

Anti-epithalamia are found as well in influential prose narratives. The story of Cupid and Psyche in Apuleius's *The Golden Ass,* a compendium of Neoplatonic philosophy, includes an anti-bridal procession:

> The hour came when a procession formed up for Psyche's dreadful wedding. The torches chosen were ones that burned low with a sooty, spluttering flame; instead of the happy wedding march the flutes played a querulous Lydian lament; the marriage-chant ended with funereal howls, and the poor bride wiped the tears from her eyes with the corner of her flame-coloured veil. Everyone turned out, groaning sympathetically at the calamity that had overtaken the royal house, and a day of public mourning was at once proclaimed. But there was no help for it: Apollo's oracle had to be obeyed. So when the preliminaries of this hateful ceremony had been completed in deep grief, the bridal procession moved off, followed by the entire city, and at the head of it walked Psyche with the air of a woman going to her grave, not her bridal bed.⁴

Like Psyche, Proserpine and Eurydice are brides of "dark descent and gloomy wedding" whose stories "Eleusis . . . silently conceals."⁵ Medieval and Renaissance commentators, to whom all of the poets of this chapter were heir, made of these myths an allegory of the progress of the soul.⁶ Blake draws upon this tradition when he formulates, in a brilliant paradox, the oxymoron "marriage hearse," his term for the descent into generation through sexual desire.⁷ The mixing of epithalamic and elegiac modes here points forward as well to Richard Crashaw's baroque inversion of marriage song into funeral elegy, S. T. Coleridge's development of the mariner's rime against the nuptial convention of its opening, Stéphane Mallarmé's crowning of a wedding song with a ceremonial decapitation, and Paul Celan's parody of the bridal preparations of Song of Songs in his elegy for victims of the death camps. The presence of both modes in these poems survives the conventional demise of either and lends resilience and longevity to the generic commerce between them.

Poets write anti-epithalamia for a range of reasons, from interest in the sweet conceit of shroud and veil to desire for full-scale parody of a source like Spenser. Spenser too has his own anti-nuptial poem in *Prothalamion,* an allegory of the decline of the poetic imagination at court, played out against the virgin's fear of marriage. Spenser's poem draws, not only upon the classical elegiac overlay of bridal and funeral ritual, but also upon the whole medieval anti-nuptial tradition: courtly love's rejection of marriage, erotic debate's barely disguised preference for romantic love, even prose satire's disparagement of marriage, as in the *tiers livre* of Rabelais. In this chapter we shall examine three responses to Spenser's *Epithalamion,* which in spirit claim a closer relation to his elegiac *Prothalamion.* Donne's "Epithalamion Made at Lincolnes Inne," written perhaps in the same year as Spenser's poem, bawdily pits fescennine against Spenser's high-serious epithalamium, competing directly with the earlier poem in a broadly parodic manner. Crashaw's "Epithalamion" knows little of the odic publicity of Spenser's hymn; his metaphysical lyric turns on the mystic marriage/death collision, boldly mingling traditional imagery of the epithalamium with elegy's funereal symbols.[8] Finally, Blake's *Visions of the Daughters of Albion* is so fully a commentary on Spenser's *Epithalamion* that it echoes ironically, two centuries later, that poem's orphic refrain: "The Daughters of Albion hear her woes, & eccho back her sighs."[9]

II

Donne's "Epithalamion Made at Lincolnes Inne" was the first written of his epithalamia and the only one to lack a dedication. In fact the poem's focus on Spenser's nuptial hymn is so steady, its mock-staging of that work so thoroughgoing, that Spenser's poem and no marriage of friend or patron may be deemed its occasion. The poem remains an enigma to the readers of Donne—neither a date nor ceremonial pretense can be named for certain—and the poem appears to elude the critics as well.[10] In fact this early poem not only announces the differences between Donne's and Spenser's poetry, it calls upon a different audience, and it points forward to the brilliant verbal play of Donne's later poetry. An odd epithalamium, ending with the violent disemboweling of the bride on the altar of love, the poem was written in response both to the conventions of Elizabethan love poetry and to the sensibility which produced it—neither of which Donne could share.[11] Spenser's sense of himself as a professional poet charged with a sacred duty—to gain for the rich heritage of classical civilization an English hearing—and his confidence in his place at the altar of such celebration could produce a poem like the *Epithalamion:* a work intensely private, yet so public it could embrace mythological characters, Christian personages, and the general attendant public alike. In Donne's poem we find a wry diminishment of epithalamium's panegyric scope: if Spenser felt himself another Orpheus, imaging the relation of the poetic imagination to its public in nature's echo of his song, Donne appears a caustic undergraduate, engaged in sophisticated wordplay before a rather restricted coterie of initiates.

If career aspirations and poetic program are terms too deliberate for Donne, at least we can say that this early poem uses the form of the epithalamium to announce its creator's very different sense of the poet's place in the world. The poet of "Epithalamion Made at Lincolnes Inne" is hardly that harmonious center out of which the marriage ceremony emanates, the bridegroom of Spenser's poem. Donne's master of ceremonies is an implied presence: deliberately keeping himself at a remove, he manipulates the scene, makes broad sexual jokes, stretches the Petrarchan play on love and death into a particularly arresting image of sacrifice. Donne's epithalamium makes no other claim than to entertain its limited audience. In this connection, Novarr's hypothesis that the poem was Donne's contribution to the Midsummer revels of his fellow law students, written while he was a twenty-three-year-old law student at Lincoln's Inne, offers a convincing explanation for much of the puzzling imagery of the poem. Whereas I agree with Novarr's statement that "Donne's canticle here sings a song of sacrilege" and remain persuaded by his explanation of the poem's play with hermaphroditism in terms of the mock-wedding performed by the male law students, I feel he ultimately misreads the poem. Donne's overt attention to the sexual significance of the occasion is not, I think, "crude and tasteless," "crass and vulgar."[12] The shock value of Donne's imagery was to become the trademark of his poetry and should not be mistaken for tastelessness. Here the sexual explicitness functions to undermine some of the seriousness of the earlier poem. That Donne could not share Spenser's sense of poetry as a kind of secular priesthood can be illustrated by a comparison of the two poems.

Donne's desanctification of a rival poem, particularly one which had met with such unprecedented literary success, is accomplished two ways. First he apes the form of Spenser's poem, approximates its stanza form and mimics its refrain. With the other two poems of this chapter, this "Epithalamion" signals its debt to Spenser by borrowing its refrain. Donne's "To day put on perfection, and a womans name," repeated at the end of each stanza of the poem, is, like Spenser's last line, a long line of twelve syllables. Although most epithalamia are shorter than Spenser's 365-line poem, Donne works a comic foreshortening of the *Epithalamion*. Reducing the number of stanzas to eight and changing the content of the refrain after four from "To day" to "To night," he renders Spenser's lengthy, luxuriant ceremony with irreverent brevity. The night is as long as the day in Donne's poem, and even during the description of the day's events Donne's epithalamist cannot keep his mind off the "wish'd bed" (l. 63), itself a parodic echo of the original "wish'd day" (*Epith.*, l. 31). Spenser's lover longs for the consummation that night will bring on that longest day of the year, whereas Donne's laments that this day is not short like "winter dayes" and impatiently awaits Phoebus's steeds' lively gallop "downe the Westerne hill" and "other disports than dancing jollities" (ll. 49, 58, 52). The use of Spenser's word here is telling: "iollitie," or nuptial revelry and fellowship merely, will not be enough in Donne's poem. From opening lines—in which conventional language the bride is commanded to leave her "solitary bed" now that the sun has risen—to close, the poem never allows the reader's attention to stray from that "warme balme-breathing thigh" which is promised the lover (ll. 2, 7). The best example of Donne's exuberant sexual punning is the *double entendre* of the refrain: "To day put on perfection, and a womans name." Jay Halio argues convincingly in "*Perfection* and Elizabethan Ideas of Conception" that to the contemporary expression "women receive perfection by men" Donne joins Aristotelian reference to conception and generation.[13] At the end of each stanza for the duration of the poem, we are reminded of the impending sexual encounter.

The second way that Donne deflates Spenser's poem is by imputing less than romantic motives to the groomsmen wanting to marry the wealthy Senators' daughters and to the fathers hastening to make rich matches for their girls. Lest we be tempted to allegorize a marriage of Church and Christ here, or even body and soul, Donne reminds us that these motives are mortal and materialistic: Spenser's mythological female choruses and their counterparts in the present, "merchants daughters" (*Epith.*, l. 167), are replaced here with "Daughters of London" desired for their "Golden Mines, and furnish'd Treasurie"—the images are sexual as well as financial (ll. 13, 14). Called "Angels," they are also worth a dowry of gold coins to their bridegrooms on their wedding day. The "frolique Patricians" who wait upon the groom are would-be "Sonnes" of the rich "Senators" who seek to marry off their daughters, and like suns seek to dry up the oceans of their wealth (ll. 25, 26). Even the bride's description reeks of opulence and licentiousness: "As gay as Flora, and as rich as Inde," she may not even be a virgin:

> Loe, in yon path, which store of straw'd flowers graceth
>   The sober virgin paceth;
>   Except my sight fail, 'tis no other thing;
>
>   (ll. 32–34)

Two other fully developed conceits of the poem deserve further explanation, in part because they account for much of the critical censure of the poem. Neither Tufte's view of sacrificial imagery as inherent in wedding poetry, nor Novarr's assumption that these bald images were invented by Donne to parody Spenser, seems satisfactory.[14] In fact both conceits—the likening of church architecture to the bride's genitals and womb, the superimposition of bridal rite and ritual disembowelling—have antecedents in the erotic imagery with which Church mystics attempted to express the ineffable. Blake too would draw upon the tradition that called the Blessed Virgin the "domus aurea"; in a plate for *Vala*, Blake outlines a shrine to the virgin on the exposed genitals of a nude woman.[15] In Donne's version of the image, the "two leav'd gates" and "sacred bosome" of the "faire Temple" which will contain the lovers "mystically joyn'd" in marriage metamorphose into a "leane and hunger-starved wombe" which, like a "tombe," will enclose the lovers and their parents when they die (ll. 37–41). This extraordinary collision of images not only foreshadows Donne's later experiments with the language and symbolism of mysticism, it answers the philosophic base of Spenser's poem in the present. Where the debate between body and soul for Spenser could be resolved by a Renaissance marriage of earthly nuptials with irradiating Platonic significance, Donne utterly collapses the distinction. Body is soul, he seems to tell us here: the essence of Godhead after which the mystic lusts is none other than the naked genitals themselves.[16] A related, but more impressive, conceit of the poem, however, is Donne's mystic equation of marriage and death, an axis which Crashaw will explore with even more precision and control. Viewing the conversion of virgin into wife as a kind of death runs through medieval literature. In *Prothalamion* Spenser plays on the *Romaunt*'s Danger, that stout protector of virginity which can only be overcome by the arrows of love. Donne makes of the virgin's impending wifehood a mystic rite of passage which entails necessary but "pleasing sacrifice" on "loves altar" (ll. 74–75). He too exhorts his bride to leave the "solitary bed" of virginity:

> Leave, leave, faire Bride, your solitary bed,
> No more shall you returne to it alone,
> It nourseth sadnesse, and your bodies print,
> Like to a grave, the yielding downe doth dint;
> You and your other you meet there anon;
>
> (ll. 2–6)

As in Blake's *The Book of Thel*, sexuality or generation involves a descent to the grave; it "nourseth sadnesse" because it requires that the virgin die a ritual death, both psychological and spiritual. The conceit is further elaborated by the reference to "sheets": the bed can become the nuptial couch or it can remain a grave, depending on how the word is read. The reference to smothering in the sheets when next the bride goes to bed had a range of meanings at Donne's time: fornication, of which this bride might be guilty, was punishable by enclosure in a sheet; a sheet might also figure the shroud in which her dying virginity smothers, or the sheets of conjugal bedding between which her nascent sexuality smoulders and her natural fecundity rests in potential:[17]

> This bed is onely to virginitie
> A grave, but, to a better state, a cradle;
> (ll. 79–80)

The exchange this poem ostensibly promotes of "this life for a better" (l. 86) is called into question by the mocking tone of the whole. Yet Donne was perfectly capable of conceiving of epithalamium and elegy as dynamic and related opposites. A sermon written a few years before his death welcomes their mystic chiasmus and harkens forward to the heavenly nuptial vision at the close of Milton's elegy for King:

> HEAVEN is Glory, and heaven is Joy; we canot tell which most; we cannot separate them; and this comfort is a joy in the Holy Ghost. This makes all Jobs states alike; as rich in the first Chapter of his Book, where all is suddenly lost, as in the last, where all is abundantly restored. This consolation from the Holy Ghost makes my mid-night noone, mine Executioner a Physitian, a stake and a pile of Fagots, a Bone-fire of triumph; this consolation makes a Satyr, and Slander, and Libell against me, an *Ave*, a *Vae* an *Euge*, a *Crucifige* an *Hosanna;* It makes my death-bed, a mariage-bed, And my Passing-Bell, an Epithalamion.[18]

These lines might serve as a gloss to the vision bestowed upon the resurrected Lycidas, helping the reader to decipher the emblem of Blessed Troops wiping tears from his eyes and welcoming him to Divine Presence with a nuptial anthem. In turn, the initiation scene enacted in *Lycidas* may make sense of this early poem of Donne's. Whatever irreverences "Epithalamion Made at Lincolnes Inne" commits, it provided the early Donne with a conventional stage on which to exercise his poetic voice; it allowed him to dialogue with a formidable literary opponent; and it permitted him to lay aside the student years of his own poetic virginity in the course of an increasingly vigorous literary career.

III

Richard Crashaw's "ingenious arabesque" of an "Epithalamion" is interesting less as evidence of "epithalamic decline" than as a particular and idiosyncratic response to Spenser's poem.[19] As in the case of Donne's anti-epithalamium, the occasion of the piece remains obscure; evidence suggests that it was written some forty years after Donne's and Spenser's poems when Crashaw was in his early twenties; the identity of the pair for whom it might have been written has not been conclusively established.[20] But the covert imitation of Spenser's *Epithalamion* which "Epithalamion" affects suggests literary rivalry with that poem. Formally it follows the bare outline of *Epithalamion*: beneath the twelve stanzas of Crashaw's poem, each ending with a long line reminiscent of Spenser's refrain, and the closing allusion to Spenser's envoy—a conventional prayer for the longevity of the "well sett song" (l. 143)—is the coy invitation to compare the two poems. But the resemblances end here. Spenser's panegyric appears almost a masque in comparison with this self-enclosed, compressed lyric. Instead of an orphic courtier directing the progress of a well-attended wedding, we hear the voice of a mock-monodist: by a striking inversion, Crashaw presents his nuptial hymn as a half-serious elegy on the death of a "maydenhead" (l. 11). "Marriage bed," in this poem, becomes explicitly "funerall pyle" (ll. 66, 65).

The essential conceit of the poem is established in the earliest stanza by a curious translation of epithalamic imagery into that of elegy. First "virgin tapers of pure waxe / . . . all white / as snow, and yet as cold" (ll. 1–3)—those conventional symbols of virginity—are exhorted to "come" participate in a ceremony which looks increasingly like a funeral, in much the way that nymphs are invoked to share the pastoral dirge. That virgin tapers are to become votive candles becomes clear in the last line of the first stanza, lifted practically verbatim—with one witty emendation—from the April blazon of the *Calender*: "helpe me to mourne a matchlesse maydenhead / that now is dead" (ll. 11–12). By converting Spenser's line—"Helpe me to blaze / her worthy praise" (Variorium, "Aprill," ll. 43–44)—into an elegiac injunction to participate in the dirge, Crashaw begins to supply an undertext of elegy to the wedding song.

The bride of Spenser's poem, that radiant presence, undergoes as well a parodic diminishment. Represented only by the synecdochic maidenhead, she entertains a range of shapes borrowed from medieval and Elizabethan love poetry. Since virginity signifies unfulfillment and infantilism for the poet, the maidenhead is figured in turn as a bud whose "blooming kisses" still lie in "Rosy sleepe" (ll. 5, 8)—a "froward flower" whose "peevish pride / within it selfe, it selfe did hide" (ll. 21–22); next as the hesitant eagle of Chaucer's *Parlement* who declines to choose for yet another year, preferring to serve as a virgin instead; finally as a phoenix, that traditional symbol for the combustion consummation produces and the progeny which rise on its ashes. But this phoenix is a hunted bird—of "Cupids shafts afraid" (l. 37)—whose Danger can only be overcome by love's arrows. And in a dainty allegory which looks forward to Pope's *The Rape of the Lock,* "poore Loue" finally invades that impenetrable "Christall castle" by setting up "fort" in "noble Bramstons eyes" (ll. 49–58). The conceit is an old one: medieval mysticism and secular love lyric both claim the eyes as that instrument by which Divine Love's fire is communicated to the human heart. "Ayming thence," Cupid finds his spot and "this matchlesse maydenhead / was soone found dead" (ll. 59–60). Readers of Crashaw will recognize in the sexually charged imagery of "shafts" (l. 53) and penetration the complex mystical legacy of his poetic patron saint, Teresa.

Superimposing the image of the phoenix upon the virgin's maidenhead, Crashaw suggests, of course, that annihilation will be a fecund death, a complex analogy he develops in a short Latin poem, "Phaenicis Genethliacon & Epicedion." In that poem as in this, loss of virginity is a *mors obstetrix* (*Poems,* p. 224). In the phoenix's "funerall pyle"—an image of "Hymens holy heate"—the virgin's coldness is subsumed in the "mutual fire" of conjugal love (ll. 65, 4, 34). The eulogy for the dead maidenhead is a mock one:

> With many pretty peevish tryalls
>   of angry yeelding, faint denyings,
> melting No's, and milde denyalls,
>   dying liues, and short liued dyings;
>   with doubtfull eyes,
>   halfe smiles, halfe teares,
>   with trembling joyes,
>   and jocund feares;
> Twixt the pretty twylight strife
> of dying maide and dawning wife;
> twixt raine and sun-shine, this sweet maydenhead
>   alas is dead;
>
> (ll. 73–84)

The seventh stanza, bringing the poem to two-thirds completion, sings the dirge for the lost virginity. The "turn," or upward movement of consolation, begins with the recognition of "riche loss" (l. 86) in the exchange of "dying maide" (and the conventional pun on death and orgasm is intended) for "dawning wife" (l. 82). Crashaw expresses the paradox of this fortunate fall here and elsewhere in a brilliant sequence of contraries and oxymora: smiles and tears, ice and fire, joys and fears, rain and sun, "sweet brine" (l. 103), "sighed smile" (l. 67), "loue in death" (l. 80), and "jocund feares" (l. 80). "Short liued dyings" may signify all-too-brief orgasms, but "dying liues" seems to confer, in the terms of mock-elegy to be sure, something of that immortality that Milton claims for the reborn *Lycidas* in the formulation: "sunk low, but mounted high."

Imagery of consolation is, in the poetry of Crashaw, rigorously predictable. It issues from his Mariolatry and focuses, in this case, on the maternal attributes and capacities of his "sweet . . . mother phaenix" (l. 71)—her spiced "neast" which offers shelter and refuge (l. 72) and the "Cradles where her kindred flamed," and the nurturing bosom she offers to her supplicants. In fact the consolation Crashaw offers to this dying virgin is a "well fledged neast / of winged loues" to be maintained in the "breast" of each marital partner (ll. 129–30): the aggregative complex of nuptial (and increasingly nurturing) imagery which accompanies the consolation of pastoral elegy. The ninth, tenth, and eleventh stanzas of the poem effect a mystical allegory of the soul in small, couched in nuptial terms but drawing for its imagery upon Crashaw's baroque mystic vocabulary. The ninth features an exchange of pure liquids: "raine" and "deaw" from the Heavens elicit life-giving seminal fluids from the "Blessd Bridegroome" (ll. 97, 105, 97)—those "dropps that wash away the maide / shall water your warme planted loues"—and tears of joy and penitence in the bride. The tenth converts water into wine as in the marriage at Cana. Marital couple is imaged in the traditional symbiosis of vine and oak: "clusters" of grapes are held up for sustaining kisses. As consummation approaches, erotic love is figured in the filling of cups "to the brimm" with the aphrodisiac vintage of sexual passion. The eleventh stanza is a mystic benediction which ends upon the eternally held mutual gaze of the couple. But Divine Love is not merely seen; it is heard as well. The last metaphor the poem offers us is that of the concert of spheres:

> May their whole life a sweet song proue
>   sett to two well composed parts,
> by musickes noble master, Loue,
>   played on the strings of both their harts;
>   (ll. 33–36)

Thus may earthly lovers and singers attune their sensibilities to the "unexpressive nuptial song" of the heavenly troops.

Most Crashaw poems end here, with the attainment of mystic ecstasy;

but this "Epithalamion" brings us roundly back to Spenser in its final lines. In fact Crashaw's borrowed use of the canzone technique here echoes Spenser's envoy in two important ways: it emphasizes the literary antecedent of this otherwise unconventional poem, playing up what I have called its artifactual nature; it also enforces the contrast between these two poems by turning upon Spenser's short/long play in a much-altered tone. In Crashaw's poem the lovers' "mutual sound" is "not short though sweet" (l. 140). And the poet tunes his song to theirs, hoping heaven will "think its short though it bee long," a "well sett song indeed, which shows / sweet'st in the Close" (ll. 142–44). There is something precious in this elaboration which makes of Spenser's direct yet delicate claim—"Be unto her a goodly ornament, / And for short time an endlesse moniment"—a rhetorical exercise. Critics have suggested that although they were rough contemporaries the Metaphysicals were temperamentally alienated from Spenser's rich Renaissance poetics: "sensuous ecstasy," writes Ruth Wallerstein, "was as it were a short circuit blocking out the ampler vision."[21] Crashaw's anti-epithalamium, far from a failure, is evidence for me that his sense of poetic vocation was already much more personal and idiosyncratic, though not a whit less "religious," than Spenser's. Rhetorical excellence becomes itself a *raison d'être* for the poet. As Marc Bertonasco and A. Alvarez rightly remind us: "Just as [le jongleur de Notre Dame] offers his lowly skill to the honor and glory of God, so the baroque poet 'performs' out of reverence, offering his talents up to God."[22] Crashaw's "Epithalamion," making of Spenser's marriage ode a mock-elegy upon a maidenhead, is just such an offering: rhetorically sophisticated, formally self-conscious, yet utterly sincere.

IV

Blake's *Visions of the Daughters of Albion*, written two centuries after Spenser's poem, is no less an ironic epithalamium than Donne's or Crashaw's. But Blake's long perspective on the *Epithalamion* lends to his late-eighteenth-century parody an effect less localized, less trivializing, and more complex than that of the baroque poems. Critics of Blake have long thought *Visions* to be a satiric epithalamium not unlike his *Marriage of Heaven and Hell* and have read the poem's peculiar imagery and cast of characters in terms of Blake's canon.[23] But few have considered the implications of comparing it to the *Epithalamion* it so passionately rewrites. Blake's subversion of Spenser's imagery and refrain, philosophical predisposition and literary ethos, is total, and reflects as well upon the Metaphysical poems: loss of virginity still entails the necessary death of passage, but sexuality is extramarital here. Oothoon's search for love and sensual pleasure takes her beyond the "frozen marriage bed" and costs her no less than rape and psychic divorce (Pl. 7, l. 22). And in response to her terror, the orphic refrain of Spenser's poem becomes a tragic chorus: "The Daughters of Albion hear her woes, & eccho back her sighs" (Pl. 2, l. 20). In *Visions,* Blake invokes the form of Spenser's Renaissance epithalamium to stage his own alternate allegory of the soul: but in this anti-epithalamium, the bride's death into generation and her ascent into Higher Innocence of awakened consciousness are predicated upon the double betrayal of jealous, enslaving husband and lustful, yet limiting lover.

Like all of Blake's poems, *Visions* has met with a range of critical approaches. The poem has been described variously as a political allegory of the American Revolution, an indictment of the industrial revolution and the slave trade,[24] as a vindication of the rights of women,[25] and as an account of the soul's progress on its Neoplatonic journey of spiritual generation.[26] The last approach to my mind offers greatest scope for translating Blake's idiosyncratic imagery and helps to explain the relationship between Blake's theology and that of the Christian mystic poetry discussed above. In fact, as Kathleen Raine and others have demonstrated, Blake was a rapt student of the Neoplatonic Revival of the 1790s, deriving from Thomas Taylor's works on Orphism and the Eleusinian Mysteries both a vocabulary and a philosophical system that have much in common with those of the other poems of this chapter. But whereas Crashaw's virgin soul dies that she might marry in the image of Divine Love, Blake's dialectic between the world of Innocence—out of which one descends into the "grave" or "cave" of this world—and that of Experience is ongoing. *The Book of Thel* (an elegy on the failure to descend, to be discussed in a later chapter as a response to Milton's *Lycidas*) and *Visions of the Daughters of Albion* are thus counterparts in Blake's early theology: *Thel* chronicles the first fall of the soul into the world, or incarnation; *Visions* details the consequences of that fall and envisions options in the world of experience. Thel refuses generation because she views the soul's death into mortal body as a lapse from eternity too terrifying to contemplate. In *Visions,* however, Blake turns his back on the Orphic view of the body as a tomb. Not only does Oothoon actively choose generation by plucking the flower of carnality, she celebrates in this hymn to love—as commanding in its different registers as Spenser's *Epithalamion*—full participation in the soul's progress of that problematic body electric.

Blake's quarrel with the Neoplatonists and thus with Spenser issues from his belief in the body's divinity and his rejection of the doctrine of corporeal enslavement, and helps to explain his dramatic reshaping of the

Epithalamion. In place of Orpheus and Eurydice, Blake figures a cast of three—jealous bridegroom, oppressive lover, and bride-to-be—locked in eternal combat. The narrative of the poem, so far as it can be charted, begins with Oothoon's desire for generation, her subsequent response to a bridal invitation, and her movement hence from Leutha's vale. Between this expectant virgin and her bridegroom, however, comes the roaring Bromion, agent, paradoxically, of both Oothoon's sexual awakening and her brutal rape. Theotormon's resultant jealousy becomes manifest in his deaf refusal to hear his bride's cries and his autoerotic denial of healthy sexuality. Caught between Theotormon's "self-love" (Pl. 7, l. 21) and Bromion's repressive morality (he is outraged at Oothoon's sexual awakening and enjoyment), Oothoon casts off each of their false moralities in turn, renounces the double bonds, and energetically proclaims her new-found imaginative freedom. Students of Blake will recognize in the characters of Oothoon, Bromion, and Theotormon the familiar polarization of female emanation and repressive, Urizenic male.[27] But the centrality of the bride in this satiric epithalamium, wholly consistent within Blake's wider symbolism, is an intriguing inversion of Spenser. This poem, too, for all its anti-nuptialism, is an initiation poem. Far from a transcendent symbol or a passive character in the drama, Oothoon not only wills her own marriage here, but she suffers the consequences of its bondage and imaginatively effects her own release. For the generative principle of the soul was, for Blake, eternally feminine: the bride of this poem must protest the fetters of traditional marriage, refuse the bonds of misdirected lust, and make of the loss of virginity an imaginative triumph over conventional morality.

Formally, Blake reproduces only the refrain of Spenser's poem. In *Visions,* however, the refrain is repeated only three times: unvaried, it is purposely drained of that incremental, celebratory force lent it by successive variations in the commanding song of the orphic courtier. Blake's chorus of weeping, sighing daughters not only chants an elegiac refrain, but sings as well a static round against which Oothoon's song works and evolves. The use of the refrain for the last line of the poem sets Oothoon's imaginative achievement in a timeless perspective: against the linear progression of Spenser's Christian wedding ceremony, we have the cyclic, endless oscillation of Blake's dialectic, couched here in the terms of an eternal marriage of contrarieties.

The thrice-repeated refrain divides the poem into three parts and punctuates the stages of Oothoon's evolving vision. The first part of the poem finds Oothoon wandering in that state of receptivity to dream vision which the narrator of *Prothalamion* experienced. But her embrace of that eroticism which "my whole soul seeks" mistakenly fastens on Bromion, who brands her with the name of harlot, demonically parodies the annunciation as he impregnates her, and consumes her in the "burning fires of lust" (Pl. 1, ll. 13, 18). The end of the first section finds Oothoon accepting the denunciations of her lover and husband; offering her "defiled bosom" to eternal Promethean torture, she asks only to reflect Theotormon's severe smile. "The Daughters of Albion," at this point, "hear her woes. & eccho back her sighs."

In the second movement of the poem, Oothoon begins to sense that she is not fallen but renewed. In the language of Canticles she heralds the morn and invites her bridegroom to meet her. "Arise my Theotormon I am pure" (Pl. 2, l. 28). Refusing any psychic imprisonment—"they told me that I had five senses to inclose me up. / And they inclos'd my infinite brain into a narrow circle" (Pl. 2, ll. 30–33)—she does her spiritual ablutions. In fact this knowing virgin—"how can I be defild when I reflect thy image pure" (Pl. 3, l. 16)—puts marvelous words into the mouths of Spenser's swans, for unlike the birds of *Prothalamion*, she welcomes sexuality:

> Sweetest the fruit that the worm feeds on. & the soul
>   prey'd upon by woe
> The new wash'd lamb ting'd with the village smoke &
>   the bright swan
> By the red earth of our immortal river: I bathe my wings.
> And I am white and pure to hover round Theotormon's breast.
>   (Pl. 3, ll. 17–20)

Her answer to Spenser's swans might be that of the chorus of "A Song of Liberty": "Nor pale religious letchery call that virginity, that wishes but acts not! / For everything that lives is Holy."[28] But the remainder of the section remains inconclusive. Oothoon listens to Theotormon and Bromion in turn and is silenced by their contrary speeches. Renewing the "lamentation," she hears the echoes of the Daughters of Albion.

The third section of the poem opens with Oothoon's exuberant recognition of the Urizenic in what her imaginatively inadequate lovers have to say. She renounces their "cold floods of abstraction" (Pl. 5, l. 19) and "forests of solitude" (Pl. 5, l. 19), because the "wheel of false desire" (Pl. 5, l. 27) will produce a horrible abortion of the fetus. Against this "unripe birth" (Pl. 5, 1. 27), she images the soul's rebirth into higher innocence, an unsheathing which removes layers of repressive clothing. First to be transcended is "subtil modesty," that enemy of sensuality which catches "virgin joy / And brand[s] it with the name of whore" (Pl. 6, ll. 7, 11–12). The second error is masturbatory self-enclosure: the "self-enjoyings of self denial" (Pl. 7, l. 9). The third is jealousy, a "creeping skeleton / With lamplike eyes watching around the frozen marriage bed" (Pl. 7, ll. 21–22). All three reverse the process of generation, leaving the newborn soul "a solitary shadow wailing on the margin of non-entity" (Pl. 7, l. 15). To generate, by contrast, is to accept fully and joyously the sexuality of the mortal body. Passionate engagement in ebullient "copulation" Oothoon images thus:

> I'll lie beside thee on a bank & view their wanton play
> In lively copulation bliss on bliss with Theotormon:
> Red as the rosy morning, lustful as the first born beam,
> Oothoon shall view his dear delight, nor e'er with jealous cloud
> Come in the heaven of generous love; nor selfish blightings bring.
> (Pl. 7, ll. 25–29)

But the tragedy of *Visions,* for all Oothoon's imaginative self-projection, is that there will be no marriage in this poem. At the close of this section we learn that "thus every morning wails Oothoon," but her husband cannot transcend his repressive morality: "Theotormon sits / Upon the margind ocean conversing with shadows dire" (Pl. 8, l. 12). Beulah, the "married land," promises improved sensual enjoyment but requires submission of imaginative self to a fall from the garden—full participation in sexual intercourse: "the youth shut up from / The lustful joy, shall forget to generate" (Pl. 7, ll. 5–6). Theotormon's reluctance as a bridegroom limits eternally the growth of his soulmate; but their failure to connect in no way negates her imaginative self-transformation. Oothoon's love song—"I cry, Love! Love! Love! happy happy Love! free as the mountain wind!" (Pl. 7, l. 16)—for its failure to awaken Theotormon, remains one of the most poignant pleas for the soul's unshackling in all of Blake's poetry. Blake's *Visions of the Daughters of Albion,* an answer to Spenser in the form of anti-epithalamium, is no less a hymn to love than that Renaissance poem; but where the earlier poem marches with considerable ease and confidence toward the symbolic altar of marriage, Blake's ceremony marks a difficult passage, emblematic of the soul's difficulties in the crucible of Experience.

V

By arresting an epithalamium short of conventional transcendence, ritual aggregation, and projection of issue, Blake re-establishes a tension with epithalamic tradition. *Visions of the Daughters of Albion* is a wedding poem only by inversion and negative reference: at best it remains a tenuous, passionate bridal invitation perched eternally between potential acceptance and frustrating unfulfillment. In the end, Spenser's

Epithalamion remains a negative model for Blake's poem, since it is sensual happiness—at odds with the repressive institution of marriage—into which Oothoon must be initiated. Here and elsewhere, the gold wedding ring symbolizes iron bands of domination for Blake, explaining his particular response to the nuptial genre. That Blake had even in his earliest lyrics an acute sense of epithalamic convention can be seen in the following poem from *Poetical Sketches*:

> O thou, with dewy locks, who lookest down
> Thro' the clear windows of the morning; turn
> Thine angel eyes upon our western isle,
> Which in full choir hails thy approach, O Spring!
>
> The hills tell each other, and the list'ning
> Vallies hear; all our longing eyes are turned
> Up to thy bright pavilions: issue forth,
> And let thy holy feet visit our clime.
>
> Come o'er the eastern hills, and let our winds
> Kiss thy perfumed garments; let us taste
> Thy morn and evening breath; scatter thy pearls
> Upon our love-sick land that mourns for thee.
>
> O deck her forth with thy fair fingers; pour
> Thy soft kisses on her bosom; and put
> Thy golden crown upon her languish'd head,
> Whose modest tresses were bound up for thee![29]

The spring ode in the seasonal group contains all the traditional elements of the epithalamic genre. Beginning quite conventionally with an invitation to "turn / Thine angel eyes upon our western isle," it summons up all the anticipation of the wedding day: the modestly attired bride, the sense of participants, the "approach" of the bridegroom which is "in full choir" hailed by the waiting earth. The poem restages the springtime renewal heralding the wedding in Song of Songs. It evokes a natural world wholly harmonious with this celebration of unity: hills and valleys echo the singer's orphic song in a long line imitating Spenser's refrain. This wedding poem also describes the decking of the bride, appreciation of her beauty by the bridegroom, and finally the consummation of sexual desire in an image of "languish'd head" and loosened hair. That Blake chose to parody the form in *Visions* rather than imitate it straightforwardly is evidence of his increasing suspicion for the imagery of the wedding poem—a poetic form celebrating stasis, harmony, reconciliation in marital terms had become by the time of *Visions* incompatible with his mature poetic vision. In fact, among Blake's best poems, *The Marriage of Heaven and Hell* and *Visions* parody the epithalamium, emptying it of its former content and using it to describe the healthful tension of opposites which can never meet, the full ambivalence of the soul's life in the world of Experience.

A certain kind of wedding poem written after Spenser's *Epithalamion*—and here called anti-epithalamium—challenges our notion of generic development. More interesting than Masefield's "Prayer for the Royal Marriage of Princess Elizabeth and Lieutenant Philip Mountbatten, R.N. Westminster Abbey, 20th November, 1947"[30] or the recent epithalamia for the marriages of English Princes Charles and Andrew is a whole range of anti-nuptial poems whose relation to the pastoral genre of epithalamium is perhaps once removed but vital and sustaining nonetheless. In general these poems invert the traditional imagery of the wedding poem: a bride's veil becomes a shroud; nuptial rite becomes funeral service; marriage ceremony is consummated by rape, decapitation, or worse. Heinrich Heine's "Ritter Olaf" is just such a wedding poem, commemorating a marriage of a knight sentenced to die for seducing the king's daughter: ceremonial refrain—perhaps the single most imitated convention of the epithalamium—becomes in this black rendering fairly a death knell: "Der Henker steht vor der Türe" ("The Hangman stands at the door").[31] So too in Salvador Díaz Miron's "Nox," the wedding preparations become dire auguries: singing birds are replaced by squawking flocks of cranes; rising day-star becomes a comet which "figures a note, depicts a tear."[32] Here bridal veil portends death:

> Nubecilla que flota,
> que asciende o baja,
> languidecida y floja,
> solemne y blanca,
> muestra señal simbólica
> de doble traza:
> finge un velo de novia
> y una mortaja!
>
> A hovering cloudlet,
> rising, falling,
> languid, flaccid,
> solemn, white,
> feigns in doubly symbolic aspect
> the bridal veil,
> the winding sheet.

The epithalamium remains to this century a compelling form for poets, not in its conventional manifestation as an occasional piece, but rather as a negative model: the anti-epithalamium, in its counter-generic, even elegiac form, has lent longevity and resilience, paradoxically, to a literary genre virtually defunct by the close of the seventeenth century.

5

"Unexpressive Nuptial Song": Milton's *Lycidas*

I

Rilke's Ninth Duino Elegy, debatably pastoral but unmistakably Miltonic in its verbal evocation of the "unsägliche," is a contemporary heir to that literary tradition, rooted in the pastoral, which both forces upon poets the awesome burden of the inexpressible and allows them poetic access to it.[1] Like *Lycidas*, Rilke's elegy draws poetic strength from the recognition of mutability and the inexorable fact of death. He, like Milton, calls himself a newcomer, "ein Neuling" at "klagende Leid."[2] The striking similarity between the poems, however, is the angel featured at the center of each—an angel who mediates between this world and the next by interceding for the initiate. Milton's angel is Michael himself, who bestows Christian vision upon the swain; his verbal presence in the poem, if we accept William Madsen's reading, brings about the "turn" from mourning to consolation.[3] Rilke's angel, on the other hand, is the oracular voice within, an alter ego with whom the poet dialogues, against whom he defines himself. In either case, the poet receives from the shaman/angel what Rilke calls sacred revelation, "heiliger Einfall": Milton's heavenly nuptials, at which tears of lamentation are washed away along with worldliness, and Rilke's "vertrauliche Tod," which charges life with piercing urgency and demands of the poet in the present "Verwandlung" of what is before him. The former is perhaps our classic expression of Christian revelation and consolation; the latter is a modern lyric on death with no pretense of pastoral corpse. Yet each, in its celebration of the "unexpressive,"[4] in its dialogue with the angel, acts out an initiatory scenario. Apprehension of a mystery, however transvalued, lies at the heart of each.

What is inexpressible in Milton's funeral elegy for King is, of course, a "nuptial song" (l. 176), and for this reason, the poem must be placed next to even less likely companions, Spenser's *Epithalamion* and *Prothalamion*. It is not enough, I think, to note that Milton's tortured eleven stanzas are metrically related to Spenser's experiments with the canzone in his two nuptial poems. "They were not elegies," writes John Crowe Ransom, "but at least they were marriage hymns."[5] In fact, Milton's allusion, in his quintessential pastoral elegiac statement, to certain conventions of the wedding poem and his explicit celebration of the consolation in nuptial terms do not interest the critics sufficiently.[6] Classification of *Lycidas* as the "ideal type" of English elegy obscures its vital commerce with the opposing, but related, genre of epithalamium. The context of *Lycidas* must be widened: to the whole sweep of pastoral learning from Theocritus to Phineas Fletcher's piscatorials written only a few years before *Lycidas*, we must add both the initiatory pattern derived by pastoralists from Plato's *Phaedrus,* and the nuptial odes of Milton's English predecessor.

Writing on *Lycidas* "yet once more,"[7] the critic himself experiences a curious sense of "belatednesse."[8] It is a critical truism to write that the poem is about Milton since E. M. W. Tillyard pronounced the poem a literary gesture and the poet its true subject.[9] Any reading of *Lycidas* must now similarly go beyond celebration of the poem as apex of a mode destined to die upon its publication.[10] For explicators of the poem, Arthur Barker's work on the three crescendos of *Lycidas* provides one important account of its structure and shape.[11] And M. H. Abrams's recognition that *Lycidas* divides into speeches, modified by William Madsen's suggestion that Michael speaks his own, accounts for the proliferation of voices in what professes to be a "monody."[12] The bibliography of the poem is so extensive that one is called upon to provide a fresh context for the work.[13] Here I should like to show that the poetic reciprocity of epithalamium and elegy—which Virgil discovers in the fifth eclogue, which Spenser experiments with in the "Aprill" and "November" poems and later in the *Prothalamion,* and whose opposing psychologies Milton first explored in the pair of poems on mirth and melancholy[14]—achieves consummate expression in his *Lycidas* and, more overtly but less successfully, in the *Epitaphium Damonis*. The "unexpressive nuptial song" of the first poem, so long resisted by the elegiac occasion and form of the work, gets sung in spite of formal constraints. The rolling measure of the panegyric, its peculiar imagery and range of related allusions and poetic effects, are repeatedly deflected during the progress of the poem but effectively dominate its ending. It becomes clearer in the *Epitaphium Damonis,* where the progress toward sacred nuptials is taken for granted, that Milton is drawing—for initiatory purposes—on Spenserian as well as more general cultural symbolism of marriage. In *Lycidas,* that consummate English elegy, epithalamium successfully, if covertly, invades elegy's borders.

II

Spenser offered Milton two things crucial to the composition of *Lycidas.* One was the possibility of writing in English a poem that was at once intensely private and resolutely public. Milton learned from Spenser how to make of an occasion piece a private meditation with a public purpose, naturally, of self-announcement.[15] Both poems are lyrics, written for one very self-serving voice, yet each manages to project the most populated of pastoral landscapes. Each poem records a private initiation ceremony, but each manages to convince as well that the event is truly of public record. Here, of course, epithalamium and elegy achieve common ground: the odic possibility of commemorating lyrically an occasion of public importance. The ode's strophic divisions, its intellectual movement, and its choral effects lie beneath Spenser's epithalamic and Milton's elegiac pronouncements and link them to poems less obtrusively indebted to either tradition. Wordsworth's Immortality Ode is Romanticism's answer to both of these canonical poems: the lines of wedding and funeral poems inform its structure, and the publicity of the ode form lends a private lyric the illusion of an audience.

The second thing Milton learned from Spenser is how to borrow and transform the obsessive image of Orpheus—protagonist of the ceremonial poem in classical to contemporary poetry. The archetypal bard was, of course, no stranger to the elegiac tradition. But the allusions to him in Moschus's "Lament for Bion" and Sannazaro's eleventh eclogue, among other pastoral elegies, recall his legendary poetic power over nature and commemorate his sad attempt to retrieve his wife through song.[16] Spenser, of course, invokes Orpheus's power to sing for his own bride, deliberately reversing, by medieval convention, the bard's unsuccess. Even Milton's own early references to Orpheus, in *L'Allegro* and *Il Penseroso,* both allude to his attempt to regain Eurydice: in the poem on mirth, Orpheus awakens from "golden slumber" to sing his gorgeous "strains" at Pluto's door; in the ode on melancholy, the reference is identical in content if sadder in tone. Here Orpheus's "note" drew "iron tears" from the god.[17] It is not until *Lycidas* that Orpheus appears in ritual guise—as an initiate undergoing spiritual trial. In one vivid visual image, Milton pictures the violent death of Orpheus, emblem of the impending death of the arts and of their potential rebirth on other shores.[18]

> What could the Muse herself that Orpheus bore,
> The Muse herself, for her enchanting son
> Whom universal nature did lament,
> When by the rout that made the hideous roar
> His gory visage down the stream was sent,
> Down the swift Hebrus to the Lesbian shore?
> (ll. 58–63)

Even more significant, however, is the initiatory motif this version of the Orpheus myth sounds. Like the flaying of Marsyas, the dismemberment of Orpheus signals a ritual experience. And the interpretation of the reference in this manner also explains the placement of the so-called digression on fame which follows immediately upon Orpheus's watery death within the poem. A later reference to Orpheus in Milton's corpus, coming midway through *Paradise Lost,* indicates the degree to which the archetype of that drowned poet becomes linked with his sense of his own career:

> Still govern thou my song,
> Urania, and fit audience find, though few.
> But drive far off the barbarous dissonance
> Of Bacchus and his revelers, the race
> Of that wild rout that tore the Thracian bard
> In Rhodope, where woods and rocks had ears
> To rapture, till the savage clamor drowned
> Both harp and voice; nor could the Muse defend
> Her son. So fail not thou who thee implores;
> For thou are heav'nly, she an empty dream.
> (*Paradise Lost,* VII. 30–39)

By this time in Milton's life, the Restoration had denied his hopes for reformation; blindness and failing health were taking an increasing toll on the physical man; doubt had beset the writer. No longer, as in Spenser's *Epithalamion,* does Orpheus announce the initiation drama of a young poet dreaming of literary immortality. By the end of *Paradise Lost,* Milton's unresponsive world becomes the "wild rout" which so effectively silences Orpheus; here dismemberment figures at face value—as an image of violent death with no promise of renewal.

Honing the image of Orpheus for *Lycidas,* Milton may have drawn upon another poem of Spenser, and less directly upon the initiatory drama of Plato's *Phaedrus.* "The Ruines of Time," which numbers among Spenser's *Complaints,* is a work obsessed with "vitall breath" and poetic power. That *Lycidas* echoes the poem has been adequately demonstrated by ample citation from both works; Milton draws mostly on this poem in his fame passage.[19] Here and elsewhere, Spenser's allusion to Orpheus invokes his civilizing power of song to "moderate stiffe minds, disposd to striue" as Spenser puts it in *The Faerie Queene* (*Variorium*, IV, 219), and the "sad wayment / Which *Orpheus* for *Eurydice* did make" ("Ruines," ll. 390–91). But Milton did learn from this poem and the *Epithalamion* the central place of Orpheus in a meditation on literary fame, whether epithalamic or elegiac. That he knew as well the *Phaedrus*, its Orphic analogy for initiation and its metaphoric description of the soul's proper progress heavenward, we can ascertain from a lettter to Diodati written in 1637: "You ask me what I am thinking of? So help me God, an immortality of fame. What am I doing? Growing my wings and practising flight. But my Pegasus still raises himself on very tender wings. Let me be wise on my humble level."[20] Even this passage betrays an ambivalence toward earthly recognition that the fame passage in *Lycidas* echoes. Clearly Milton is as ambitious as he is circumspect about poetic recognition. But that the immortality so aspired to here is literary, rather than philosophical or religious, only a reading of *Lycidas* can establish conclusively.

III

Milton's occasion poem for King, claiming to be an elegy and asking to take its place within this highly conventional tradition, is perhaps our most complex pastoral initiation poem. Like Theocritus's first idyll, it announces the poet's program for a new poetics and signals his first important appearance on a literary stage. Like Virgil's tenth bucolic, *Lycidas* constitutes a leave-taking from the pastoral world, with all the ambivalence that this rite of passage implies. In fact the poem telescopes an entire tradition into a single poem (during the course of which its writer becomes master of the mode and transcends it), a single ceremonial formality which claims a place for the poet in a literary tradition dating from the ancients. In rising to the occasion of King's death, Milton not only presents himself as rightful heir—successor to Theocritus, Virgil, and that self-promoting "new poete" of the *Calender*—he also gestures forward toward the moment when a future poet will "with lucky words favor my destined urn" (l. 20). The poem's oldest ancestor may be the *Phaedrus*, the initiatory scenario of which it mimics and boldly inverts: unlike Phaedrus, who willingly submits to an orphic trial at the knee of father Socrates, Milton's swain interviews a virtual procession of potential father figures, chooses the angel Michael, and enlists his participation; in short, he controls the very conditions of his own initiation ceremony.

A range of conventional elegiac elements informs *Lycidas*'s structure, but the manner in which these conventions serve is striking for its unconventionality. The traditional despoiling of nature, figured in the opening lines of the poem, for example, cuts two ways: rape of nature to symbolize her participatory sadness in the untimely death of a friend here suggests as well (with all due false modesty) Milton's fear that his untried poetic voice may be unable to command echoes, may not rise to the "occasion dear" in Spenserian, that is, orphic, registers (l. 6). Yet the violence done to nature by the poet also expresses great self-confidence. Plundering the literary store, Milton plans to subvert it for his own purpose: the favors of "some gentle Muse," the sound of "rural ditties," the refrain-like complaint at the absence of nymphs, the catalogue of flowers and the cast of mourners, even the final upward movement of consolation—cribbed from every practitioner of pastoral until Milton's time—the poet comes with "forced fingers rude" to shape anew. For a poem begun so auspiciously, asking to take its place in the tradition by co-opting a convention, it voices rather quickly its doubts that pastoral will be adequate to it:

> Alas! what boots it with incessant care
> To tend the homely slighted shepherd's trade,
> And strictly meditate the thankless Muse?
> (ll. 64–66)

And whereas in the sixth eclogue of Virgil, Apollo checked the poet's arrogant desire to abandon pastoral for martial themes, Phoebus touches Milton's "trembling ears" to remind him that fame awaits the aspiring Christian poet. In fact the most important pastoral motifs in the poem are present only by virtue of negative invocation, a technique which does not bar the poet from enjoying the use of them: the "rural ditties were not mute" (l. 32), "Satyrs" and "Fauns" would "not be absent long" from the "glad sound" of "th'oaten flute" (ll. 33–35). "Neither were" the nymphs "playing on the steep" when the waters closed over Lycidas (l. 52).

Except in the repetitions—"for Lycidas is dead, dead ere his prime" (l. 8)—and the chiasmus—"Together both, ... both together" (ll. 25, 27)—gone is the amoebean structure of pastoral elegies as in the first idyll of Theocritus.[21] Transformed as well is the role of the procession of visitors. In Idyll I, mourners are puppets of the unnamed goatherd; they taunt the dying Daphnis with their version of a more relaxed *otium*. In *Lycidas* the swain himself interviews a stream of potential mentors. Old Damoetas, pastoral singer of Eclogue III and judge of the "October" poem in the *Calender,* is the first initiator to be passed by. Next Phoebus is dutifully listened to and dismissed. The pagan gods of wind and sea are questioned and released. Camus, representing the University, slowly shakes his "reverend" but ineffectual head and passes on (l. 103). "The Pilot of the Galilean lake" is the first mediator who might effect the swain's passage beyond novitiate, but his "dread voice" precludes dialogue (ll. 109, 132). An authoritarian and "stern" speaker, Saint Peter delivers the sermon on the hypocritical clergy; he is a law-giver and not a bestower of visions. Not until the end of the flower passage does the swain's attention turn to "the great Vision of the guarded mount" (l. 161). Michael's voice not only effects the swain's transcendence of his pastoral apprenticeship, it also projects an audience of right witnesses—"solemn troops and sweet societies" (l. 179)—at the poet's literary ascension to mature poetic stature. In Daniel 10:7–17, Michael is simply called the "vision" who intercedes for the prophet, restoring the "strength" and "breath" to him which apprehension of the mystery had drained and returning "voice" to him after he had been struck dumb.[22] In *Lycidas* it is Michael's compassion, his almost female ability to "melt with ruth," that in fact consoles the initiate and empowers him to rise above "Doric lay" (l. 189). Access to the "unexpressive" by means of a ritual exchange with the angel is consolation enough for the "uncouth swain" (l. 186). The *locus amoenus* is not merely the natural opulence of Elysian Fields, as in Spenser's "November" elegy for Dido; it is the wedding feast of the Lamb of Revelation 19:9, the hierogamy climaxing the Mystery festivals, Orpheus's failed wedding song for his bride challengingly evoked in Spenser's *Epithalamion*.

> Where other groves, and other streams along,
> With nectar pure his oozy locks he laves,
> And hears the unexpressive nuptial song,
> In the blest kingdoms meek of joy and love,
> There entertain him all the saints above,
> In solemn troops and sweet societies
> That sing, and singing in their glory move,
> And wipe the tears forever from his eyes.
> (ll. 174–181)

The epithalamic close so effectively reverses the course of elegy in Milton's poem of poetic incarnation, merging with and capping the Virgilian convention of elegiac consolation, that we must trace its increasingly felt presence in the poem. A study of the Trinity manuscript version of the poem reveals that the Orpheus and the flower passages underwent the most revision; Milton clearly took great pains with their composition. These passages, the opening rape of nature, and the final projection of wedding ceremony and choral surround shall concern us as we trace the interpenetration of epithalamium and elegy in this poem. In fact *Lycidas* begins with a rape, and ends with an achieved marriage, symbolic, as in Spenser, of professional stature won. If Spenser's *Epithalamion* records continuous natural echoing of the poet's song in the incremental repetitions of its famous refrain, the opening of Milton's poem has the opposite effect. It does not posit nature's cooperation with the human singing voice; it marks instead a rupture. Milton's task is the greater: hoping to sing with some of Spenser's epithalamic confidence in the availability of a witnessing surround, he has to reverse completely the course of elegy by the close. To end *Lycidas* with a vision of "all the saints above," like the "blessed Saints" of Spenser's poem (*Epith.*, l. 423), he has to come full circle—from mourning to panegyric. The hope covertly expressed in these opening lines, that violence may yield something of enduring value, is echoed in the Orpheus passage some fifty lines below. As poetry survives the dismemberment of its creator at the hands of the Bacchic maidens, so Milton hopes his unseasonable rape of nature may result in the kind of immortality solemnizable by a heavenly nuptial choir.

Reference to Orpheus's marriage to Eurydice—the standard portrait of him in English poetry until Milton—is so conspicuously absent in *Lycidas,* and so determinedly denied by the first half of the poem, that the reader wonders whether this and not the marriage of Revelation is the first meaning of "unexpressive nuptial song." In fact the dismemberment, drawn from Ovidian and Virgilian accounts of Orpheus, is the opposite of a bridal ritual and points to an ellipsis, or what George Steiner calls in another context a "silence" in the poem, which the undertext of epithalamium will eventually fill.[23] During the course of his elegy for King, Milton matches the achievement of Spenser's *Epithalamion:* an orphic initiate, he celebrates his own poetic coming-of-age in the terms of a final, sacred marriage.

The Orpheus passage begins and the flower passage ends similarly, suggesting that they share a function in the poem. "Ay me, I fondly dream" (l. 56) introduces the first; "to interpose a little ease" concludes the latter (l. 152). The idea of unexpressed marriage which both passages convey is until this point in the poem a "false surmise" (l. 153). Until the swain's attention turns to Michael at the end of the flower catalogue, it looks as if Eurydice is not to be rescued; wedding references are subtly deflected. Three times, then, marriage is invoked by its absence: in the ravishment of nature, in the unexpressed part of the allusion to Orpheus, and in the double function, both nuptial and funereal, of flowers used to "strew the laureate hearse" (l. 151).[24] These passages, which have given critics trouble for their seeming lack of integration with the movement of the poem, cannot be labeled digressions without missing an important structural feature of the poem. The Orpheus passage, offering a model for literary initiation and giving rise to a meditation on literary fame, and the flower passage, invoking a predecessor's marriage poem and inducing inexplicably the "great Vision of the guarded mount" to turn homeward and intercede for the singer of pastorals—in short, to mediate a wedding—prepare carefully for the ceremony to come.

Earlier versions of the Orpheus passage stress even more than the final text the ritual aspect of initiation.[25] "Inchaunting," with its root suggestion of incantation, is foregrounded. Orpheus's "gorie visage" is called "divine head" at first, which overtly links the reference to rituals in honor of the dying god. Also, as the portrait of Orpheus sharpened in these lines, Milton stressed Calliope's identity as a Muse, breather of poetry into Orphic souls. "Divine head" finally became "gorie visage," better to bring out the violence of "rout" and "roare." One early deletion is particularly telling:

> whome universal nature
> might lament
> and heaven and hel deplore

The reference to Hell's refusal to listen here, invoking Orpheus's tearful plea for restoration of his bride, is carefully expunged in later reworkings of that line.

The flower passage, clearly an afterthought, is similarly crucial to interpretation of the poem in final form. If taken at face value, it amounts to no more than a "soothing fantasy"[26] or a sentimentally "consoling fiction,"[27] a pleasant interlude in an otherwise-directed elegy. In fact the catalogue, as we have seen, has a history in pastoral poetry, both elegiac and epithalamic: associated with "ideas of surviving fame, memorial tribute, and the possibility of resurrection,"[28] it only becomes a loaded reference in English poetry. Classical precedents for Milton's flower passage include the list in Virgil's second eclogue and the mention of ritually strewing leaves at the end of Mopsus's song in the fifth bucolic. But the real source for the passage is not even the "November" elegy for Dido in Spenser's *Shepheardes Calender,* but the "Aprill" blazon, the epithalamium of the group and rehearsal for Spenser's own initiation poem.[29] Appropriating the catalogue for a funeral poem, Milton strews the bier with flowers here. Once again, previous drafts of the passage are telling:[30] note the careful erasure of even negative reference to marriage in the replacement of "unwedded" with "forsaken." "Uninjoyd love" is similarly revised. The omission of intrusive words, indicating Milton's familiarity with the dual function of flower catalogues, suggests another source for these lines—the confusion over flowers in Shakespeare's *The Winter's Tale*. In this scene Perdita wishes for a spring posy for Florizel, who confuses her catalogue with funeral wreathing:

> Perdita: Now my fair'st friend,
> I would I had some flowers o' the spring that might
> Become your time of day; and yours, and yours,
> That wear upon your virgin branches yet
> Your maidenheads growing: O Proserpina,
> For the flowers now, that frighted thou let'st fall
> From Dis's waggon! daffodils,
> That come before the swallow dares, and take
> The winds of March with beauty; violets dim,
> But sweeter than the lids of Juno's eyes
> Or Cytherea's breath; pale primroses,
> That die unmarried, ere they can behold
> Bright Phoebus in his strength, a malady
> Most incident to maids; hold oxlips and
> The crown imperial; lilies of all kinds,
> The flower-de-luce being one! O, these I lack,
> To make you garlands of; and my sweet friend,
> To strew him o'er and o'er!
>
> Florizel: What, like a corse?
>
> Perdita:
> No, like a bank for love to lie on and play on;
> Not like a corse; or it, not to be buried,
> But quick and in mine arms.[31]

Two traditions of flower-strewing coalesce here, one epithalamic, one elegiac,[32] and Milton was as aware as Shakespeare of the poetic possibilities for superimposing one upon the other. The love-death association is highly erotic in both passages, but its exaggerated presence in Milton's funeral elegy provides a transition to the nuptial choruses of the conclusion.

Michael, who becomes the swain's true intercessor, mediates by his actual verbal presence the widest gap of the poem: his vision spans the distance between the flower catalogue, offering the possibility of singing an epithalamium, and the memory of Lycidas's drowned body sinking forever to the "bottom of the monstrous world" and needing a proper burial (l. 158). The poem's pagan and Christian frames of reference, its division between elegy and epithalamium, come together in Michael's great hymn of aggregation. The vision to which Michael admits the swain is, in fact, a kind of translation: Orpheus's gory head becomes the revived head of Lycidas (and the immortally raised head of the Son as well); the immortal bard's watery dismemberment is answered by Lycidas's own resurrection—accomplished by the "dear might of him that walked the waves" (l. 173); the destructive waters of the Hebrus become the nourishing ablutions of baptism.[33] The culmination of these transvaluations is the final, explicit evocation of marriage: Orpheus gets his bride in the pastoral fields of the Christian heaven. In fact the wedding ceremony—public, ritualized, divine—is the Christian poet's way of imaging admission to the sacred company.[34] All the soaring rhetoric of the close culminates in the anagogic vision Christ gave to man: the marriage between the human soul and Heavenly Love. In Daniell's fine pictorial analysis of the lines, mystic initiation figures at its core:

> Now indeed the full Baroque space of celestial joy and beatitude would seem to open above us. But as we look up it narrows strangely into a sight of the dead shepherd washing his locks in nectar. Thus purified he is surrounded by troops of saints singing the unexpressive nuptial song. The vision approaches mystical insight.[35]

Lycidas is, of course, in Milton's marvelous paradox, "not dead," because he is now a bridegroom. And in more ways than that merely does *Lycidas* imitate all the coy avoidance of the impending wedding in Song of Songs. Just as ecstatic union, deliberately withheld, is approached by means of overlapping imagery in the alternate speeches of bride and groom, so in *Lycidas* is the temptation of singing a nuptial anthem purposely resisted until it is merited by the swain's apprehension of converging significance in Michael's speech. Only then does marriage become the proper metaphoric conclusion for elegy. Geoffrey Hartman argues in addition that Michael's knighting of Lycidas as the "Genius of the shore" (l. 183) is a "sacred marriage: that of the poet's genius with the *genius loci*," reminding us of the word's derivation from the genius who guards and fructifies the marriage bed as in Spenser's *Epithalamion*.[36] "Sacred marriage" too is the climax of the Orphic initiatory ordeal. In Michael the swain has found his true spiritual and poetic father: making Lycidas guardian of the shore, the angel awards his earthly role to the initiate, recognizes the claims of the successor, admits him to the ranks.

At the close of *Lycidas,* Milton mounts skyward with the resurrected singer. He would hardly claim orphic voice for the dead King; clearly his own fortunes as a poet (and his future plans as a Christian) rise in that last figured ascent. To read the conclusion otherwise prompts the regressive view that the poem returns to pastoral and "swainishness" at the end.[37] Such interpretation results from a misreading of the coda, that much-discussed stanza which so radically alters the tone of the poem. To term it a mere "baroque extravagance"[38] or to wonder that Milton includes only half of the pastoral frame, the return to dialogue and fellowship,[39] is to slight its function in the poem. In fact Milton imitates a precursor here: the coda of *Lycidas* might be read as a rewriting of the envoy of Spenser's *Epithalamion*. As in Spenser's address to his own work, Milton's coda reaffirms the artifactual nature of the poem, places its achievement in the real world of literary careers, gestures in the direction of higher, more enduring song, and provides a sense of closure. As in Virgil's tenth eclogue and Spenser's "December," pastoral apprenticeship is decidedly ended.

When Milton shifts to the third person in the coda ("I" had come to pluck nature's berries in the invocation), the poem effectively unsheathes itself. The "uncouth swain" will continue to sing "Doric Lay" long after Milton has stopped (ll. 186, 189). Viewing the coda as Milton's self-separation from the singer of pastorals also helps to explain all the apologies and ironies pastoral imagery provokes during the course of the poem. The tone of the last lines is purposely reduced, unoracular, properly pastoral, for it is no longer Milton, self-celebrant, who sings. When Milton does return to pastoral elegy in the *Epitaphium* a few years later, he gives no evidence of his earlier ritual and mystically charged use of elegiac and epithalamic modes. The effect of the *Epitaphium*—Latin and effete, mannerist in its pastoral affectations—achieves none of the vatic register of *Lycidas*.

IV

Written to commemorate the death of Milton's dearest friend, Charles Diodati, the *Epitaphium Damonis* is a better example than *Lycidas* of the sort of elegy which, as Ellen Lambert would have it, consoles a human speaker. The *Epitaphium* is in no measure a literary gesture: an unfortunate mix of art and life, it approaches instead confessional lyric. Sincerity of grief no doubt earned the *Epitaphium*'s reputation as Milton's most moving poem, a memorial to a friendship as dead to him as the adolescence he celebrates so elegiacally. In fact the occasion of this poem, its overtly personal tone, and the limited range of its allusions and significance are utterly at odds with the elaborate pastoral machinery it musters. The poem has little of the literary, even careerist, investment of *Lycidas*: the dominant presence of first-person verbs and possessives, the localized history of mourning, the contemporary horizon of the poem, all limit its scope. In contrast to the successfully epitaphic poems we have been reading, the *Epitaphium Damonis* never reaches odic, orphic registers, never makes of the confrontation with death an initiatory scenario.

The elegy for Diodati borrows freely from the pastoral store—its nearest ancestor is Castiglione's *Alcon*—but its use of such imagery becomes increasingly mannerist as its relation to the context obscures. The ecphrastic description of the cup in Theocritus's first idyll is most ambitiously reproduced here, yet its presence in the poem bears no resemblance to the goatherd's integral counter to Thyrsis's song in the earlier poem. Additionally, the refrain, which steadily and increasingly lent orphic pitch to previous pastoral poems of initiation, has the opposite effect here. Static and unchanging—"Ite domum impasti, domino iam non vacat, agni"[40] ("Away, my lambs, unfed: your shepherd heeds you not")[41]—and startlingly concrete in its repeated exhortation to the unruly flock, the refrain is reduced to ornamental effect, which too becomes tiring. Rand's famous gibe is clearly merited: "There is one tremendous infelicity, the refrain: 'go to your folds unfed, my lambs, your master has not time for you'; this is well enough for three times or even four, but lambs that have to be liturgically shooed away seventeen times are either unusually hungry or unusually inquisitive; at any rate they have become monotonous."[42]

Milton's farewell to the pastoral mode—he selected the poem to close his 1645 volume of early poems—deliberately echoes Virgil's tenth bucolic, yet with little of the power of that poem. Virgil's appreciation, in his last eclogue, for what he is leaving is keen, even affecting; Milton's attention is hardly focused on the Arcadia he leaves behind. Thinking ahead to specific epic projects with British themes, and welcoming the "harsher speech" (l. 186) of the English language, he is only too happy to hang up his "shepherd's pipe" and renounce at last "classical cadence" (l. 186).

The *Epitaphium*'s relevance to Milton's literary career—and the reason for invoking it here—is a function of its "astonishing" conclusion.[43] Honoring Diodati with admittance to the kingdom of the elect, Milton is compelled to restage the nuptial tableau of his earlier poem. But the song that was barely expressible in *Lycidas* becomes in this poem a full-scale orphic hymn:

> Quod tibi purpureus pudor, et sine labe iuventus
> Grata fuit, quod nulla tori libata voluptas,

> En etiam tibi virginei servantur honores;
> Ipse caput nitidum cinctus rutilante corona,
> Laetaque frodentis gestans umbracula palmae
> Aeternum perages immortales humenaeos;
> Cantus ubi, choreisque furit lyra mista beatis,
> Festa Sionaeo bacchantur & Orgia thyrso.
>
> (ll. 212–19)

> Thine was untarnished youth, the flush of honour
> Untouched by wantonness: and now to thee
> The glories kept for virgin souls are given.
> Upon thy radiant head a glittering crown,
> And in thy hand the joyous green of the palm,
> Thou goest deathless to the immortal feast,
> Where the sound of the lyre and the voice of singing
> Kindle and quicken the dancing feet,
> Where the Bridegroom's feast is toward,
> And the mystic wine is poured,
> The madness and ecstasy of Heaven.
>
> (ll. 242–52)

The "unexpressive" quality of the "nuptial song" in *Lycidas*, which achieves fullest articulation in the final lines of Milton's *Epitaphium*, is decidedly of mystical origin, arising perhaps from the sacredness of such imagery for the poet-initiate. As Sidney had written in *A Defence of Poetry*: "there are many mysteries contained in poetry, which of purpose were written darkly, lest by profane wits they should be abused."[44] Flavia Alaya too notes that "pastoral is that valuative mode of expression that asserts for us the sacredness of the inexpressive. It is mythic in the sense that, as we know it, it is undoubtedly but a recorded variation on a mythology more ancient still that gave full religious significance to the humility of man in the face of this sacredness."[45] No doubt the satisfactions of *Lycidas*'s close are a direct result of the poem's obsessive obscuring of its covert epithalamic purpose: to generate a poetic analogue for the *hieros gamos* that ended the Mystery initiations and the marriage supper of the Lamb; beneath the epithalamic climax of that poem's conclusion is also the erotic power of withholding wedding until such vision has been earned by the novice experiencing passage to maturity. Now party to the company of initiates, the Milton of the *Epitaphium* no longer felt its sacredness so fully. In his last pastoral, the full poetic richness of "immortal nuptials," no longer "unexpressive," could at last be given utterance.

V

The Orphic myth lies at the heart of *Lycidas* both as evidence of the poet's centrality to his world—Orpheus was, even before Spenser, the perfect courtier-bridegroom—and as proof of the literary immortality conferred upon the initiate once the orphic image is fulfilled by "the dear might of him that walked the waves" (l. 173). I should like, by way of conclusion, to measure the distance between this evocation of Orpheus's symbolic power and the two poems which preface the *Collected Poems* of W. B. Yeats. There can be no doubt that Yeats intended the companion poems "The Song of the Happy Shepherd" and "The Sad Shepherd" to serve as a pastoral preface to his volume of works and to reflect an attitude toward pastoral in general. In the juxtaposition of these poems, Yeats was thinking of Blake's dual perspective in the matching *Songs of Innocence* and *Songs of Experience*, who in turn knew this pastoral dualism from Spenser's pair of poems, the "November" elegy and the "Aprill" epithalamium, each with its own conventions and related imagery. But taken together, the two Yeats poems compose an elegy on pastoral's demise. Even the happy shepherd's song begins by mourning the passing of pastoral forms and immediacy: "The woods of Arcady are dead, / And over is their antique joy."[46] Miltonic and Spenserian forms of truth are then evoked in their own language and rejected. These two, and here Yeats uses Milton's word for the angel's pity, "shall singing fade in ruth / And die a pearly brotherhood." Determining to "nowise worship dusty deeds," the singer of the first poem decides not to follow Milton on Galileo:

> New dreams, new dreams; there is no truth
> Saving in thine own heart. Seek, then,
> No learning from the starry men
> Who follow with the optic glass.
>
> (p. 7)

nor Spenser:

> Seek, then, for this is also sooth,
> No word of theirs—the cold star-bane
> Has cloven and rent their hearts in twain,
> And head is all their human truth.
>
> (p. 8)

The most that this poem can offer in terms of consolation is a return in dream to Arcadia, where the pastoral singer might still "please the hapless faun, / ... With mirthful songs before the dawn" (p. 8). Here the poet pictures himself briefly with the power of another Orpheus:

> And still I dream he treads the lawn,
> Walking ghostly in the dew,
> Pierced by my glad singing through,
> My songs of old earth's dreamy youth.
> (p. 8)

Ultimately, however, orphic command is not seized by these singers. The first poem ends inconclusively and leads into the sorrowful lament of the sad shepherd. In the second poem the singer is no longer able to sing or dream. The song of the sad shepherd takes the form of a lament by the sea—"*Dim sea, hear my most piteous story!* / The sea swept on and cried her old cry still" (p. 9)—which ends in failure of imagination rather than reactivation of poetic power as in *Lycidas*. Whereas in the happy shepherd's song the poet tells his story to an "echo-harboring shell" by the "humming sea," in its companion piece the sea is indifferent and the "*heavy story*" whispered into a shell reverberates until "my own words, *re-echoing, . . . send* / *Their sadness through a hollow, pearly heart*" (p. 9). Instead of deriving power from the exchange by seaside, a feature of a certain kind of elegy written in the wake of Sannazaro's piscatorials and Milton's *Lycidas*, the poet is reduced to a self-mirroring solipsism. This diminished Orpheus hears only the echo of his own voice:

> Then he sang softly nigh the pearly rim;
> But the sad dweller by the sea-ways lone
> Changed all he sang to inarticulate moan
> Among her wildering whirls, forgetting him.
> (p. 9)

In a later chapter, "Sea-Changes: The Incarnational Ode and Ceremonial Modes," we shall return to initiation poems by seaside which respond to Milton's piscatorial of self-announcement by means of a generative parody. Whitman's "Out of the Cradle" and Crane's "Voyages," Hopkins's "Wreck of *The Deutschland*" and Eliot's "The Dry Salvages," are, like Yeats's poems, seashore incantations, but these poems do not end with a bleak portrait of Orpheus stammering his song into a self-echoing shell. In these poems the poet-initiate receives a secret word from the sea, and a knowledge of death that enables him to transcend fear of it. In each case the word he learns to utter gives him orphic stature and marks his ascension to the company of poets.

6
Failed Elegies: Blake's *The Book of Thel* and Shelley's *Alastor*

I

Historians of the elegy generally concede that the mode reaches its apex in Milton's *Lycidas*—that supreme collation of classical myth and Renaissance symbolism acclaimed for its successful distillation of an entire tradition into a single lyric poem—then declines ignobly in the obsequies of its eighteenth- and nineteenth-century imitators. As consensus would have it, "one finds after Milton only an aftermath."[1] Ellen Lambert's study of the pastoral elegy virtually ends with *Lycidas*, and T. P. Harrison's anthology, *The Pastoral Elegy*, includes only five poems after Milton's: the derivative pastorals of Pope and Philips, Gay's parodic "Friday" from his *Shepherd's Week*, and the two singularly wooden pastoral elegies which the English tradition hails as responses to *Lycidas*, Shelley's *Adonais* and Arnold's *Thyrsis*.[2] The implication of such editorial choice is that only poems which profess outright dependence should be read as imitations of *Lycidas*, limiting that poem's resonance to tinny comparison with later academic exercises.

In fact *Lycidas*, like Shakespeare's *Hamlet*, dominates in less visible ways the poetic imagination of the past few centuries. In the first instance, poets have responded to its symbolism and language in lyric forms other than elegiac. As A. Reeve Parker convincingly demonstrates in "Wordsworth's Whelming Tide," Wordsworth and Coleridge dialogue by means of a double imitation of *Lycidas* in parallel passages from the former's *The Prelude* and the latter's "To William Wordsworth."[3] Additionally writers have mimicked the form of *Lycidas* for purposes other than funereal: Marvell's "The Nymph Complaining for the Death of her Faun," for example, published forty years after Milton's poem, is an elegy on the death of innocence. But the nymph's tears, unlike those of *Lycidas*, are for a historical situation so irrevocably changed that pastoral is no longer able to comfort. The statue into which she metamorphoses is a powerless relic memorializing a literary tradition which has lost its power to console. In Geoffrey Hartman's analysis of this "idyll of idylls," poetry responds to invasion of the "wanton Troopers" by gathering to itself "the vision of lost and original unity." Yet the poem cannot be more, he continues, than a "perennial monument of tears." Instead of figuring admittance to the heavenly company, the poem "ends with an image of exquisitely fashioned grief."[4]

Other less overt tributes which I want to consider more fully in this chapter similarly document failure when placed next to Milton's *Lycidas*. As Marvell's poem may be seen as a counter-elegy to the monody for King, one beweeping its estrangement from the sources of consolation available to the earlier poem, so Blake's *The Book of Thel* and Shelley's *Alastor* must be read as deliberately flawed artifacts which imitate *Lycidas*'s form for the express ironic purpose of reversing its conclusion.[5] Both poems reproduce the searching rhythms of *Lycidas*, its sequential interview of prospective mentors, and its symbolic debate between points of view. Both record a journey, described in allegorical terms as a progress of the soul undertaken by the poetic imagination in its attempt to incarnate. As every poem inspired by *Lycidas* cannot help seizing upon its watery context or piscatorial nature, so these two Romantic poems are fairly drenched in the moisture of generation. But the conclusion of each work roundly inverts the consolation of Milton's poem: Thel refuses the necessary descent of the initiate soul upon which transcendence is predicated and regresses back to her infantile paradise with the shriek of a picked flower. Shelley's *Alastor* is an attenuated elegy, a little epic of the soul, which records the death of the imagination as a result of excessive solitude and, in the words of the poem itself, "self-centred seclusion." Neither *Thel* nor *Alastor*, then, ends with that rising movement of consolation or *anagnorisis* which has been characteristic of pastoral elegy since the fifth bucolic of Virgil. No nuptial metaphors appear in the final lines of either poem to represent admittance of the *mystes* to the community of initiates. Instead each poem offers only the dirge—in bleak, but rigorously honest, response to Milton.

Milton's Romantic heirs felt as keenly as he did the pastoral injunction to begin one's literary career with pastorals, in proper Virgilian sequence, before attempting the somewhat higher strain. It is no surprise to find, then, that the corpus of each of the English Romantics contains an initiatory collection of pastorals, however idiosyncratic the interpretation of that prescription might be. An early poem of Keats, "Sleep and Poetry," for example, will suffice to record the poet's sojourn in the "realm . . . / Of Flora, and old Pan," and announce the author's literary ethos and intentions.⁶ Blake's *Songs of Innocence* and *Songs of Experience,* the fulfillment of his early pastoral *Poetical Sketches,* and Wordsworth's and Coleridge's lyrical balladry, including *The Rime of the Ancient Mariner,* represent more extensive pastoral apprenticeships: the poetic programs they announce differ vastly, but their initiatory inspiration is wholly pastoral. Finally, after reading *The Book of Thel* and *Alastor* next to Milton's *Lycidas,* we might be better disposed to think of Byron's *Childe Harold* and Keats's *Endymion* as quest-elegies, pastoral rites of passage.

II

The Book of Thel is perhaps Blake's first prophetic book; but its imagery, theme, timing (dated 1789, but probably contemporary with *The Marriage of Heaven and Hell* and *Visions of the Daughters of Albion,* Blake's experiments with epithalamic forms), and placement (it precedes the *Songs* in Erdman's edition) link it firmly to Blake's pastoral output. Students of Blake, initiated into his peculiar pastoral vision by *Sketches* and *Songs,* will recognize the childlike context, the mythological condensation, the pastoral nonchalance, the imaginative play between contrasting states, and the garden landscapes of innocence in its overture. The title page pictures Thel in shepherd's garb, holding a crook, and the poem itself opens by describing the pastoral activities of Mne. [*sic*] Seraphim's daughters—counterparts of Albion's tragic chorus, much as Thel is a younger, less knowledgeable Oothoon—as they lead about their "sunny flocks." Only Thel, like Oothoon, is perceptive enough to see beyond the round of eternity.

> All but the youngest. she in paleness sought the secret air.
> To fade away like morning beauty from her mortal day:
> Down by the river of Adona her soft voice is heard:
> And thus her gentle lamentation falls like morning dew.
> (Pl. 1, ll. 2–5)

The poem exists in embryo in these opening lines. The river of Adona is probably derived from Milton and Spenser. Milton's "smooth Adonis," who "from his native Rock / Ran purple to the Sea, suppos'd with blood of Thammuz yearly wounded" (*Paradise Lost,* I. 450–52), combines the pastoral Adonis, nature-cult hero Thammuz, and dying Orpheus into a complex association of death and rebirth ritual which Blake, in his brief allusion, clearly intends to invoke. Spenser's Garden of Adonis, a kind of waiting room for unborn souls not unlike the vales of Har, is similarly invoked by the reference.[7] The river of inspiration, like the "morning dew" of Thel's awakening vision, supplies the necessary moisture of Neoplatonic generation to which nascent souls are attracted, as infants move instinctively toward nourishing milk.[8] Thel's impulse to generate is fueled not only by this liquidity; it issues from her recognition that mutability haunts even her pastoral preserve. The poem, then, will chart Thel's passage from the realm of pre-existence into a more demanding imaginative life, and record her eventual refusal to make the leap. Although the poem's fiction of a "virgin" on the brink of sexuality and marriage would seem to call for an epithalamic form, Thel's failure to generate ultimately calls for elegy instead: the poem classes itself in its fifth line as a "lamentation."

The reading of Thel I want to advance here has roots in Northrop Frye's description of the "elegiac mood of Generation"[9] and David Wagenknecht's work on elegy and Blake's poetics in the first sections of his *Blake's Night*.[10] For Frye, the "elegiac" is often accompanied by a "sense of the passing of time, of the old order changing and yielding to a new one."[11] The passage into generation is a fall from Eternity, infused, for Frye, with all the double-edged poignancy of the elegiac. Wagenknecht's sense of the pastoral-elegy tradition is more restricted; although he classes *Thel* with *Lycidas*, he does not read Blake's poem as a commentary on Milton's.

Formally and thematically, Blake's *Thel*, like Wordsworth's Immortality Ode, clearly has *Lycidas* in mind. Milton's poem begins with the poet's self-characterization as an unripe elegist, and starts with consciousness of dissonance between the fact of Lycidas's death and the possibility of consoling balm caught up in the oxymoronic formulation of "melodious tear." *Thel*, too, begins with isolation of the elegist—that youngest daughter's separation from her sisters by virtue of her superior imaginative scope—and issues from her growing sense, couched in natural metaphors, of mutability even within "O life of this our spring!" (Pl. 1, l. 6). Milton's poem begins with a description of pastoral seedtime, during which kindred souls battened flocks and tempered rural songs to the oaten flute. Thel, too, inhabits a world of lower innocence, an unfallen garden of ephemeral delights, in which she is content to pasture flocks. Finally, both poems turn upon the possibility of a fortunate fall from this state: Lycidas, as we know, is "sunk low" but will be "mounted high." Thel, presumably, must descend into the generated world of fallen perceptions in order to achieve a state of improved vision.

The problem enacted in both poems is the search for a proper mentor, an imaginative guide capable of conducting the initiation ritual. We have seen in *Lycidas* how a profusion of characters renders a pastoral lyric dramatic: pastoral Damoetas and Muses, Phoebus and Neptune, hoary Camus, finally the "dread voice" of that "pilot of the Galilean lake," cross Milton's cluttered stage before the angel is persuaded to "look homeward . . . now, and melt with ruth," effecting the elegist's transforming vision. Blake telescopes the procession of mourners into a symbolic tripartite visitation: Thel, the immortal soul hovering on the brink of incarnation, engages in three symbolic debates, during the course of which she discovers first her similarity to, then her distance from, the speaker. Lilly, Cloud, and Clod of Clay offer Thel increasingly complex versions of the same story—inclusion in a cyclic order of material metamorphosis. Her refusal to espouse the reasoning of her symbolic visitants is, however, as I shall hope to show below, not the "spiritual failure" critics have made it out to be.[12] Her resistance to absorption in the higher order of the consoling vision constitutes a kind of triumph: Thel as initiate has access to the vision and she refuses it.

Part of that refusal involves a retreat from the (increasingly insistent) epithalamic imagery which Thel's situation seems to demand. Blake's Lilly offers Thel the chance to incarnate, to take her place as a nurturer in the cyclical round of nature, an unassuming place in the world of matter. Lilly cannot understand why "should Thel complain" since she herself is content to be "clothed in light, and fed with morning manna / Till summers heat melts [her] beside the fountains and the springs / To flourish in eternal vales" (Pl. 1, ll. 23–25). Thel recognizes Lilly's innocence and knows that it is not enough for her: unlike the plants, she yearns for transcendence. Lilly does not mind being food for animals, but Thel—proto-embodiment of the soul—has to remind herself that transience is only a property of the body. She is not replaceable in the way that Lilly is: "I vanish from my pearly throne, and who shall find my place" (Pl. 2, l. 12). As a result, Thel pointedly ignores aspects of Lilly's speech. For one she refuses to acknowledge a whole complex of imagery in Lilly's language which adumbrates the potential bride's passage from virgin to mother—the epithalamic time of year, "Summer"; the white gown ("milky garments") and "perfume" of the bride, the duties of the future mother ("thy breath doth nourish the innocent lamb"); the "wine" and "honey" of the bridal feast[13]—and she steadfastly fails to acknowledge the sexuality implicit in images of generation: "contagious taints," "fire-breathing steed." Thel refuses the role of nourisher that Lilly represents and ignores the consequent sexual references. Calling herself a "faint cloud kindled at the rising sun," she envisions her next visitor by aligning herself symbolically with the "little Cloud" (Pl. 2, l. 11).

The virgin soul's dialogue with Cloud continues the body-and-soul debate she has begun with Lilly. Thel fears above all imprisonment in a mortal body, and wonders why Cloud "complainest not when in one hour thou fade away" (Pl. 3, l. 2). The answer, of course, is that Cloud is content to feed flowers with moisture, and he offers Thel a place in the life cycle analogous to his. But Cloud's participation in the natural round is more involving than Lilly's, and his epithalamic imagery is more overt than hers. He explicitly seeks a "partner" and pictures marriage in sexual terms Thel is not likely to like: he imagines arriving at the "shining tent" where:

> The weeping virgin, trembling kneels before the risen sun,
> Till we arise link'd in a golden band, and never part
> But walk united, bearing food to all our tender flowers.
> (Pl. 3, ll. 14–16)

Cloud hits, in this passage, the precise target of Thel's fear of generation. She in turn deflects his pitch by refusing to hit it head-on. Stating defensively that "I fear I am not like thee" (Pl. 3, l. 17), she speaks only to Cloud's parental image of feeding birds and flowers.

> I hear the warbling birds,
> But I feed not the warbling birds. they fly and seek their food;
> But Thel delights in these no more because I fade away,
> And all shall say, without a use this shining woman liv'd,
> Or did she only live. to be at death the food of worms.
> (Pl. 3, ll. 19–23)

A second time, then, Thel projects imagistically her next conversation, the "Worm upon its dewy bed," whose physical appearance leaves Thel "astonish'd" (Pl. 4, l. 1). She, of course, wants to see the Worm as a feeder upon corpses, deliberately avoiding Cloud's implication that Worm too might seek a partner in this "pensive queen" (Pl. 3, l. 29). Harold Bloom is not the only critic to see in Worm a "phallic emblem of Generation."[14] But Thel instantly defuses the image: "dewy bed" becomes a cradle, and the phallus becomes an infant wrapped in a cocoon, a weeping babe whom Thel leaves to Matron Clay to nourish.

The Clod of Clay is the last visitor to engage in symbolic debate with Thel, and she represents Thel's most formidable opponent. Clay, of course, explicitly symbolizes generation by her association with the red clay from which Adam was formed. But she is, unlike Cloud, a female; she is, unlike Lilly, a bride; she accepts, unlike Thel, potential maternality. Clay articulates most convincingly of the three a developed epithalamic vision:

> But he that loves the lowly, pours his oil upon my head.
> And kisses me, and binds his nuptial bands around my breast,
> And says; Thou mother of my children, I have loved thee.
> And I have given thee a crown that none can take away
> But how this is sweet maid, I know not, and I cannot know,
> I ponder, and I cannot ponder, yet I live and love.
> (Pl. 5, ll. 1–6)

Thel is wise enough to know the limits of this state—it precludes passage to Higher Innocence because it is ignorant of an imaginative state beyond generation—but she is also wise enough to know that it is the fullest consolation likely to be offered to her. For a moment the promise of *Lycidas* is held out: Thel wipes her "pitying tears with her white veil," the veil of the potential bride, and considers the fall from Eternity:

> . . . Alas! I knew not this, and therefore did I weep:
> That God would love a Worm I knew, and punish the evil foot
> That wilful, bruis'd its helpless form: but that he cherish'd it
> With milk and oil. I never knew; and therefore did I weep,
> And I complain in the mild air, because I fade away,
> And lay me down in thy cold bed, and leave my shining lot.
> (Pl. 5, ll. 8–13)

She contemplates momentarily the epithalamic vision of the heavenly troops, bending as in *Lycidas* to transform tears of grief into the balm of consolation. Matron stands at the gates and like the archangel welcomes the initiate inside:

> Wilt thou O Queen enter my house. 'tis given thee to enter,
> And to return; fear nothing. enter with thy virgin feet.
> (Pl. 5, ll. 16–17)

But the veiled references to epithalamium in *Lycidas,* culminating in the "nuptial song" of the celestial choir, do not have an analogue in Blake's poem. The last section of the poem, during which Thel peers down upon the cemetery of generated souls—to the unborn soul generation is a kind of death—inverts the conclusion of Milton's poem. As in *Lycidas,* the final section of *Thel* constitutes a commentary on the poem itself. Instead of espousing the heavenly nuptial vision and commemorating passage to "pastures new," however, Thel looks down through the northern gate upon a Urizenic acceptance of experience and declines to descend.[15] Ignorant acceptance of the fallen condition is death to Thel:

she rightly sees the "couches of the dead" in a "land of sorrows & of tears where never smile was seen" (Pl. 6, ll. 3, 5). As much as she might wish to be planted, a seedling in a bed of earth, that she might transcend her condition, the vision of "her own grave plot" promises nothing more than death. And all the references in the poem to the waters of generation, tears of consolation, "fail"—in Wagenknecht's fine expression—"to prefigure resurrection; oozing nourishing milk for the child of Generation, they only moisten the lip of the girl's grave, making it easier for her to slip in."[16] From the "hollow pit" of her open grave comes a prophetic "voice of sorrow":

> Why cannot the Ear be closed to its own destruction?
> Or the glistning Eye to the poison of a smile!
> Why are Eyelids stord with arrows ready drawn,
> Where a thousand fighting men in ambush lie?
> Or an Eye of gifts & graces, show'ring fruits & coined gold!
> Why a Tongue impress'd with honey from every wind?
> Why an Ear, a whirlpool fierce to draw creations in?
> Why a Nostril wide inhaling terror trembling & affright
> Why a tender curb upon the youthful burning boy!
> Why a little curtain of flesh on the bed of our desire?
> (Pl. 6, ll. 11–20)

The voice that issues from the grave, of course, is Thel's own experiential voice, and its rises, during this final visionary incantation, to the pitch of a dirge. Thel's questions and catalogue in this passage, lamenting limitation of the senses and celebrating the sweep of their power, illustrate her imaginative growth since the beginning of her quest. But the sequence is self-indicting: when she comes to the fifth sense, touch or sexuality, she faces her own fears intently, and with the "shriek" of a plucked flower rather than the birth-cry of a newborn, she retreats to the "vales of Har."

Thel is sexually regressive, but she is imaginatively mature. I do not think that her flight condemns her to Bloom's "dungeon of Ulro";[17] nor does it earn her the sentence of Robert Gleckner: "The final tragedy of the poem springs from Thel's vanity."[18] It is true that she is not prepared to accept along with resurrection of the body sexual involvement of the body, and she shrinks from the commitment of Beulah, that "married land" which forms the lower paradise and promises sensual enjoyment. Even if she fails to compromise her "shining" or immortal nature by descending into physicality, she preserves the integrity of her position by refusing to incarnate in those terms offered her by Lilly, Cloud, and Clay.

As her questions in the visionary passage show, she is capable of envisioning what her visitors do not know exist: imaginative passage to Eden, the upper paradise, in which eternal dialectic reigns.[19]

The Book of Thel "fails," as the critics would have it, only in conventional terms. It fails as elegy in Miltonic terms, paradoxically, because it does not close with an epithalamic chorus, however much it might marshall epithalamic imagery in the service of compensatory vision. *Lycidas* ends with the nuptial choir's celebration of reconciled worlds, human and divine, and the hymn of aggregation welcoming the newcomer to the transcendent realm of the elect. *Thel* ends instead with steady contemplation of the "couches of the dead" and a solitary retreat from that vision. Instead of the snowballing rhetoric of *Lycidas*, its incremental infusions of nuptial imagery, we find in *Thel* refusal of epithalamic symbols and inversion of its premises. Thel does not find, like the poet of *Lycidas*, an angel to guide her spiritual progress; instead she learns that she is wiser than the guides available to her. To my mind Blake's *Thel* challenges *Lycidas* by means of a sophisticated parody: for Blake the imagination's journey is a solitary one, and the descent into generation arduous in intensity. Giving us a portrait of its very difficulty and an emblem, in Thel, of refusal to descend, he calls upon elegy ironically to puncture the hypocrisy of the Christian consoling vision—admittance to which requires passive acceptance, submission of self—and that of any such absorbing vision which does not originate in the human breast.

III

Shelley's *Alastor*, like Blake's *Thel*, is an early poem in the poet's corpus. In fact *Alastor* was included in the first volume of poetry Shelley published with his name on the title page.[20] The book constitutes a record of literary apprenticeship: containing lyrics on death, translations from Moschus, poems addressed to Shelley's immediate predecessors, Coleridge and Wordsworth, it launches Shelley's career as a poet. And *Alastor*, even more than his *Adonais*, sets itself up as a poem of passage. Beginning with a Miltonic invocation and the poetic trappings of pastoral elegy, it seeks the pastoral resolution of epithalamium. But like Blake's *Thel*, Shelley's *Alastor* is deliberately catalectic: ending with negation of nuptial imagery, it eschews the consolation of panegyric and valorizes the solitary lament.

Criticism on *Alastor* ranges from reductive exegesis to officious condemnation of the poem as an immature product of the poet's youth. *Alastor* has been read as a romantic drama and as a voyage poem;[21] it has been judged derivative, along with Blake's *Thel*, of Johnson's *Rasselas*.[22]

An ongoing critical debate attempts to identify the poet of *Alastor*.²³ But the worst disservice is committed by those who persist in viewing the poem as a "dead end," a "premature vision of despair."²⁴ By way of answer to critics who call the poem "vague literary melancholia, an indistinct idyll of social failure,"²⁵ I offer the following reading of *Alastor* as a response to *Lycidas*. It is not my intention merely to furnish parallels between the two works; Shelley's *Alastor* actually reworks the form of Milton's elegy and inverts the rising rhythm of its conclusion.

In two important ways the beginning of *Alastor* recalls the opening of Milton's *Lycidas*. Both poems start with a ritual invocation to nature upon the memorializing occasion of elegy. Although Milton's very literary call to the sisters nine is naturalized in Shelley's poem—in which Mother Nature herself is enjoined to "Favour my solemn song" (l. 19)—the nature of the elegiac quest remains the same: Shelley asks nature to "render up the tale / Of what we are," to reveal her "deep mysteries" and unveil "thy inmost sanctuary" (ll. 28–29, 23, 38). As in *Lycidas,* such questions are prompted by the "untimely tomb" of a young poet, and are followed by announcement of the writer's literary intention to deck that bier with the proper poetic encomium (l. 50). In the opening sixty-five lines of the poem, the initiatory pattern—invocation, definition of quest, expression of desire for spiritual guidance, undertaking of ritual task of elegy—begins to establish itself along the lines of *Lycidas*. But the breath of inspiration Shelley awaits as confirmation of his task, auspicious breezes, is wholly Wordsworthian and will be discussed in more detail in the following chapter:²⁶

> I wait thy breath, Great Parent, that my strain
> May modulate with murmurs of the air,
> And motions of the forests and the sea,
> And voice of living beings, and woven hymns
> Of night and day, and the deep heart of man.
> (ll. 45–49)

The next sixty-five lines of *Alastor* share more than placement with the pastoral flock-battening passages in *Thel* and *Lycidas*. Shelley's technique is to draw out the ten-line section of *Lycidas* into a comprehensive catalogue of the ways in which his "infancy was nurtured" (l. 68): "divine philosophy," "strange truths," "Nature's most secret steps," "the awful ruins of the days of old," "memorials / Of the world's youth" made up the "strong inspiration" of his apprenticeship (ll. 71, 77, 81, 108, 121–22, 127). This section of *Alastor* echoes as well the language of Milton's seedtime passage and his invocation to absent nymphs:

> A lovely youth—no mourning maiden decked
> With weeping flowers, or votive cypress wreath,
> The lone couch of his everlasting sleep:—
> Gentle, and brave, and generous,—no lorn bard
> Breathed o'er his dark fate one melodious sigh:
> (ll. 55–59)

Not only in his use of the Miltonic negative, to make present in the poem what is patently missing, but in the very diction, "melodious sigh" for "melodious tear," Shelley invites comparison with *Lycidas*.

Like Milton's elegy and Blake's *Thel, Alastor* features a series of experiential visits. But whereas Milton's technique in *Lycidas* called for mythic condensation of a range of pagan and Christian poetic fathers—a necessarily populous pastoral scene of instruction—and whereas Blake dramatized a series of stylized symbolic conversations of soul with generated self, Shelley sends his poet on an equivalent, but very different, topographical journey of self-discovery: substituting vast geographical distance, poetic narrative, attenuated descriptions, a profusion of natural sites for the populated gardens of Milton and Blake, he supplies the effect if not the actual content—dialogue, conversation—of those symbolic visits. There is no character other than the poet in the whole poem; Shelley's point, of course, is that his poet "lived, he died, he sung, in solitude" (l. 60). In fact a similar poetic technique propels his *Prometheus Unbound:* all characters in that lyrical drama are allegorical of aspects of the human mind. By creating a host of intermediary voices, choruses, geographical journeys, Shelley fosters the illusion that something like drama is being enacted on the stage. Here the poet will seek initiated vision in increasingly remote settings, until, like Narcissus, he confronts the solipsistic image of his own face and comes to know the limit of his quest.

The first of the poet's encounters marks his only exchange with another human being—and even here the connection is so tenuous that the visitor might be a figment of the poet's imagination. Shelley describes the ministrations of an "Arab maiden" on his behalf: she "brought his food," "spread her matting for his couch," watched his nightly sleep, finally "to her cold home / Wildered, and wan, and panting, she returned" (ll. 129, 131, 138–39). Interestingly enough, the poet does not figure, except as passive recipient of her gifts, in these lines at all. The poet refuses, like Byron's Manfred, the companionship of the extended human hand; he chooses to ignore the maiden's love and deliberately avoids the possibility of human and earthly marriage. When the poet dreams later of a "veiled maid," he projects in her an image of his own self (l. 151). The poet seeks professedly an ideal soul-mate—the Neoplatonist machinery and symbolism cannot be ignored—and wishes for the death that generation brings. His search is for communication and debate, but that quest takes him farther and farther from human society. Nihilistic confrontation with the "spirit of solitude" becomes the existential problem of the poem.

The poet's next two stopping places are recognizable literary landscapes. The symbolic topography of each spot suggests, by its disposition and composition, possible initiatory sites. The first is a lonely dell:

> where odorous plants entwine
> Beneath the hollow rocks a natural bower,
> Beside a sparkling rivulet he stretched
> His languid limbs.
> (ll. 146–49)

Shelley's *locus amoenus*—natural bower, trees, sparkling brook—offers comforting support to the hollow of his back. But what is missing is the companionable figure of an unnamed goatherd, the piquant conversation of a knowing Socrates. Instead of spiritual guidance, Shelley's poet receives in the bower the awful visitation of the "veiled maid," in quest of whom he will eventually die. He pauses a second time in a piscatorial version of the pastoral garden: on the "lone Chorasmian shore" (l. 272), a "strong impulse urged / His steps to the seashore," where he watches the flight of birds and pictures the return of one to its "sweet mate" (ll. 274–75, 282). It is but a step here to Whitman's poetic incarnation by water in "Out of the Cradle Endlessly Rocking": shore, birds, water, initiation to the vision by means of that secret word *death*. Conditions are ripe for generation in Shelley's poem too, but the possibility for initiation is once more deflected:

> Startled by his own thought he looked around
> There was no fair fiend near him, not a sight
> Or sound of awe but in his own deep mind.
> (ll. 296–98)

Neither the pastoral vale, nor the seashore—traditional sites for pastoral initiation scenes—offers the poet a way out of the consuming solitude of his spiritual quest. Finding a "little shallop" "floating near the shore," he embarks on two voyages by water (ll. 299–300): the first is a sea voyage on open ocean, a miniature restaging of the journey of Coleridge's mariner, about which I shall have more to say below. The second follows a winding stream past increasingly remote glens, dells, and forest clearings to the starkest poetic translation of the *locus amoenus* we have yet to witness.

The second voyage itself is composed of two parts, the first of which culminates in a failed initiation scene, the second of which ends with the grave. In the first of these, "some more lovely mystery" draws the poet to a "secluded dell," at the center of which figures a well, a "liquid mirror" (ll. 454, 462). Here too the features of the classical *locus* appear—the "motion of the leaves," the "grass" and the "sound / Of the sweet brook," "undulating woods"—in tandem with "some unaccustomed presence" (ll. 475–78, 484). The "Spirit" who "seemed / To stand beside him" only gazes upon him with "intense pensiveness": the potential initiator—clothed in "no bright robes / Of shadowy silver or enshrining light"—"held commune" with him momentarily but could not effect passage of the initiate. The Spirit, of course, is a reflection of the poet himself. When the poet looks into the well, he finds—like Narcissus—his own image there:

> His eyes beheld
> Their own likeness through the reflected lines
> Of his thin hair, distinct in the dark depth
> Of that still fountain; as the human heart,
> Gazing in dreams over the gloomy grave,
> Sees its own treacherous likeness there.
>   (ll. 469–74)

It comes as no surprise, then, that—his "frail exultation" nearly "spent" (l. 521)—the poet "descend[s]" finally to the "one silent nook" which will hold his grave. The elements of the *locus* figure once again, but their aspect is strangely foreboding: a "solemn pine" and "torrent" define the hammock perched precariously at the "edge of a grey precipice" (ll. 571–72).

> It was a tranquil spot, that seemed to smile
> Even in the lap of horror. Ivy clasped
> The fissured stone with its entwining arms,
> And did embower with leaves for ever green,
> And berries dark, the smooth and even space
> Of its inviolated floor and here
> The children of the autumnal whirlwind bore,
> In wanton sport, those bright leaves, whose decay,
> Red, yellow, or ethereally pale,
> Rivals the pride of summer.
>   (ll. 577–86)

The components of the above scene suggest a parallel with Milton's ravished landscape at the beginning of *Lycidas*. Shelley's allusion to that landscape—ivy, berries, evergreens, shattered leaves, summer giving over to mellowing year—in his description of the poet's grave creates the expectation in the reader of a parallel close as well. Instead *Alastor* ends with lyric evocation of the poet's death and a deeply ambiguous dirge. In an inversion of pastoral elegiac machinery, the *locus amoenus* becomes the poet's grave:

> He did place
> His pale lean hand upon the rugged trunk
> Of the old pine. Upon an ivied stone
> Reclined his languid head, his limbs did rest,
> Diffused and motionless, on the smooth brink
> Of that obscurest chasm;
>
> (ll. 632–37)

In this final "green recess" composed of tree and ivied stone, all the initiatory landscapes of the poem coalesce (l. 625); the potential self-discovery and visionary access to the Mystery invoked at the outset of the poem are deflected for the last time.

The passing of the poet from the earth prompts a dirge every bit as vatic as that of *Lycidas,* but wholly devoid of its consoling vision. Even the orphic echoes—"many-voiced waves"—are not borne out. Lest the reader be tempted to view in the overlay of grave and initiation site a too-quick equation of them, Shelley goes to great pains to suggest that his poet will not find there an immortality unknown in earthly existence:

> Even as a vapour fed with golden beams
> That ministered on sunlight, ere the west
> Eclipses it, was now that wondrous frame—
> No sense, no motion, no divinity—
> A fragile lute, on whose harmonious strings
> The breath of heaven did wander—a bright stream
> Once fed with many-voiced waves—a dream
> Of youth, which night and time have quenched for ever,
> Still, dark, and dry, and unremembered now.
>
> (ll. 663–71)

Suspect, too, is the power of art to reclaim for the poet any existence beyond the grave, or for the mourner any guarantee of literary attention for his pains:

> Let not high verse, mourning the memory
> Of that which is no more, or painting's woe
> Or sculpture, speak in feeble imagery
> Their own cold powers. Art and eloquence,
> And all the shows of the world are frail and vain
> To weep a loss that turns their lights to shade.

In fact, like Blake's *Thel*, Shelley's *Alastor* is an *élégie manquée,* in Potts's phrase; "it is without new light or new life."[27] In each case the imagination or soul seeks a principle of immortality; in each case these hopes are seen to be delusive:

> It is a woe "too deep for tears," when all
> Is reft at once, when some surpassing Spirit,
> Whose light adorned the world around it, leaves
> Those who remain behind, not sobs or groans,
> The passionate tumult of a clinging hope;
> But pale despair and cold tranquillity,
> Nature's vast frame, the web of human things,
> Birth and the grave, that are not as they were.
> (ll. 713–20)

Consolation in Christian terms, no longer a believable fiction, is here more than pastoral elegy can muster. Instead, in these Romantic poems, it becomes the particular function of elegy to convey a vision of truth not necessarily consoling.

IV

The ironic term of my title, "failed elegy," requires qualification by way of conclusion. A work which fails to meet conventional expectations does not, needless to say, always fail in artistic terms. Blake's *Thel* and Shelley's *Alastor* stop short of "fresh woods and pastures new," but each offers, with considerable integrity, a record of the imagination's search for enduring incarnation in all its difficulty. Blake's poem is a delicate elegy on the pressures of generation, a tribute to a shadowy soul which yet fears to experience sexuality in the fallen world. Shelley eulogizes, it becomes increasingly clear, the disappointed literary ambitions of his own youthful poetic self. For all the critics' attempts to see the poet of *Alastor* as the dying spirit of a hardened Wordsworth or Coleridge, Shelley's fortunes and his future are bound up with what "art fled": "The brave, the gentle, and the beautiful, / The child of grace and genius" (ll. 689—90). Shelley's *Alastor*, like other Romantic odes—Wordsworth's Immortality Ode, Coleridge's *Dejection*, Keats's *Ode to a Nightingale*—is an attempt to allay a peculiarly Romantic lack of confidence in the longevity of the poetic imagination. Each records a sense of falling away from a golden age which promised immortality in a range of literary forms. Each mourns the lack of poetic succession and records the imagination's journey as a solitary and perilous voyage.

Blake's Thel and the elegy-maker of Shelley's *Alastor* are condemned to an eternal round of solitary wandering, and for this reason should be placed next to the mariner of Coleridge's *Rime* by way of conclusion.[28] In all three poems, the landscape and imagery of elegy overshadow those of epithalamium: Thel, we recall, views steadily and then refuses the ominous nuptial imagery—restrictive bands, glittering jewelry—tendered by Lilly, Cloud, and Clay. *Alastor*'s poet considers marriage in earthly and transcendent forms, but never achieves union with his dream spouse. This poem does not end with absorption in something higher, the communal vision that epithalamic imagery supports; instead the searching poet consciously seeks out increasingly unpeopled landscapes against which to measure the isolation of his poetic voice.[29] *The Rime of the Ancient Mariner*—whose ocean voyage *Alastor* imitates even to writhing snakes, horned moon, driving winds—offers itself similarly in the stead of a wedding poem. Wrongly interpreted by Bloom and Penn Warren as a prothalamion preliminary to eventual reconciliation, the poem is played out *against* the safe harbor of the wedding imagery. Roundly preventing celebration of the marriage feast, detaining its guest, inverting its imagery, the poem is perhaps not a pastoral poem but a response to a pastoral poem: like *Thel* and *Alastor,* the *Rime* comments harshly on a peculiarly pastoral convention by deflecting the wedding feast. If in fact, as Richard Cody maintains, pastoral's consummate form of expression is epithalamium, a reconciling fiction toward which all pastorals, *Lycidas* included, tends, then each of these poems is profoundly anti-pastoral, preferring the honesty of an unfinished chord to a perfect third, a bleak truth to a consoling fiction—in a peculiarly modern form, elegy to epithalamium.

7

"A Wedding or a Funeral": Wordsworth's Immortality Ode

I

Falling chronologically between the poems of the preceding chapter, Wordsworth's *Ode: Intimations of Immortality*—a generically complex pastoral initiation ode incorporating elegiac and epithalamic elements in its evolution of consolation for a lost faculty of the soul[1]—is profitably read next to Blake's and Shelley's versions of the same problem.[2] Like Blake's *The Book of Thel*, the Great Ode depends for its central fiction upon a myth of Neoplatonic pre-existence; like Thel, Wordsworth's child descends from its infantile paradise trailing clouds of glory into a world of reflections, shadows, tarnished images. But Wordsworth attempts the transcendence—that *tertium quid* of Higher Innocence—that Blake's Thel finds not such an easy leap. It is just this recompense of the "philosophic mind"[3] that Shelley conclusively calls suspect in his *Alastor*, a criticism of both *Lycidas* and the Great Ode.[4] The externalized quest of the inquiring soul in Shelley's poem issues from Wordsworthian directives—"obstinate questionings," "natural piety," "Whither have fled / The hues of heaven that canopied his bower," "but thou art fled," "It is a woe 'too deep for tears' when all / Is reft" (*Alastor*, ll. 26, 196, 695, 713)—as fully as it is patterned on Miltonic form and imagery. But neither Blake nor Shelley inherits the consoling symbolism of Milton's mystical wedding feast, emblem of Christian admittance to the Kingdom, nor Wordsworth's analogous pastoral *peripeteia* crowning "thought," "faith," and "primal sympathy" as intimations of an immortality. Wordsworth's singular achievement in the Great Ode is his translation of the initiation scenario. In a faithless age, in an age self-confessedly cut off from literary tradition, Wordsworth writes a profoundly traditional poem: seasoning the poetic imagination at Nature's knees, he celebrates its transcendence of the fear of death in a participatory sacramental vision—allusively elegiac and epithalamic—wholly his own.[5]

The Immortality Ode is strong evidence that Wordsworth's most interesting poems are not those of plainstyle balladry, but rather those of much-censured "poetic diction."[6] For all Wordsworth's claims for a conspicuous departure from traditional poetical language, the Ode claims a startling number of literary antecedents. In Frances Ferguson's reading of the poem, the Ode is a birth announcement: "Wordsworth is writing a nativity ode upon himself" in the style of Virgil's Pollio eclogue and Milton's *On the Morning of Christ's Nativity*.[7] Geoffrey Hartman calls the poem "a dialogue of the soul with itself in the presence of nature" and links it to other works which chart the career of the soul.[8] Additionally the Ode borrows more than a myth of pre-existence from the philosophical meditations of Plato; like the *Phaedrus*, the Ode looks back elegiacally upon a prior sense of immediacy, on unmediated contact with origins, and celebrates a compensatory vision—here Wordsworth's "philosophic mind" gains particular resonance—which is held to supersede the former. But the sharpest modal orientations beneath the Ode's structure and movement are those of funeral obsequy and spousal panegyric. Epithalamium and elegy lend characteristic energy and pattern to the finished form of the Immortality Ode and enforce the central conflicts of the poem: the gap between loss and gain, between solitude and community, between mourning and panegyric.

A cipher, or key to the poem's self-expressed registers, appears in the description of the child's activities:

> A wedding or a festival,
> A mourning or a funeral;
> And this hath now his heart,
> And unto this he frames his song:
> (ll. 94–97)

The pigmy darling, of course, pursues his unthinking course of "endless imitation"; his "whole vocation"—lacking in self-consciousness—is a parody of the poet's ceremonial activity. What the poem taken as a whole will deliver, however, is an overlay of elegiac and epithalamic conventions so complete that the Ode oscillates between the two more completely than any other poem of this study. The initiatory subtext of Spenser's marriage hymns and Milton's elegiac *Lycidas* frames this song: subsuming their differences in a speculative lyric mode that draws upon the structures and imagery of each, Wordsworth answers Spenser and Milton with a single poem.

II

From Spenser's marriage hymns, Wordsworth borrowed not only the suggestion of shape—stanza form, long concluding line, even specific rhymes—but a rhythm and vocabulary for nuptial panegyric as well. Wordsworth had, in fact, made a study of Spenser in the late fall of 1801; he read *Prothalamion* in April 1802 during the time of the Ode's composition.[9] The epithalamium, and its attendant panegyrical imagery, were to exert a strong influence on Wordsworth's poetics: from Spenser he borrowed a literary vocabulary of self-celebration to commemorate that "marriage"—of "individual Mind" and "external World" (ll. 63, 65)—upon which the production of poetry depends.

> Paradise, and groves
> Elysian, Fortunate Fields—like those of old
> Sought in the Atlantic Main—why should they be
> A history only of departed things,
> Or a mere fiction of what never was?
> For the discerning intellect of Man,
> When wedded to this goodly universe
> In love and holy passion, shall find these
> A simple produce of the common day.
> —I, long before the blissful hour arrives,
> Would chant, in lonely peace, the spousal verse
> Of this great consummation:[10]

The Prospectus to *The Excursion* quoted above is a kind of prothalamion, a song preliminary to a wedding. In fact the lines generate a formulation, "spousal verse," which characterizes most of Wordsworth's pronouncements upon his poetic endeavor. To this extent the opening books of *The Prelude* and "Lines Composed a Few Miles Above Tintern Abbey" might also function epithalamically, staging as they do that marriage song of mind with the other that confronts it, a wedding which the poet-initiate always affirms as vision.

The Immortality Ode draws upon generic conventions of the *Epithalamion* in two crucial places. The tone and imagery of Spenser's nuptial ode infuse the first four stanzas of Wordsworth's poem—in which he conjures retrospectively the harmony of the child's world in a manner comparable to the function of epithalamium—and the last two—in which he celebrates a restored version of that festival atmosphere.[11] All the pastoral images of the Ode, in fact, are drawn from that catalogue, Spenser's nuptial procession. The "birds" which "sing a joyous song" (l. 19) recall the "birds louelearned song" of *Epithalamion*; the "gay girlands" and "coronall" of Spenser's poem find an analogue in Wordsworth's "pansy" and "coronal" (l. 40); a chorus of shouting boys appears in each work; "fresh flowers" abundantly perfume each (l. 48); finally, even the exhortative refrain of Wordsworth's last stanza, announcing the panegyric—"And O, ye Fountains, Meadows, Hills and Groves"—is learned from Spenser's strong first lines, and may even allude to the echoing natural surround of Spenser's epithalamic refrain. The whole "sweet May-morning" note of Wordsworth's poem is borrowed from the *Epithalamion* to figure forth the "simple creed / Of Childhood" and adult resurrection of that epithalamic and panegyrical vision (ll. 44, 137–38). The nuptial close marks the triumph of communal celebration over solitary song. It celebrates the joining rather than the severing "of our loves" (l. 189). It concludes with a difference the Immortality Ode: consolation, as in Milton, takes on overtly epithalamic contours.

But the Great Ode taps as well the elegiac tone of Spenser's *Prothalamion*.[12] Like that poem—"Calme was the day" (l. 1)—it opens with a retrospective observation: "There was a time" (l. 1). Like that poem, it begins with a dream vision: "To me did seem / Apparelled in celestial light, / The glory and the freshness of a dream" (ll. 3–5). It even consciously imitates the archaism of Spenser's poem:

> It is not now as it hath been of yore;—
>   Turn wheresoe'er I may,
>   By night or day,
> The things which I have seen I now can see no more.
>   (ll. 6–9)

Like the singer-witness of Spenser's poem, Wordsworth finds himself alienated from the wedding celebration at the outset: "sullein care" keeps Spenser's poet from sharing in the "Brydale day" (ll. 5, 17); Wordsworth calls it an "evil day" because he is "sullen / While Earth herself is adorning, / This sweet May-morning" (ll. 142–44). In both cases wedding preparations enforce the singer's recognition of loss and distance: Spenser's poet, travelling down the river with his "two Swannes of goodly hewe," is forced to acknowledge the decay of Templer Knights and his own analogous fall from "goodly grace" (ll. 37, 138); so intent is he upon his bid for patronage that he hands the nuptial song over to an attendant nymph. The *Prothalamion,* as I have suggested, is a song preparatory to a wedding undercut by its elegiac preoccupation with the poet's decline at court. Wordsworth borrows this poem's fixation upon loss and decay to render the pigmy child's declining state of grace. But he, like Milton, wants to see an epithalamium at the close: the nuptial chorus of *Lycidas* and the confident panegyrical measure of the *Epithalamion* hover behind the Ode's final stanzas and lend to the consoling vision of the "philosophic mind" an epithalamic frame.

Wordsworth's most interesting borrowing from Spenser—and it amounts to a borrowing from Milton as well—is the twice-mentioned pansy: a condensation of the profuse and variegated flower catalogue of the blazon and *Prothalamion*, the consoling pastoral bouquet of Milton's poem. In the Ode, the flower not only prompts the dirge— "Whither is fled the visionary gleam? / Where is it now, the glory and the dream?" (ll. 56–57)—and introduces the long middle section, a meditation on the poet's childhood fall from a state of instinctive imaginative grace, it also becomes the agent of consolation. The pansy, an analogue for thought, or *pensée*, becomes guarantee for Wordsworth of the mind's adult access to the imagination's store, Nature. The symbolic flower, linked inextricably to the flower catalogues in Spenser's and Milton's odes, has an equally conventional function in Wordsworth's poem: it reminds us of the poem's ancestry; it reminds the poet of his elegiac task; and at the close figures, by transvaluation, reversal and consequent *peripeteia*.

For Wordsworth's documentation of progressive states of consciousness indeed calls for an elegiac form: it is specifically "grief" for loss of "primal joy" he seeks to assuage (l. 26). The Ode, like Blake's *Thel* and Shelley's *Alastor*, records a linear journey of the soul and depends, as do these poems, upon Milton's *Lycidas* for its characteristic movement. It shares with that poem a peculiar use of pastoral imagery to render an idyllic childhood from which the singer is now, by the thought of death, irreparably distanced. In both poems a kind of untimely loss imposes a burden on the mind which wrongs the season—a technique Milton and Wordsworth both knew from Spenser. The "sad occasion dear" compels Milton to disturb Nature's "season due." Wordsworth, conversely, determining to recover primal joy, or evolve compensation for it, insists: "No more shall grief of mine the season wrong" (l. 26). A second similarity between the two poems, and, for that matter, Spenser's *Epithalamion*, is the solar cycle upon which each is structured.[13] In the precursor odes, as in *Lycidas,* movement of spirit is identified with the passage of the sun across the sky. The epiphanic moment in the elegiac works, however, comes at sunset. The day's decline and implied sunrise, against which Lycidas's ascension is played out, match that of the swain:

> And now the sun had stretched out all the hills,
> And now was dropped into the western bay;
> At last he rose and twitched his mantle blue:
> Tomorrow to fresh woods, and pastures new.
>
> (ll. 190–93)

Wordsworth's youth, "who daily farther from the east / Must travel," follows a similar course. Here is the Ode's version of the Miltonic close:[14]

> The Clouds that gather round the setting sun
> Do take a sober colouring from an eye
> That hath kept watch o'er man's mortality;
> Another race hath been, and other palms are won.
>
> (ll. 197–200)

A difference in tone can be discerned between these two passages: Milton's final vision—that nuptial tableau of heavenly proportions—emphatically replaces earthly sunsets, offering eternal consolation for earthly loss. Wordsworth's sunset has a distinctly compensatory feel to it: working backward from the state of childhood grace, he has to evolve a man-made vision powerful enough to sustain poetic endeavor, a vision which he too images in nuptial terms. The solar passage in both poems recalls that of Spenser's bride, who awakens with the "worlds light giuing lampe" and sets her pace by its passage across the sky. Initiatory passage—Wordsworth's youth is "Nature's priest, / . . . [who] by the vision splendid / Is on his way attended"—is in all three poems a solar movement (l. 75).

From Milton Wordsworth knew a special sort of initiation poem, one which brilliantly served its pastoral apprenticeship and demonstrated the poet's readiness for epic projects. As much as *Lycidas*, then, the Great Ode dramatizes its author's literary initiation—here, characteristically, the scenario is given by turns cosmic scope (a small voice gains orphic pitch by commanding echoes from a vast landscape)—and outlines a theory of the imagination and attendant poetics designed to guarantee future literary productivity. As Harold Bloom suggests, the Ode was "written directly in the shadow of Milton, and may be called a misprision or powerful misreading of *Lycidas*."[15] But his literary Freudianism—"As a defense, this reaction-formation wards off instinctual impulses by means of that mode of distrust that creates the superego"—never transcends diagnosis and weary prognosis. Bloom concludes: "Wordsworth can live more 'normally' as a man by contenting himself with internal returns to his 'oceanic sense.' " To my mind, Wordsworth identified his own literary initiation with that of his predecessor, and modelled his elegiac "appearance" on the epithalamic resolution of *Lycidas*. Wordsworth's great interest to us as a writer of displaced elegy is precisely his determination to make elegy work traditionally at a time when conventional consolation was no longer buttressed by a significant pattern of belief. If we recall that the first epigraph of the Immortality Ode was those words that foreshadowed epic projects in Virgil's fourth eclogue, "paolo maiora canamus,"[16] then the project of the Immortality Ode is to achieve and signal the end of pastoral apprenticeship. Blake and Shelley avoid the rising rhythm of consolation at the risk of writing what critics call failed poems, but Wordsworth recasts conventional imagery and generic form, not only to bring the Ode to a satisfying formal conclusion, but to celebrate, if compensatorily, the imagination's resurrection in adult form—and its possible immortality through literary products—in a manner designed to sustain the creation of poetry. By ritually reenacting the death of the imagination, Wordsworth's greatest fear as a poet, and singing a dirge for its loss in the inherited form of the pastoral elegy, he earns the right to reverse its generic course by means of an epithalamic close.

In one final way Wordsworth exploits an elegiac tradition—by his related interest in the epitaph. Frances Ferguson, in her appropriately titled "Wordsworth's Epitaphic Mode" in *Language as Counter-Spirit*, locates in Wordsworth's own "Essay Upon Epitaphs" a specific procedure for defusing death that she also finds in his poetry:

> The poet's spiritual autobiography virtually constitutes a series of epitaphs spoken upon former selves, "other Beings," who can be approached only across vacancies almost as wide as those between the living and the dead. And Wordsworth's revisions substantiate this link between autobiography and epitaph which implies that the themes of growth and immortality never stand far from the theme of death.[17]

In the serial "fallings from us, vanishings" which the Ode records (l. 144), Wordsworth pronounces elegies upon the "many miniature deaths" which the soul or imagination undergoes in a lifetime. For Ferguson, the obsession with epitaphs, the doubling of consciousness through memory and anticipation, the persistent reenactment of the impossibility of constructing a surviving essence of self, suggest in Wordsworth's poetry that "neither human incarnation nor linguistic incarnation can be arrived at and sustained."[18] I believe, with Ferguson, that the Ode attempts to come to terms with lack of connections and assurances, but it seems untenable to me that it "affirms these connections in a rhetoric which suspends itself over a gap in demonstrable truths."[19] The Immortality Ode is in fact one of the last great poems to use elegiac and epithalamic conventions straight, and it does so with the conviction that the modal force of these ceremonial forms can still support the new poet's self-presentation as a singer of pastorals. The Great Ode does not parody by manipulating or reversing epithalamium and elegy, but it exploits the consoling, aggregative effect each traditionally achieves both to confront and to master the fear of engulfment which threatens the poetic imagination periodically and incrementally throughout its hazardous career.

III

It is not my intent in the following brief reading of the poem to depart substantially from standard analyses of the poem, but to supply a new context for the poem by reading it, as I have Spenser's *Prothalamion* and Milton's *Lycidas,* as a healthy amalgam of ceremonial modes. I hold, for example, to the tripartite division of the poem supported by most readers;[20] I note, with others, its antiphonal pattern approximating the effect of dialogue. I read the poem, along with most critics, as a pastoral having transcendence of that mode very much on its mind. But I propose here to chart the poem's oscillation between epithalamic participation in the natural community and elegiac, even alienated, speculation, and its eventual resolution of diametrically opposed rituals into an integrated whole.

The first four stanzas of the Ode project the undifferentiated bliss of the innocent child at play, establish the poet-observer's present alienation from it, and conclude with the delineation of a pastoral scene of instruction—a spare, stylized *locus*—and the onset of the visionary's dirge. In fact each attempt at epithalamic celebration is matched with elegiac recognition, much as the poet of *Prothalamion* hesitates between those poles of articulation; for four stanzas the poem hovers between panegyric:

> Ye blessed Creatures, I have heard the call
> Ye to each other make; I see
> The heavens laugh with you in your jubilee;
> My heart is at your festival,
> My head hath its coronal,
> The fulness of your bliss, I feel—I feel it all.
> (ll. 36–41)

and its counterpart:

> The sunshine is a glorious birth;
> But yet I know where'er I go,
> That there hath past away a glory from the earth.
> (ll. 16–18)
>
> Now, while the birds thus sing a joyous song,
> And while the young lambs bound
> As to the tabor's sound,
> To me alone there came a thought of grief.
> (ll. 19–20)

In each of the first four stanzas, the procedure holds: the first moves from light to darkness, from "There was a time when meadow, grove, and stream" to "The things which I have seen I now can see no more" (ll. 1, 9). The second draws upon Genesis and Blake's *Songs of Innocence* for an allegorical landscape of the unfallen condition, yet it too ends with an adversative "but" and elegiac concern for that glory's passing "from the earth" (l. 18). The third turns on the contrast between "heart of May," "tabor's sound," and shouting boys, and the poet's "thought of grief," his Miltonic apology for wronging the season with his elegiac meditation (ll. 32, 21, 22). In the fourth stanza, the adversative is harsh and abrupt. After the plurality of natural description—"In a thousand valleys far and wide, / Fresh flowers" (ll. 47–48)—and the moment of fullest participation in that nearly epithalamic scene—"I hear, I hear, with joy I hear!" (l. 50)—the singularity of the elegiac landscape stands out in sharp contrast:

> —But there's a Tree, of many, one,
> A single Field which I have looked upon,
> Both of them speak of something that is gone:
> The Pansy at my feet
> Doth the same tale repeat:
> Whither is fled the visionary gleam?
> Where is it now, the glory and the dream?
> (ll. 51–57)

"Meadow, grove and stream," the shorthand classical *locus* invoked in the first lines of the poem, is assigned to the prior paradise of the child's world, a realm of pre-existence buttressed by Neoplatonic myth. Its analogue in the present is the "parodically attenuated counter-image" quoted above.[21] As Shelley's questing poet rejected a series of conventional loci in favor finally of a stark hollow on the brink of a precipice, so Wordsworth particularizes a Golden Age landscape. At the moment when tree, "single

Field," and pansy prompt meditation upon "something that is gone," the scales tip: panegyric suddenly yields to the elegiac measure of the long middle section. The *locus amoenus,* personalized and transformed by Romantic sensibility, yet recognizable by its components, signals once more a possible initiation scene.

The four middle stanzas—tonally very different from the first—do describe an initiatory journey: one beginning with "birth" and sunrise and "light" and moving inexorably "daily farther from the east" (ll. 58, 70, 72). The Neoplatonic imagery of the fifth stanza links this birth to the fall into generation of Blake's Thel. Both leave behind the glory of an immortal paradise to descend into this world of deceptive appearances. Drawing upon a myth of pre-existence, both Blake and Wordsworth give us a record of human history in a reduced, symbolic, deliberately miniature form. Wordsworth's "Boy," "Youth," and "Man," however, lacking Thel's wisdom, only too willingly submit to the ritual eastward movement, an initiatory journey linked, by virtue of its association with the sun's trajectory, to the symbolic wedding day of Spenser's bride and the emblematic pastoral day of Milton's swain. But sunset, through the eighth stanza of the poem, has none of the culminating significance that it has in Spenser and Milton. Wordsworth's poetic rendering of generation is as double-edged as Blake's.

For the portrait we are given of initiation in the Immortality Ode is an ironic one indeed.[22] It is a retrospective and regressive journey *away* from immortality: the Youth, "Nature's priest," walks paradoxically away from the light, leaving the "vision splendid" behind him as he goes (l. 73). Earth too is an untrustworthy guide, doing "all she can / To make her Foster-child, her Inmate Man, / Forget the glories he hath known" (ll. 82–84). Like London, Spenser's "most kyndly Nurse" in *Prothalamion* (l. 128), whom he contemplates in retrospect, so Earth in the Ode proves only a foster mother. Furthermore the child unthinkingly contributes to his own inevitable decline: "Why with such earnest pains dost thou provoke / The years to bring the inevitable yoke" (ll. 124–25).

I have argued earlier that often allegories of the soul record the journey of the poetic imagination in its search for a principle of permanence, its quest for a stay against mortality. Wordsworth's generated soul similarly enacts an allegorical descent: the newborn soul, by its proximity to the "imperial palace," is the "best Philosopher" (ll. 85, 111); it is an "Eye among the blind," a distillation of the five senses into one transcendent all-seeing Eye. It enters the "darkness of the grave" which is our "earthly freight" (ll. 118, 127). But the Neoplatonic imagery of the eighth stanza gives way to imagery of another kind of journey, that of the nascent literary sensibility, the incarnated imagination. Drawing upon imagery of the theater—"newly-learned art," "song," "fit his tongue / To dialogues," "little Actor," " 'humorous stage,' "[23] "part" (ll. 93, 97, 98–99, 103, 104, 103)—Wordsworth works a biting parody of the poet's "vocation," a process which he must reverse unless it is to culminate in the sterility of "endless imitation" (ll. 107–8). Throughout his corpus, Wordsworth uses the child's unmediated contact with nature, the model epithalamic harmony expressed by such a marriage, as an analogy for the connection the mature imagination seeks with Nature. In fact it becomes the work of the literary imagination to sing a compensatory "spousal verse" for that loss. What the remainder of the poem attempts to do, in the form of consolation, is to eulogize that death which "custom," lying upon us with "a weight," brings to the imaginative store we are given at birth (l. 128).

The "O joy" which punctuates the turn in the Immortality Ode has a direct literary antecedent: it is as sudden in its way as the shift from "O carefull verse" to "o ioyfull verse" in Spenser's "November" elegy for Dido. What follows there, as here, is an orphic paean to Nature's restorative powers and a celebration of the mind's newly reestablished dominion over its world. In the early stanzas, echoes were forthcoming and effortless: "I hear the Echoes through the mountains throng, / The Winds come to me from the fields of sleep" (ll. 27–28); in the concluding stanzas, the poet tries out his voice again, hoping for echoes of a different sort. The closest line to Spenser's orphic refrain comes at the head of the final stanza: "And O, ye Fountains, Meadows, Hills and Groves" is an orphic appeal to an imaginatively transformed landscape.

Of the final three stanzas, one outlines the nature of consolation and provides a transition between the ironies of the middle section and the exhortative measure of the last. Two are choral in nature, providing the ceremonial *peripeteia*. For Spenser, of course, Dido's death is neutralized by her ascension, with all its allegorical possibilities. In Wordsworth we have no corpse to mourn but a faculty of the mind itself. It is thus no wonder that memory becomes the means by which Wordsworth retrieves an epithalamic sense. Dido and Lycidas attain certifiable heavenly immortality for the poets who raise them; Wordsworth is happy to locate "intimations" even of immortality in what we have learned to call visionary or imaginative experience. Not for recovery of "the simple creed / Of Childhood" and its attendant joys does he raise "the song of thanks and Praise" (ll. 137–38, 141), but for the mental processes—"thought of our past years," "obstinate questionings," "high instincts," "shadowy recollections" (ll. 134, 142, 147, 150)—which guarantee the literary imagination a kind of longevity long after the immediacy of the natural world and literary traditions have ceased to do so. Yet for all Wordsworth's disclaimers he writes a very traditional poem at the end of the experimental lyrical balladry: the content of consolation—"truths that wake, / To perish never" (ll. 156–57)—has changed and interiorized, but the form of consolation, however obscurely Wordsworth mimics the pastoral elegy, still carries recognizable and predictable force. The vision which brings the ninth stanza to a climax and introduces the epithalamic chant recalls Lycidas's retrieval from the waves and Milton's seaside moment of initiated vision:

> Hence in a season of calm weather
> Though inland far we be,
> Our Souls have sight of that immortal sea
> Which brought us hither,
> Can in a moment travel thither,
> And see the Children sport upon the shore,
> And hear the mighty waters rolling evermore.
> (ll. 162–68)

There is more than regressive compulsion toward "oceanic sense" in this passage. The compensatory language—"though inland far we be"—is learned from Milton; borrowed as well from that predecessor is the watery context of incarnation, the baptismal sea-change which the dying god suffers and experiences. But "Children sport" in Wordsworth's poem where "Blessed Troops" sing a nuptial hymn in Milton's: for the latter, Paradise is figured in imagery of Christian mysticism; in Wordsworth, as in Blake, epithalamic imagery coalesces with that of the child at play.

The last two stanzas of the Ode sing a "spousal verse" in exactly these terms. As Geoffrey Hartman reminds us, life "for Wordsworth is the freeing of his soul from solipsism."[24] And, he continues, "the mature man . . . bases his faith in self-transcendence on the ease of unconsciousness with which the apocalyptic imagination turned in childhood toward life. Then the crisis was to go from self-love (unconscious) to love of nature, and now it is to go from self-love (conscious) to love of man." In this sense, of course, as Wordsworth writes in the Ode's final epigraph, "Child is father of the Man." For Wordsworth it became the work of the mature imagination to celebrate poetically that extensive network of linkages by which love of nature might produce love of man. The Ode, of his lyric works, takes a first step in that direction, drawing upon epithalamium's orphic management of Nature to produce the illusion of echo or response:

> Then sing, ye Birds, sing, sing, a joyous song!
>   And let the young Lambs bound
>   As to the tabor's sound!
> We in thought will join your throng,
>   Ye that pipe and ye that play,
>   Yet that through your hearts to-day
>   Feel the gladness of the May!
>   (ll. 169–75)

Wordsworth is more than an observer in these final stanzas. At the outset of the Ode the poet peered into a scene from which he was eternally barred readmittance; by the close he is a participant, joining "in thought" at least the celebration that modulates grief:

> We will grieve not, rather find
> Strength in what remains behind;
> In the primal sympathy
> Which having been must ever be;
> In the soothing thoughts that spring
> Out of human suffering;
> In the faith that looks through death,
> In years that bring the philosophic mind.
>   (ll. 180–87)

If Wordsworth's vision seems somewhat "sober"[25] next to Milton's apocalyptic close—"Another race hath been, and other palms are won" in the Immortality Ode[26]—it seems important to remember that what is being recommended in the last lines is not faith in a transcendent creed, but self-confidence in a state of mind, all the more powerful because resurrection of that diminished and unpredictable power takes place at the panegyrical close of this elegy for poetic youth. By his formal imitation of Spenser and Milton, Wordsworth is trying to claim some of their confidence in the orphic initiate's control of his world. Rainer Maria Rilke makes the same procedure explicit in his twenty-sixth sonnet to Orpheus: dramatizing the nature of our response to primal joys, birdsong, and the cries of children playing, Rilke ends the sonnet with an exhortation to Orpheus to arrange those criers, that constellation of natural imagery, into a current which might bear his head and lyre upon its shoulders. The implication, as in Wordsworth's Ode, is that the poet's stay against annihilation—the river-borne head remains an emblem of immortality—is his own power to interpret and organize nature's manifold voices into an echoing choir.

8

Epithalamia Awry: Mallarmé's *Hérodiade* and Hart Crane's "For the Marriage of Faustus and Helen"

I

The English epithalamium became an object of parody, as Donne's and Crashaw's poems attest, almost as soon as it was recognized as a legitimate, if minor, genre. For the most part anti-epithalamia appear in dramatic works—Shakespeare's *Romeo and Juliet* and Webster's *The Tragedy of the Dutchesse of Malfi,* for example—hinting, by their inversion of conventional epithalamic imagery, at impending doom. But satiric epithalamia in verse, particularly after the Restoration and through the eighteenth century, usually pointed to as evidence of "waning epithalamic tradition,"[1] do much to keep the tradition alive. To be sure Richard Duke's "Epithalamium upon the Marriage of Captain William Bedlowe" and William Wycherley's "An Epithalamium upon the Marriage of Two Very Ill-Natured Blacks" have an admittedly limited appeal. A more interesting branch of this family of poems, including Blake's and Wordsworth's experiments with the form, claims its epithalamic ancestry less broadly. Beginning with the nineteenth century and the concomitant decline of close and conscious imitation of forms, a new kind of epithalamium makes its appearance. It will be the purpose of this chapter to bring up to date the history of the anti-epithalamium: an analysis of Stéphane Mallarmé's *Hérodiade* and Hart Crane's "For the Marriage of Faustus and Helen" affords the opportunity to comment upon a range of related experiments with the genre.

The poems of this chapter, like Donne's and Crashaw's mystic anti-epithalamia, gain their peculiar force by inversion of epithalamic convention: marriage as metaphor no longer signifies public recognition of a private ritual, but stands instead for the tense yoking of opposites. As might be expected, epithalamic imagery is infused with violence in such works. In most cases an evening or lunar landscape replaces the often spring or summer setting of the wedding poem. Instead of the communal celebration of restorative ritual, these poems feature ceremonial sacrifice, death, solitude, rupture. T. S. Eliot's "East Coker" of the *Four Quartets* illustrates just this process. Beginning with evocation of a wedding feast and allusion to the possibility of dynastic and historical succession, the poem ends as a meditation on death, bleakly elegiac:

> On a Summer midnight, you can hear the music
> Of the weak pipe and the little drum
> And see them dancing around the bonfire
> The association of man and woman
> In daunsinge, signifying matrimonie—
> A dignified and commodious sacrament.
> Two and two necessarye coniunction,
> Holding eche other by the hand or the arm
> Whiche betokeneth concorde. Round and round the fire
> Leaping through the flames, or joined in circles,
> Rustically solemn or in rustic laughter
> Lifting heavy feet in clumsy shoes,
> Earth feet, loam feet, lifted in country mirth
> Mirth of those long since under earth
> Nourishing the corn. Keeping time,
> Keeping the rhythm in their dancing
> As in their living in the living seasons
> The time of the seasons and the constellations
> The time of milking and the time of harvest
> The time of the coupling of man and woman
> And that of beasts. Feet rising and falling.
> Eating and drinking. Dung and death.
> . . . .
> The houses are all gone under the sea.
>
> The dancers are all gone under the hill.
> . . . .
> And we all go with them, into the silent funeral,
> Nobody's funeral, for there is no one to bury.[2]

The hallmark of the modern elegy and epithalamium, paradoxically, is that there is no one to bury and no wedding to commemorate. In Eliot's poem, a lyric meditation on death borrows elegiac form—hesitating rhythms, odic antitheses of thought, final rising movement of consolation—inverting nuptial imagery at the outset and then returning to it in the transvaluations of the close: "neither gain nor loss" is Eliot's subject, but lyric search for "another intensity," "a further union, a deeper communion." Without a specific occasion for mourning, Eliot attempts to come to terms with the historical and literary past—"a lifetime burning in every moment / And not the lifetime of one man only"—in much the way that Milton and Wordsworth did in their own great odes. In Wordsworth and Milton, however, the fading of the epithalamic vision and the descent into death are rewarded by a compensatory and transcendent hymn of aggregation. In Eliot's poem, as in other modern poems of its caliber and intent, the movement away from the communal wedding feast is replaced, at best, with a defined search for a heightened personal vision.

Similarly, neither Mallarmé's nor Crane's cryptic epithalamia celebrates a real-life marriage; if a wedding takes place at all in these poems, it is a Blakean marriage of abstract contraries, a difficult, tension-filled wedding of abstract principles. Mallarmé's poem turns on the biblical myth of Salomé, daughter of Herodias, and her imperious demand for the head of John the Baptist, whose authoritative opposition to the marriage of Herod and his sister-in-law prevented her mother's happiness. The *noces,* between loyal daughter and condemned saint, take place between odd marriage partners indeed. Crane's epithalamium draws upon Goethe's *Faust*—and that couple's holy partnership of creative spirit and ideal beauty—for the characters of its drama. In an ironic parallel of myth and present moment learned from Eliot, Crane both ennobles and diminishes the stature of his lovers languidly listening to jazz in a smoke-filled New York nightclub. In fact the two poems make for surprisingly interesting comparison. Each work is in finished form a triptych.[3] Each asks in its title to be read as an epithalamium. The "wedding" projected in each work, however, is repeatedly foiled, viewed as suspect. The marriage which finally occurs in each is achieved through violence—decapitation, rape—and antithesis. Consummation, in both works, is tenuous indeed: in *Hérodiade* it depends upon one piercing gaze between virgin and decapitated head; in "Faustus and Helen" the poem's synergy rests upon possession of the "saddled sky" by "eternal gunman,"[4] an image as startling in its way as Donne's disembowelling of the bride on love's altar. Finally, each satiric epithalamium marks a turning point in the poet's career. Both Mallarmé and Crane work a new poetics into this ritual marriage of principles: the nuptial altar and marriage ceremony provide a conventional stage for the enactment of rites wholly literary.

Emptied of its social value and imitated for parodic purposes, the wedding poem remains in modern form, oddly enough, as allegorical as its Renaissance original: Spenser's lovers were Orpheus and Eurydice, two sides of the soul, whose marriage resolved the relation of worldly to divine, of secular to sacred, of literary to public life. In Mallarmé and Crane, the marriage partners are just as symbolically abstracted: in each work a male creative principle, cerebral and potent, attempts to unite with the elusive feminine spirit of beauty. The wedding might be imaged otherwise as the union of the poet with his muse. Difficult as this marriage is to sustain—and the indirections of both poems do much to convey this very difficulty—it allegorizes the incarnation of the poetic imagination in a satiric wedding drama, modern counterpart of that Renaissance hymn of self-celebration, the poet's ode to "endlesse matrimony."

II

Mallarmé began *Hérodiade* in 1864 during a period of spiritual and metaphysical crisis, intending to invent "une langue qui doit nécessairement jaillir d'une poétique très nouvelle" as he wrote to Cazalis,[5] but we know the work was on his desk incomplete when he died in 1898. Only "Scène," the long middle section, was published during his lifetime—in the *Poésies* of 1887. Preceded by "Ouverture ancienne d'Hérodiade" and followed by the "Cantique de Saint Jean," it is usually published as a trilogy. The first section, the nurse's incantation, sets the scene as a prelude to the dialogue of the center section. The "Cantique," abrupt, short, and terse, opposes the "Scène" in every way. If any fertile union emerges from this marriage of contraries, it proceeds, in nice Hegelian fashion, from the negative. The poem has been read variously as a Jungian marriage of *anima* and *animus*,[6] with *L'Après-midi d'un faune* as a failed approach to the mystic state of *hieros gamos*,[7] as a psycho-sexual allegory of Mallarmé's own oedipal drama—according to Charles Mauron, the decapitation/castration of Saint Jean is punishment for the violation of an infantile taboo[8]—and as a revision of scriptural models of apocalypse.[9] I prefer to read it, with Crane's "Faustus and Helen," as a peculiarly modern challenge to the genre of the epithalamium. As in Crane's poem, the implied machinery and symbolism lend to *Hérodiade* a ritualized form. As in other parodies of the epithalamium, elegiac imagery—tombstones, funeral pyres, etc.—is superimposed upon nuptial symbolism. Finally, like Crane's "Faustus and Helen," Mallarmé's *Hérodiade* is a parable of the poetic imagination in its attempt to achieve communion with an impossible principle of beauty and purity. Mallarmé wrote to Villiers de l'Isle-Adam on December 31, 1865, that the subject of the poem was "la Beauté" and that "le sujet apparent n'est qu'un prétexte pour aller vers Elle . . . C'est, je crois, le mot de la Poésie."[10] The union projected in the work, from which poetry results, is between male principle—abstract, creative, and intellectual—and the feminine incarnation of beauty, ephemeral and unknowable. This allegorical fusion of abstractions, the "gala intime" of the soul, he has called in *Crayonné au Théâtre* a "rite . . . de l'Idée."[11] Crane too had written that "the very real and absolute conception of beauty," evocation of which obsessed him as a poet, was symbolized for him by the Greek goddess Helen. His marriage poem is a study of "the more imponderable phenomena of psychic motives, pure emotional crystallization," an exploration of poetic consciousness in the presence of abstract, tantalizing beauty.[12] Either Mallarmé or Crane could as easily have chosen Orpheus and Eurydice as his pair of lovers. Both poets, as I shall hope to show by way of conclusion, conceived of poetic creation as an orphic task: as a death-marriage with a tormenting female principle, a *katábasis* requisite to the recovery of song.

The "Ouverture" of *Hérodiade,* narrated neither by the princess nor her groom, sets the tone of the poem and establishes its contexts of imagery. In fact spoken by the nurse—who in her own person suggests all that Hérodiade will not be, fertile, nourishing, maternal—the incantation serves an ironic end. Instead of an epithalamic hymn on the morn of a wedding, we have instead an elegiac prothalamion sharing something of Spenser's sense of foreboding in his poem of that name. On this cold dawn "tout est présage et mauvais rêve": the landscape is, as usual, one of absence; dawn itself is "abolie"; "un bel oiseau" has fled the "lourde tombe" of Hérodiade's tower, "tour cinéraire et sacrificatrice" in which some strange rite will take place. In the "pâle mausolée" of these landscapes "déchus et tristes," the nurse appears to announce a dirge: "Crime! bûcher! aurore ancienne! supplice!" (p. 41). In fact she waits for death, as the imagery of her speech reveals. The "incantation" she articulates is a prelude to odd "noces" indeed: "ostensoirs refroidis," "suaire," are the attendant symbols of this rite "á l'heure d'agonie et de luttes funèbres!" (pp. 42–43). The nurse's terrible survey of the scene is fraught with tensions, which in fact it is the purpose of the overture to establish: Hérodiade's conflict between desire for marriage (and the consequent destruction of purity by sexual intercourse) and instinct for self-preservation, sterile, aloof, abstract, is suggested in the overture by the tension between "aurore" burning with "plumage héraldique" in the mirror of the pool and the autumnal mood of the dying season, between the "diamant pur de quelque étoile" and the darkness of one which "ne scintilla jamais."

In a similarly anti-epithalamic gesture, perfumes, candles, flowers, empty beds are qualified negatively as soon as they suggest a bridal chamber.[13] The nurse underlines the importance of this "jour dernier qui vient tout achever," the momentousness of "ce temps prophétique," by means of a gesture backward—at Hérodiade's father; the "cadavres" resulting from his reign; his cold, deaf refusal to succor his daughter in the present—and an implied gesture toward the future. The whole tone of impending apocalyptic crisis in the "Ouverture" points toward passage for Hérodiade out of solitude, absence, and negation by means of marriage. We are left with a portentous image, that of Mallarmé's famous swan-soul, eyes hidden in its feathers, wrapped upon itself in absolute solipsism and caught between two extremes: between distress and "l'éternelle allée / De ses espoirs," between an agonizing "étoile mourante" and "diamants élus." Will dawn bring with it passage to womanhood for the resisting Hérodiade? Will this day constitute a fulfillment of the father by the son, a replacement of distant, unknowing father by the all-seeing gaze of a bridegroom? Repeated references to rite and "mystère" suggest the possibility of a successful initiation, both of bride and of son. But the "Ouverture" does no more than set the scene for this occurrence by dramatizing the soul's division between emergence into life *out* of the white chrysalis and further retraction into the folds of the self.

The second part of the trilogy, "Scène," is a dialogue between Hérodiade and her nurse which confirms the fears of the initiate on the brink of spiritual passage. In fact Hérodiade's "horreur" of the flesh, her fierce devotion to a sexually naive but deathless state, her determination to preserve a purity which precludes incarnation, recall that of Blake's Thel perched on the lip of the generated world. The nurse's invitation to her charge to "essayer la vertu / Funèbre," that is, the necessary death that sexual involvement entails, mortality, recalls Matron Clay's assurances to Thel. Hérodiade's nurse might as easily describe Thel as that "triste fleur qui croît seule et n'a pas d'autre émoi / Que son ombre dans l'eau vue avec atonie" (p. 46). Both virgins know that marriage is tantamount to death: each is, in that sense, a "victime lamentable à son destin offerte!" Three times the nurse bends over Hérodiade to perform a nuptial toilette, the decking of the bride, and three times she is repulsed: first she seizes the girl's fingers and is order to "reculez"; next she offers to anoint the girl with myrrh and attar of rose, only to be told to "laisse là ces parfums! ne sais-tu / Que je les hais"; finally she moves to adjust a plait of hair and is commanded to "arrête dans ton crime." The crime, of course, is fleshly contact and all that it forebodes. Hérodiade is a warrior princess. She prefers the imagery of ice, dull pallor of metal, weapons, urns, the barren chill of gems, to all the transient beauty, flowers and perfumes, erotic imagery of the epithalamium. The nurse's touch foreshadows the ritual to follow:

> Ce geste, impiété fameuse: ah! conte-moi
> Quel sûr démon te jette en le sinistre émoi,
> Ce baiser, ces parfums offerts et, le dirai-je?
> Ô mon coeur, cette main encore sacrilège,
> Car tu voulais, je crois, me toucher, sont un jour
> Qui ne finira pas sans malheur sur la tour . . .
> Ô jour qu'Hérodiade avec effroi regarde!
> (p. 46)

> This act, this scandal: ah! now tell me what
> Demon—it must be—casts you in this state,
> This kiss, these scents offered and, shall I say?
> My heart, this hand still full of blasphemy,
> For you, I think, wanted to touch me, are
> A day destined to end upon the tower
> In grief . . . O day Herodias holds in dread!
> (p. 107)

Acknowledging that the "temps" are indeed "bizarre," the nurse mistakes Hérodiade's apprehension for pre-nuptial fear of sex. To her question—"pour qui, dévorée / D'angoisses, gardez-vous la splendeur ignorée / Et le mystère vain de votre être?" (p. 46)—Hérodiade responds with Antigone's resolve: "Pour moi." "Je ne veux rien d'humain." The passage, resonant with Hérodiade's self-claimed metallic imagery, deserves to be quoted in full:

> Oui, c'est pour moi, pour moi, que je fleuris, déserte!
> Vous le savez, jardins d'améthyste, enfouis
> Sans fin dans de savants abîmes éblouis,
> Ors ignorés, gardant votre antique lumière
> Sous le sombre sommeil d'une terre première,
> Vous, pierres, où mes yeux comme de purs bijoux
> Empruntent leur clarté mélodieuse, et vous
> Métaux qui donnez à ma jeune chevelure
> Une splendeur fatale et sa massive allure!
> (p. 47)

> For me, for me I flourish, desolate!
> Gardens of amethyst sunk far below
> In dazzled deeps of endless lore, you know,
> And you, keeping your ancient light, O gold
> Hidden in the dark sleep of primal mould,

> You stones from whence my eyes like flawless jewels
> Borrow their melody of light, you metals
> That to my youthful locks and tresses bring
> Their fatal splendour and their massive bearing!
>
> (p. 111)

The portrait of Hérodiade gazing Narcissus-like into her mirror which dominates "Scène" seems absolute until we begin to read in her speeches an ambivalent, that is, submerged but smouldering sexuality. In three places she covertly suggests, by way of imagery alone, not only possibility of sexual intercourse, but probable enjoyment of conjugal pleasures. The first is her suggestion that the "pâles lys" within her stand erect as she is welcomed by the jet of water in a fountain (p. 44); twice she seems to wish that her robe might be parted to reveal the white thrill of nakedness, and the second time she even reads it as a prophecy of Saint Jean's arrival. Finally, her exultation over the virgin state is vibrantly sexual. The symbolism in the passage needs no exegesis:

> J'aime l'horreur d'être vierge et je veux
> Vivre parmi l'effroi que me font mes cheveux
> Pour, le soir, retirée en ma couche, reptile
> Inviolé sentir en la chair inutile
> Le froid scintillement de ta pâle clarté
> Toi qui te meurs, toi qui brûles de chasteté,
> Nuit blanche de glaçons et de neige cruelle!
>
> (p. 47)

> The horror of the virgin state
> Delights me; oh to live amid the fright
> My hair inspires, and reptile-like to crouch
> Inviolate at evening on my couch
> To feel in useless flesh your pale light's chill
> Sparkle, burning to death in your chaste hell,
> O white-eyed night of frost and cruel snow!
>
> (p. 111)

There is something of the mystic's ecstasy in these oppositely charged images—an ecstatic release which she will share with the saint at the moment of his beheading.[14]

I want to argue here, against the critics who view Hérodiade's stance as repressive, static, and absolute, that although she speaks indirectly, although she never converses with her bridegroom, although she repeatedly champions the "charme dernier" of her solipsistic life in the tower, the "Scène" does prepare for some sort of consummation, however unconventional. This reading depends upon attention to Hérodiade's sexually charged language and to her excessive protestations. Robert Cohn is one of the few critics to see that "beneath her outer coldness, she is clearly trembling with sensuality about to erupt."[15] Near the end of "Scène," she seems to tire of histrionics, to resign herself to the inevitable ceremony of passage. When her nurse asks, "Madame, allez-vous donc mourir?", she responds wearily: "Non, pauvre aieule, / Sois calme et, t'éloignant, pardonne à ce coeur dur" (p. 48). The scene in the tower, that last preserve of the inviolate self, was a necessary prelude to Hérodiade's rite of passage. Her gaze is now directed outward toward that "azur" which is both feared and desired. The last lines of "Scène" convey not only resignation but also receptivity to the heretofore feared and unknown. Content now to renounce the splendor of the pure "corps solitaire" for the uncertainty of the strange rite that awaits her, Hérodiade waits for the arrival of her bridegroom.

If the "Cantique de Saint Jean" is a bridal invitation, as its title seems to suggest, it is an oblique one indeed. Although the white wintry landscape of the "Ouverture" was first intended to find its counterpart in the warm afternoon sensuality of the Faune eclogue, in final published form it is the "Cantique" and not *L'Après-midi d'un faune* which offers the swan-soul a means for transcendence of its state. The answer, however obscurely put by the poem, is a kind of marriage. Charles Mauron is undeniably right when he says that the "drama ends magnificently." But it does so only apparently by a "separation and a flight toward two frigidities."[16] In fact "Cantique," by inversion, brings the trilogy to such a climax—the moment of beheading converges with an intense sexual release—that we may view it as an epithalamium, however violent. More is involved here than the linguistic possibility of the positive result of two negations. Mallarmé, perhaps more than any other modern poet, knew the power of the negative. At the instant of Saint Jean's decapitation, as I shall hope to show, several consummations occur: the frigidities of martyr and virgin subsume one another in a mystic convulsion; at the moment of sunset, life and death embrace intensely. The experienced "frisson" is at once orgasm and death tremor. At this sacrificial altar, Saint Jean's initiation is achieved as well: he both fulfills his historical function by announcing the coming of the Son, and he gains orphic stature by his power to sing even after decapitation.[17] He becomes a figure of poetic genius in modern terms: beheaded, he sings a bridal hymn.

As a bridal invitation, the "Cantique" has several antecedents. The solar and seasonal oppositions between this poem and the two preceding poems in the triptych are like those of eighteenth-century seasonal pastorals. In Blake's season poems in *Poetical Sketches,* for example, the winter poem calls for a cold, nocturnal landscape; the spring poem, in which the sun-bridegroom visits the earth, enacts a wedding. Whereas Hérodiade's tower landscape is cold, frozen, and black, Saint Jean's hymn is spoken at the summer solstice, on the feast of St. Jean's Eve, at sunset. The seasonal fulfillment of its timing and placement effects a revolution, marks a progress. Additionally, of course, "Cantique" echoes the Song of Songs: in this bridal scenario, the young woman is also identified with darkness; she is associated with lilies and myrrh, both of which Hérodiade regards as suspect. In that strange epithalamium as well bride and groom communicate with difficulty and by indirections. The language of paradox prevails in the biblical Song—"I am sick with love"[18]—as it does in Mallarmé's—"toi qui brûles de chasteté" (p. 47). Violence is a peculiar prelude to marriage in Song of Songs, as it is in *Hérodiade*: in the biblical text, the bride is beaten and wounded by watchmen, whereas in Mallarmé's poem the bride exacts the cruel decapitation of the bridegroom she awaits. Both works open themselves to allegorical interpretation as journeys of the soul. Both approach by torturous means the mystical nuptial vision: "you have ravished my heart with a glance of your eyes," says the bridegroom of Song of Songs; Saint Jean fixes "son pur regard" upon Hérodiade in Mallarmé's poem (p. 49), and all the senses are subsumed into that supremely physical, yet transcendent, gaze. By means of decapitation, "les anciens désaccords / Avec le corps" are overcome; body and soul become one at the mystic moment. Paradoxically, as in the baroque mystic inversions of the marriage poem, spiritual transcendence is recorded in sensual terms.

As a marriage between feminine principle of beauty and masculine principle of poetic genius, the poem recalls Shelley's *Alastor,* in which pursuit of the veiled maiden, Ideal Beauty, entailed the poet's death. But death in Mallarmé's poem occurs with such a spasm of intensity that life appears to be there in all its fullness. Saint Jean's martyrdom, into which Hérodiade is drawn, is a ritual experience with an unmistakably sexual resolution: the first stanza of the "Cantique" describes not only the arc of the sun's path in the sky and the path of Jean's career, but also the diametrical opposition of erection and detumescence:

> Le soleil que sa halte
> Surnaturelle exalte
> Aussitôt redescend
>   Incandescent.
>   (p. 49)

> Supernatural
> The sun's pinnacle
> Is soon earthward bent
> Incandescent.
> (p. 115)

The "solitaire vigie" of the head, that phallic lookout, traces the same movement:

> Et ma tête surgie
> Solitaire vigie
> Dans les vols triomphaux
> De cette faux.
> (p. 49)

> While my head stuck out
> A lonely lookout
> In this flying scythe's
> Triumphal swaths.
> (p. 115)

Decapitation/castration is, for all its violence, a triumph for them both: neither is compromised by it—the fierce virgin remains intact; the saint, "de jeûnes ivre," remains celibate—and yet the act binds them into a complicity. The last stanzas of *Hérodiade* do, to my mind, constitute a bridal greeting: given the choice of adhering to their respective "froidure," they move in the direction of one another, experiencing by means of this act a ritual "baptême." In the last line of the poem, the saint's head "pènche un salut." The greeting is not only to his bride; it is a gesture toward the future.

In fact the poem does prepare, by this burning marriage of opposites, a future for bride and groom: Hérodiade leaves the cold, unresponsive kingdom of her father by her mystic union with the saint; Jean, by his collusion with the father's daughter, prepares to overtake him. Together they announce a cosmic birth, the coming of the Son. We are not far here from Spenser's preoccupation with "issue" at the end of the *Epithalamion*: new life resulting from the union is the conventional conclusion to the marriage poem. Also in Spenser, the metaphors of marriage and sexual communion have everything to do with poetry-making. The implied marriage of Hérodiade and the saint—for Mallarmé claims always to "peindre non la chose, mais l'effet qu'elle produit"[19]—has great implications for the production of poetry. This marriage overcomes sterility, fatal mirroring, autoeroticism; this union produces, in the disembodiment of the saint, the voice of poetry itself, pure and incarnate.

If the severed head of the Baptist continues to sing, it is because Jean himself is a figure of the orphic poet as Mallarmé conceived him. But Spenser's courtier-bridegroom, acting as master of ceremonies at his own wedding, gives way in this symbolist work to a conception of Orpheus, essentially inherited from Baudelaire, as a visionary who possesses "a certain key to the invisible world and accordingly speaks the language of correspondences."[20] Mallarmé preserves Jean's Christian significance—he is a precursor to Christ—but he also endows him with orphic stature: by linking him with solar myth, by abstracting him to a poetic principle, by crediting him with having found a new way of transcending the ancient antagonism of body and soul, by linking the decapitated saint with the ritually beheaded poet. Like Saint Jean, Orpheus also had a bride who exacted a grisly price, a submission of the lover to dark descent. Like him, Orpheus was rewarded with poetic immortality for his ritual death. In fact Saint Jean is a relatively early manifestation of Mallarmé's orphic poet; of the later poems, the sonnet in "yx" most explicitly delineates the orphic task: the philosophical search for beauty by descent into nothingness, by spiritual suicide, willed death of the material self.[21] Additionally, Mallarmé's own life work, the *Livre,* was understood in orphic terms:

> J'irai plus loin, je dirai: le Livre, persuadé qu'au fond il n'y a qu'un, tenté à son insu par quiconque a écrit, même les Génies. L'explication orphique de la Terre, qui est le seul devoir du poëte et le jeu littéraire par excellence: car le rhythme même du livre, alors impersonnel et vivant, jusque dans sa pagination, se juxtapose aux équations de ce rêve, ou Ode.[22]

It would become Mallarmé's life work to write an orphic cosmogony, a sequence of orphic hymns: to go beyond the obscurity of the "grimoire" by means of a universalizing and universally understood poetic language. By lending to the void ontological status, by illuminating the shadows of orphic descent, by attempting ritually to recover Eurydice and restore union with her (or at the very least sketch the void that her absence circumscribes), the poet achieves orphic stature and redeems his former sterile, self-mirroring poetics. It is particularly telling that the modern poet who most valorized exile, solitude, whiteness, absence, as in these lines from the 1885 swan sonnet:

> Fantôme qu'à ce lieu son pur éclat assigne,
> Il s'immobilise au songe froid de mépris
> Que vêt parmi l'exil inutile le Cygne.
> (p. 68)

> A ghost whom to this place his lights assign,
> He stiffens in the cold dream of contempt
> Donned amid useless exile by the Swan.
> (p. 169)

died with *Hérodiade* unfinished upon his desk. It was this marriage song for the wedding of beauty and poetic genius, two uncompromising purities, which obsessed him lifelong, this epithalamium which could only be expressed by indirections and with continual difficulty.

III

For all their differences, Mallarmé and Crane share, surprisingly, a common literary sensibility and predilection for certain recurring images. Crane, for example, believed with Mallarmé in the aggregative effect of words in a poem, in synaesthesia as a poetic principle of the first order, in associative rather than logical order of poetic elements. He too succumbed to the beauty of the "poetry of negation," while at the same time worrying about its siren-like dangers.[23] Inventory of Crane's imagery yields a Mallarméan catalogue: vortex, azure, hiatus, calyx, circles, towers, minerals, and stones. In fact the following lines from "The Broken Tower" might serve as a gloss on *Hérodiade:*

> —visible wings of silence sown
> In azure circles, widening as they dip
>
> The matrix of the heart, lift down the eye
> That shines the quiet lake and swells a tower . . .
> The commodious, tall decorum of that sky
> Unseals her earth and lifts love in its shower.
> (pp. 193–94)

It is not only the dislocation of syntax that links the two poems. Crane's work shares an apocalyptic tone with that of Mallarmé, its language of mysticism and that poem's division between dirge and panegyric. Consider as well Crane's use of an orphic cipher in "The Wine Menagerie":

> Rise from the dates and crumbs. And walk away,
> Stepping over Holoferne's shins—
> Beyond the wall, whose severed head floats by
> With Baptist John's. Their whispering begins.
>
> —And fold your exile on your back again:
> Petruschka's valentine pivots on its pin.

At the visionary center of the poem is an image of the floating head of a decapitated male poet figure exacted by an imperious female muse. The pattern recurs throughout Crane's poetry, and, although he retreats from it in "The Wine Menagerie," he often works poetic strength from the violence of the confrontation between the creative spirit of the poet and the elusive female incarnation of beauty.[24] As in Mallarmé's *oeuvre*, poetry results from the tense marriage of contraries held in equipoise, from the initiatory dismemberment of Orpheus by the maenads.

Like *Hérodiade* in the career of Mallarmé, "For the Marriage of Faustus and Helen" announced Crane's mature poetic style and celebrated his achievement of mature poetic stature.[25] I agree with Herbert Liebowitz that the poem is a "festive solemnizing of his vocation as a visionary poet," but the poem goes beyond Romantic embrace of the difficult muse.[26] "Faustus and Helen" is in every sense modern: exploiting a poetics of tension, it works technological imagery and the rhythms of modern music into a "pseudo-symphonic" arrangement of sounds.[27] Nothing of the epithalamium's stately measure, its consciously reconciling and melodic language, its appeal to a witnessing surround, characterizes this poem. In fact the cubist effect of an erotic fantasy of Helen undressed in Part I, the bizarre rooftop dance to the jarring rhythms of jazz in Part II, and the cosmic rape of "mounted, yielding cities" in the last part confound any expectation that "Faustus and Helen" is a conventional wedding song. As in Mallarmé, the bride herself is a maenad: dismembering the poet-god in the French poem, she taunts him sexually to self-abdication in Crane's, asking no less than submission from the poet-initiate. As in Mallarmé, the wedding celebrated is a "mystic consummation" of principles, drawing for its effect and vocabulary upon the imagery of baroque mysticism.[28] As in that poem much of the consummation takes place in the white space upon the page, between tense sections of the trilogy. "Faustus and Helen," like *Hérodiade*, sets up a marriage which requires of the reader that he serve as witness.

Both Crane and Mallarmé, in an oddly traditional manner, use the form of the epithalamium as a backdrop for an allegory of the emergence of the poetic imagination. The telling similarity between the two is that for each poet consummation or epiphany, the supreme poetic moment, is as brief, tenuous, passing, as orgasm itself can be. In each case it involves the ritual submission of the poet to that dark marriage, the *katábasis*. In Mallarmé's poem, Saint Jean's beheading paradoxically provides him with greatest sexual, prophetic, and incantatory strength. Crane's Faustus too finds a voice during his encounter with Helen: the experience of initiatory, even sacrificial wounding—"blamed, bleeding hands"—enables the "imagination" to "extend and thresh the height" (p. 33). Crane's poem, in its final lines, recalls the end of Mallarmé's. After a violent marriage, the singing voice soars upward toward infinity:

> The imagination spans beyond despair
> Outpacing bargain, vocable and prayer.
> (p. 33)

The mind which at the outset of the poem had "shown itself at times / Too much the baked and labeled dough" becomes during the course of a poem ritually consecrated as the "white wafer cheek of love" (pp. 27, 28). As in the poetry of Mallarmé, the metaphor is often drawn from Christian ritual—monstrance, wafer—but the intent, I suggest, is to lend appropriate formality to a secular rite, the incarnation of the literary imagination.

Part I of "Faustus and Helen" turns on the competition between two worlds within the mind and begins to effect a transcendence of the lower, unvisionary quotidian realm. What the poet leaves behind in the "stacked partitions of the day" are "memoranda," "baseball scores," "stenographic smiles," and "stock quotations" (p. 27). This "world dimensional," as Crane suggests in a prose quotation inserted after the second stanza, is for those "untwisted by the love of things irreconcilable." The poetic intelligence, on the other hand, catalyzed by the dramatic play of polar opposites, seeks its own place: an evening, even lunar, landscape, where the imagination is free to create.

> Until the graduate opacities of evening
> Take them away as suddenly to somewhere
> Virginal perhaps, less fragmentary, cool.
> (p. 27)

A halting encounter follows between the poet and Helen. "Some evening" on the subway, "lost yet poised in traffic," the poet courts her with his glance, hoping to "find your eyes across an aisle" (p. 28). He suggests by his tentativeness that, although she "turned away once," now the eyes are "half-riant," "uncontested" (p. 28). There is also a suggestion that union with her, rendered in this section in terms of a rather disembodied sexual fantasy, would be a stay against death: he would have her "meet this bartered blood . . . before its arteries turn dark"; also "the earth may glide diaphanous to death," but if "I lift my arms it is to bend / To you." The imaginative realm in which he hopes consummation will occur begins to take form "lightly as moonlight on the eaves meets snow" (p. 28).

The movement of the first section is from particular to general, from localized and individual to cosmic. Sexual intercourse is read onto a landscape as if a marriage were being consummated between sky and earth: Helen's blush is that of sunset; rainbows appear at the moment of imagined orgasm—"when ecstasies thread the limbs and belly" (p. 28). The poet here is the body of the world, self-submitted to the "hiatus" arching over him. Through this fantasized encounter with Helen, as in Saint Jean's implied marriage to Hérodiade, Faustus attains a state which transcends the "anciens désaccords" of this world.[29] Sexual imagery is gradually translated into the language of mysticism in which the terms of nuptial consummation will be couched. The exchange of interested looks on the streetcar "flickering with those prefigurations" becomes a "lone eye" fixed in positively mystic devotion upon the soul of the beloved; the warmth and effusion of imagined sexual ecstasy become the "eventual flame" in which the two will conjoin, willingly submitting themselves to "final chains, no captive then." As in the martyrdom of Saint Jean, in which Hérodiade is implicated, so in Crane's poem does consecration to a common imaginative goal gain for the poet a commanding poetic voice. Faustus's canticle, hinted at in the last line of Part I, is an orphic hymn: "One inconspicuous, glowing orb of praise."

The second poem of the trilogy, onomatopoetic of the rhythms and sounds of jazz, is a jarring antithesis to the first. A kind of *decensus,* it is Crane's version of that Blakean crucible in which souls are tried, the descent into Experience. On this dark night of the soul, brasses blare—"a thousand light shrugs balance us / Through snarling hails of melody" (p. 30). In fact the offbeat rhythms of this section threaten to undo the harmonies of the first:

> Brazen hypnotics glitter here;
> Glee shifts from foot to foot,
> Magnetic to their tremolo.
> This crashing opera bouffe,
> Blest excursion! this ricochet
> From roof to roof—
> Know, Olympians, we are breathless
> While nigger cupids scour the stars!
> (p. 30)

In spite of the "deft catastrophes of drums," however, "this music has a reassuring way." Not only does the poet contemplate taking Helen "on the incandescent wax" of the dance floor, he also invites the fantasy of taking her home with him:

> Greet naively—yet intrepidly
> New soothings, new amazements
> That cornets introduce at every turn—
> And you may fall downstairs with me
> With perfect grace and equanimity.
>
> (p. 30)

But Helen is "still so young," this seductive siren "of the springs of guilty song," so "striated with nuances, nervosities / That we are heir to," that consummation on this plane is purposely deflected. On this "metropolitan roof garden," a diminished and ironic analogue to the historical Helen's "Dionysian revels . . . and seduction," it seems as if the wedding is off.[30] Beauty in the dimensional world cannot marry Imagination. After the movement toward prayer and ceremony in the first section, the second part seems a retreat from congress.

If the third section of the triptych produces a synthesis between the first two, it does so by violent and obscure means. The backdrop of this section is, of course, the World War. "Speediest destruction" by technological means is superimposed upon the sexual possession of Helen by Faustus. In fact the entire epithalamium, if it may be called so, is shot through with contrastive imagery, oxymora: "blessing and dismay." By a curious doubling, the poet becomes both participant and observer: he becomes a "religious gunman," that "delicate ambassador / Of intricate slain numbers," who vents "repeated play of fire" upon the female sky (p. 32). And he stands back from that rape, a tragic spectator, to envision the catharsis that will follow it—"Let us unbind our throats of pity and fear" (p. 32).

As in Mallarmé's *Hérodiade,* the moment of soaring consummation in "Faustus and Helen" follows directly upon that of harshest violence. The poet of Crane's poem, unable to merge with Helen in either of two preceding poems, identifies with the destructiveness of the "capped arbiter of beauty."

> We know, eternal gunman, our flesh remembers
> The tensile boughs, the nimble blue plateaus,
> The mounted, yielding cities of the air!
>
> (p. 32)

Only by rending the skies in an airplane, "spouting malice / Plangent over meadows," does he find momentary satisfaction of the desire to possess. Then, like Saint Jean, finding a way to consummate a marriage to beauty by odd ascetic means, Crane's Faustus separates himself from the "eternal gunman" and reconciles himself to the exacting life of poetry: the wedding song is for the poet—who must practice devotion to Helen's purity to the point of renouncing fleshly union with her—and his demanding bride, the eternally tantalizing idea of beauty. As in *Hérodiade,* the imagination is subjected to privation and suffering, out of which it churns strength. In the act of martyrdom, mystic marriage of two purities, the poem is released. Crane's Faustus swells with a hymn of praise which rescues the world from destruction and lends poetic voice to the sufferer:

> We did not ask for that, but have survived,
> And will persist to speak again before
> All stubble streets that have not curved
> To memory, or known the ominous lifted arm
> That lowers down the arc of Helen's brow
> To saturate with blessing and dismay.
>
> (p. 33)

Orphic devotion to a dark bride brings with it ecstatic, if ascetic, release:

> Laugh out the meager penance of their days
> Who dare not share with us the breath released,
> The substance drilled and spent beyond repair
> For golden, or the shadow of gold hair.
>
> (p. 33)

The sexual metaphor in the foregoing lines provides the consummation that the poem appears to lack. What remains before Faustus now, as he transcends this initiatory drama, is the life of poetry. In a curiously Rilkean formulation—that of the last *Duino Elegies*—Crane's poet learns to "praise," that is, to raise the orphic song which transforms the universe. This becomes the life work of the seasoned imagination: panegyric to a world which needs its redeeming presence.

> The lavish heart shall always have to leaven
> And spread with bells and voices, and atone
> The abating shadows of our conscript dust.
> . . . .

> Distinctly praise the years, whose volatile
> Blamed bleeding hands extend and thresh the height
> The imagination spans beyond despair,
> Outpacing bargain, vocable and prayer.
>
> (p. 33)

The language is wholly Christian—where have we a better vocabulary for initiation, for rendering of the *coincidentia oppositorum*?—but the rite enacted has aesthetic and metaphysical implications. The imperative of the last lines has the force of certain of Rilke's sonnets to Orpheus in which self exhorts self to fuller participation:

> Sei immer tot in Eurydike—singender steige,
> preisender steige zurück in den reinen Bezug.
> Hier, unter Schwindenden, sei, im Reiche der Neige,
> sei ein klingendes Blas, das sich im Klang schon zerschlug.
>
> Dead evermore in Eurydice, mount with more singing,
> mount to relation more pure with more celebrant tongue.
> Here, in this realm of the dwindlers and dregs, be a ringing
> glass, which has, even though shivered to pieces, been rung.[31]

For Crane, as for Rilke in this instance, eternal marriage to Eurydice, eternal pledge to be her opposite and fulfillment, is what devotion to the literary life requires. Crane's "Faustus and Helen," like certain of Rilke's sonnets, is thus a celebration of what Walter Strauss calls the orphic ontology: "the death that must be understood and experienced as the other side of life, this fusion of death and life achieving its fullest being in pure relatedness."[32] An odd epithalamium, "Faustus and Helen" commemorates just such a marriage of opposite forces, a death-wedding which precedes song and yet prepares for it. As in Mallarmé's poem, the principles which marry are antithetical, and the progress toward union obstructed and difficult; as in Mallarmé's poem too, however, the ritual marks a passage and celebrates the very transcendence toward which the genre traditionally aspires.

IV

Mallarmé's *Hérodiade* and Hart Crane's "For the Marriage of Faustus and Helen" are linked by the parodic yet generative use they make of the epithalamium. In the case of these two works, a nuptial ceremony provides the occasion for a drama of imaginative incarnation. Wedding altar becomes, by inversion, a sacrificial block because passage to the married state decrees death to the virgin soul inviolate. Nuptials in both works are consummated by decapitation and rape. A surround of appropriate witnesses is conspicuously absent. The conventional imagery of the wedding poem is roundly inverted or denied—except in the transcendence of the close. And it is precisely in such poems as these that the epithalamium survives as a resilient literary form, a powerful allegory of the imagination's attempt at incarnation in erotic terms.

Other poems have made similar satiric use of epithalamic form and marriage symbolism. Coleridge, for instance, in his *The Rime of the Ancient Mariner,* works the mariner's journey against the wedding feast. The voyage takes him "below the kirk, below the hill," away from the safe harbor of fellowship to the uncharted region of spiritual trial. Recounting the tale causes the mariner to detain a wedding guest, preventing him from attending the ceremony as witness of communal ritual. The dice-throwing episode in the *Rime,* too, is a parody of a nuptial ceremony. For other poets, the fiction of the epithalamium provides a form for marrying psycho-sexual forces. Rilke's centaur sonnet and Eliot's "Death of St. Narcissus," featuring a hermaphroditic marriage of opposites in a single figure, are jokes on wedding poems. Finally, two poets use the form of the wedding poem ironically to convey the vast gap between conventional marriage ceremony and the values of contemporary culture. In C. S. Lewis's "Prelude to Space: An Epithalamium," wedding becomes an apocalyptic symbol of cultural imperialism: "Bombs, gallows, Belsen camp" replace conventional epithalamic imagery. Paul Celan similarly effects a grim parody of nuptial imagery, mainly that of Song of Songs, in his *Todesfuge.* In this carefully crafted work, epithalamic symbols become emblems of the gas ovens: milk, rising scent of perfumes, communal song, serve funereal purposes here. But almost in spite of Celan's black inversion of epithalamium as genre, the wedding song beneath this poem lends dignity to the camp chant of Celan's sufferers. Nuptial imagery and refrain confer sacred purpose on their round song and press panegyric upon the most inconsolable loss this century has known.

9

Sea-Changes: The Incarnational Ode and Ceremonial Modes

I

In modern poetry, in the wake of diminishing influence of the doctrine of imitation, a diffuse, but recognizable, initiation poem continues to be written. In its way, this poem is as ritualized and formal as *Lycidas*—that elegy which immortalized the form of seaside meditation upon the subject of death. After *Lycidas* poems tend to imitate its form closely and ultimately unsatisfactorily, in the end pronouncing a dirge on pastoral elegy's power to assuage. Hart Crane's most overt allusion to (and perhaps most subversive use of) the conventions of the pastoral elegy occurs in the explicitly funereal "At Melville's Tomb," a poem which embraces the same bleak sea vision as the writer it memorializes. If once death by water promised a sea-change—"Frosted eyes there were that lifted altars" echoes Ariel's song from *The Tempest*—now "wrecks passed without the sound of bells," now "monody shall not wake the mariner."[1] "Monody," of course, is the Miltonic catchword, signaling the difference between that poem and this admission of defeat, this abandonment of corpse to the "whelming tide." Crane's piscatorial, read against *Lycidas* and the classical funeral obsequy, refuses to lift the mariner's head from the waves in a modern version of Daphnis's deification or Lycidas's resuscitation. In "At Melville's Tomb," Hart Crane refuses transcendence: "This fabulous shadow only the sea keeps."

Otherwise poems respond to *Lycidas* less directly, dispensing with the elegiac fiction of singing over a bier and the Arcadian *dramatis personae* and drawing instead upon Milton's orphic ode of self-announcement for the model of literary initiation and succession it provides. These modern piscatorials tend to be lyric-philosophical pronouncements on mortality and art. They take place by water, "at least in vision, if inland far they be," writes Bloom paraphrasing Wordsworth.[2] Each of these works records an encounter with death which purges the neophyte of his fear of immersion and engulfment. Finally, each is linear and marks stages of evolving consciousness toward a vision that is transcendent, self-celebrating, and vital to continued literary productivity. They have been called, with *Lycidas,* odes of incarnation or immortality odes because, recording rising poetical character, they promise transcendence of imaginative death.[3] Paul Fussell, Jr., who briefly links some of the poems of this chapter under the heading "The American Shore Ode," supplies a context insufficiently comparative for these works. He notes that the poems take place on American beaches and that they memorialize an American initiation ritual—that of a "boy like Huck Finn . . . positioned in the midst of physical nature, [who] discovers the idea of death and then enacts some strategic ritual by which his discovery is brought into coherence with his journey toward maturity."[4] But by rooting them so firmly in American soil, Fussell denies the works a heritage and future resonance. Leo Spitzer, in an essay on Whitman, comes closer to finding a context in world literature for such works as that poet's "Out of the Cradle . . ." when he calls it a "powerful original synthesis of motifs which have been elaborated through a period of 1500 years of Occidental poetry," a democratization of the ode form.[5] I suspect with Spitzer that Whitman's "Out of the Cradle . . ." and Crane's "Voyages," and for that matter Eliot's "The Dry Salvages," have more in common with the ode's successful mix of public reference and private utterance than with American elegiac prose. I would also suggest that the iconography of these poems is rather that of Milton's "whelming tide" and Wordsworth's "immortal sea" than that of picturesque American seashores.

Before reading these poems as important transformations of the classical and Miltonic elegiac, however, I shall briefly sketch a continental context as well for the seaside setting of displaced elegy to demonstrate the complexity of modern piscatorialism. Paul Valéry's *Le Cimetière marin,* it seems to me, has a place in this tradition of dense, philosophical, sea-inspired poetry, as does St.-Jean Perse's collection, *Amers.* The former is an odic exploration of consciousness in the face of death, inspired by a constellation of sea, sky, and grave. Valéry called the work "un monologue de 'moi,' dans lequel les thèmes les plus simples et les plus constants de ma vie affective et intellectuelle . . . fussent appelés, tramés, opposés . . .Tout ceci menait à la mort et touchait à la pensée pure."[6] For all its seeming anti-pastoralism, however—Valéry ironically portrays himself as a smiling shepherd pasturing "le blanc troupeau de mes tranquilles tombes"[7]—the poem borrows certain elegiac conventions and takes up its familiar consoling statement, even if to reject it:

> Maigre immortalité noire et dorée,
> Consolatrice affreusement laurée,

Qui de la mort fait un sein maternel,
Le beau mensonge et la pieuse ruse!
Qui ne connait, et qui ne les refuse!
Ce crane vide et ce rire eternel!

Gaunt immortality in black and gold,
Consoles grimly wreathed in laurel, making
Believe that death's a warm maternal breast,
Sublime falsehood, consecrated fraud!
Who does not recognize them and reject
That empty skull, that everlasting grin!

St.-Jean Perse's *Amers,* translated by Wallace Fowlie as *Sea-Marks,* is an aggregate hymn to the sea of such dimension and power as perhaps to be the single most sustained work on the sea in the French language. It is an incarnational lyric, a ritual incantation, a Mariner's tale, a "chant d'épousailles" and a dirge, a seasonal miscellany, a monody and a choral hymn at once. Perse conceived the work "comme l'arène solitaire et le centre rituel," "la table d'autel du drame antique" of humanity.[8] The genesis of the creative Word, about which all the poets of this chapter shall have more to say, is churned out of the sea by means of a choral song. Pierre Emmanuel writes of *Amers:* "from this chorus around the sea the sea itself rises: it is the song, the energy shared by all men, the prophecy, the Supreme Word, which goes beyond them, and yet is born of them."[9]

I do not mean here to attempt an unwieldy iconography of the sea as symbol. I merely mean to remind the reader of the sea's long significance as a source of poetic power and inspiration of a tradition which comes to focus in pastoral's piscatorial corpus—Sannazaro's seaside confrontation with death during the course of an elegy for Phyllis, Milton's watery depiction of Lycidas's bier. But between Shakespeare's allegorizable notion of suffering a baptismal sea-change and Freud's initiatory immersion in the oceanic wellspring of creative power is a long-founded tradition, borrowed by pastoral piscatorialists, of viewing risk of the "open sea" as evidence of a daring and imaginative poetic life.[10] Keat's 1818 letter to James Hessey charts this shift of favor from a safe and landed pastoral "green" to a Romantic piscatorialism:

> In Endymion, I leapt headlong into the Sea, and thereby have become better acquainted with the Soundings, the quicksands, the rocks, than if I had stayed upon the green shore, and piped a silly pipe, and took tea and comfortable advice.

"Sounding seas" is a Miltonic formulation which I sense Keats intends to echo here. Braving the open sea becomes an initiatory motif which signals readiness for spiritual trial and passage to mature poetic style. Here is Whitman's version of the injunction:

> Long have you timidly waded holding a plank by the shore,
> Now I will you to be a bold swimmer,
> To jump off in the midst of the sea.

For Valéry, too, at the close of *Le Cimetière marin,* the "puissance salée" of the sea "me rend mon âme." Immersion invigorates and replenishes, even baptizes, and the sea-change experienced by the initiate makes possible the composition of the poem.

The poems of this chapter share a certain number of literary motifs which I shall trace to Milton and Wordsworth and to the pastoral elegiac tradition in general. As initiatory scenarios, each takes place by water, where, Bloom tells us, poets tend to incarnate. Each explores in this context the nature of death and rebirth. Each stages a quest for the word, that secret talisman rendered up to the *mystes* by the sea—a word that becomes incarnate during the course of the elegy. Finally, each initiate succeeds by virtue of some interceding female figure who has the power to bestow or confiscate poetic power. In Hopkins's "The Wreck of *The Deutschland*" and Eliot's *Four Quartets,* treated briefly in the conclusion to this chapter, the intercessor is Mary herself and the word out of the sea is the Word made Flesh. In the case of the latter poems, of course, the language is sacramental, the imagery devotional. But in all four cases the ritual being enacted remains the same. "A Word Out Of The Sea," Whitman's working title for "Out of the Cradle Endlessly Rocking," applies equally well to each of the four poems. We get in Whitman, Crane, Hopkins, and Eliot a sea-change "into something rich and strange" worthy of comparison with Milton's transvaluation of the drowned Lycidas, although in the later poems we witness an utter displacement of pastoral elegiac machinery. What survives the demise of pastoral convention in these modern poems, however, is a range of ceremonial forms with attendant imagery of passage from one state to another: nuptial anthems, nativity odes, funeral elegies, orphic hymns of self-announcement.

II

Whitman's "Out of the Cradle..." and Crane's "Voyages" are both initiatory experiments: each work chronicles a poetic coming-of-age which involves dissolution of personality and subsequent graduation to orphic stature. Each poem views this process metaphorically as a voyage into the sea, out of the confines of the merely personal. Each poem personifies the sea as a deeply ambiguous female figure, a mother-bride capable of maternal caresses or seductive postures—confrontation with whom, erotically achieved, is tantamount to passage to poetic manhood. Each poem locates the moment of incarnation at the point where eros and thanatos meet: the going outside oneself toward another, being laved in a lover's embrace, is—as mystic poets have always known—a kind of death. During the course of this figured *descensus* in search of a mature poetic voice, the Word is ritually bestowed upon each poet. I would suggest that each work is in this sense a pastoral, an apprenticeship work: Whitman reworks a childhood "reminiscence,"[11] during the process of which he becomes an "outsetting bard," writing a nativity ode upon his own double birth not unlike that announced by Milton in his transcendence of "swainishness"[12] in *Lycidas* or by Wordsworth in the Immortality Ode. Crane brings *White Buildings,* the important lyric *oeuvre* of his early years, to a close with "Voyages," signaling his readiness for the epic venture of *The Bridge.*

Whitman gives birth to himself during the course of "Out of the Cradle." In fact the entire progress from cradle to grave is ritually charted: in the parturition of the prologue, in the marriage song of the bird, in the dirge for separation, loss of love, rupture. The first twenty-one lines of the poem, which Whitman labeled Pre-Verse when he first published the poem in 1859 as "A Child's Reminiscence," represent the "Ninth-month midnight" of gestation, and imitate, in the repetition of phrases, the almost biblical anaphora, the expulsive rhythm of birth itself. The first lines are not only a prologue to the poem as a whole, assembling its imagery ("cradle," "shuttle," "sands," "child," "bird," "moon," "word," "sea") and initiating its rhythms, they actually generate the speaker out of the encompassing surround: prepositional phrases beginning "out of," "over," "down from," "up from," "from," literally spawn the subject "I" some twenty lines into the poem. Even the moon, late-risen and swollen with tears, is ready to parturate. The progression toward incarnation of the man/boy is, however, difficult, as if the poet fears the poem may not get written "ere all eludes me." The last word of the twenty-one-line sentence is the verb "sing," which Whitman, purposely dislocating the syntax, takes great pains to generate last. "Out of the cradle" of the sea, onto the "sand" is born a man capable of orphic song. A "uniter of here and hereafter," the bard is born who will recover from the sea the word incarnate, poetry's guarantee.

At the beginning of "Out of the Cradle" is one of those "junctions elegiac" which Crane noted in the "Cape Hatteras" section of *The*

Bridge: in the image of the singer as "a man, yet by these tears a little boy again," singing a poetic "reminiscence," we catch Whitman looking backward at Wordsworth in the first stanzas of the Immortality Ode. As Wordsworth viewed the epithalamic harmony of the child's world from a distanced adult perspective, so Whitman invokes the spring—"when the lilac scent was in the air and fifth-month grass was growing"—of a pastoral seedtime, one in which, figuratively, he watched a "he-bird" and "she-bird" marry and nest expectantly on the seashore.[13] Not only does Whitman invoke Wordsworth's lost Eden of immediacy and primal joy, he emphasizes rather pointedly in the twice-repeated "both together" his own analogue for the pastoral flock-battening scene of Milton's *Lycidas,* that time of youthful obliviousness when "both together" Milton and King kept schoolboy company.[14] The evocation of earlier—Blake would say Innocent, or ungenerated—states of consciousness is the first task of elegy; the next is to accommodate in a way that allows for future literary productivity the unalterable fact of death.

The birds' idyll, set apart from the narrative by italicization and by its assignment to another speaker, is short-lived; and the untimely separation of the couple forces upon the poet, by virtue of his identification with "my brother" the "lone singer," the confrontation with the waves of death hinted at in the prologue. We have *not,* here, a pastoral dialogue between shepherd and older goatherd as in the classical elegies of Theocritus and Virgil, but we do have an analogue to such an initiatory encounter. The child of "Out of the Cradle" recognizes immediately in the bird's song the music of mystery and entrusts himself to that spiritual mentor for guidance and direction.

The bird/boy relationship is that of shaman/initiate: the one sings a song, "pouring forth the meanings"; the other "treasur'd every note... listen'd to keep, to sing, now translating the notes." In point of fact, however, the filial relationship of swain to angel, as in Milton, or shepherd to goatherd, as in Theocritus, is replaced here with an untraditional, democratic American relationship. "Following you my brother," the boy tells the bird, explicitly labelling his mentor with a familial term suggesting equality. It is quite probable that the impulse to project a community of brothers is utterly American. Additionally Whitman, viewing himself as the first American bard and recognizing no real precursors in American literature, was privileged with the status of the "new." His evocation of that "demon or bird"—and I read this as an appeal to the Genius of the Shore, as in *Lycidas,* or the procreative father Genius in Spenser's *Epithalamion,* the daimon, or other—can afford to be tender and reciprocal rather than violent. Whitman is a father figure to American poets like Crane and Stevens; his place in American literature is analogous to that of Milton in English or Hugo in French literature, yet the lack of a strong American lyric tradition preceding him gives him greater originary stature than Milton and Hugo. His sense of competition with Milton still exists, however, and there can be no doubt that his model for elegy was Milton's own. Here is Edgar Lee Masters's record of Whitman on Milton, too thoroughgoing a dismissal not to be suspect:

> It seems to me that Milton is a copy of a copy—not only Homer but the Aeneid: a sort of modern repetition of the same old story: legions of angels, devils: war is declared, waged: moreover, even as a story it enlists little of my attention: he seems to me like a bird—soaring yet overweighted: dragged down, as if burdened—too greatly burdened: a lamb in its beak: its flight not graceful, powerful, beautiful, satisfying, like the gulls we see over the Delaware in midwinter—their simple motion a delight—attracting you when they first break upon your sight: soaring, soaring, irrespective of cold or storm. It is true, Milton soars, but with dull, unwieldy motion . . . There's no use talking, he won't go down with me.[15]

One wonders whether the bird figure in "Cradle," with whom the boy so charmingly dialogues, is not a wishful portrait of Milton within the poem itself. In any case, the bird's effect on the boy is analogous to that of Michael on the swain: in *Lycidas* the archangel projects a vision of the heavenly company as nuptial choir; in Whitman's poem, the bird sings a love song with the undertones of a dirge, a bridal invitation to his lost mate so heavily erotic, so fused with the idea and imagery of death, so enticingly pitched, that it hovers just on the line between ecstasy and despair—"a reckless despairing carol" with the force of a hymn.

When the bird's "aria" sinks, the boy experiences an epiphany or transference of poetic energy so productive of a metamorphosis that it has been likened to the sunrise of the youthful Apollo, a figure for the emergence of the poetic spirit.[16] Until this point in the poem "that lagging, yellow, waning moon" dominated the landscape. Now, with the transmission of mystical knowledge to initiate, a revolution occurs, and light replaces night. In this instant the poet achieves a second birth:

The aria sinking,
All else continuing, the stars shining,
The winds blowing, the notes of the bird continuous echoing,
With angry moans the fierce old mother incessantly moaning,
On the sands of Paumanok's shore gray and rustling,

> The yellow half-moon enlarged, sagging down, drooping, the face of the sea almost touching
> The boy ecstatic, with his bare feet the waves, with his hair the atmosphere dallying,
> The love in the heart long pent, now loose, now at last tumultuously bursting,
> The aria's meaning, the ears, the soul, swiftly depositing,
> The strange tears down the cheeks coursing,
> The colloquy there, the trio, each uttering,
> The undertone, the savage old mother incessantly crying,
> To the boy's soul's questions sullenly timing, some drown'd secret hissing
> To the outsetting bard.
>
> (ll. 130–43)

In the first lines of the poem a man is born; in the lines following the bird's dirge, a second birth of the poet as bard is projected out of that trinity there, the trio of bird, boy, and fierce mother. The birth is sexual and psychological (pent-up emotions burst forth tumultuously in tearful and ecstatic release) as well as literary: the old mother hisses "some drown'd secret" in answer to the "boy's soul's questions" and in the process acts as midwife to the birth of Whitman as poet, the "outsetting bard." At this pivotal moment in the poem, the poet literally finds his voice—"for I, that was a child, my tongue's use sleeping, now I have heard you"—and begins his poetic career:

> Now in a moment I know what I am for, I awake,
> And already a thousand singers, a thousand songs, clearer, louder and more sorrowful that yours,
> A thousand, warbling echoes have started to life within me, never to die.
>
> (ll. 147–49)

The crucial shift here is from the bird's "solitary song" to Whitman's "thousand warbling echoes" of communal, even epic, song. Vocation in the double sense makes of Whitman a bard. These lines of positive self-celebration should be compared with the following lines from "As I Ebb'd with the Ocean of Life," in Bloom's words, "Whitman's great elegy of Orphic disincarnation,"[17] in which "sobbing dirge" provides no transcendence:

> O baffled, balk'd, bent to the very earth,
> Oppress'd with myself that I have dared to open my mouth,

> Aware now that amid all that blab whose echoes recoil upon me I have
>   not had the least idea who or what I am,
> But that before all my arrogant poems the real Me stands yet untouch'd,
>   untold, altogether unreach'd,
> Withdrawn far, mocking me with mock-congratulatory signs and bows,
> With peals of distant ironical laughter at every word I have written,
> Pointing in silence to these songs, and then to the sand beneath.[18]

On this shore too he listens "to the dirge," but incarnation does not occur:

> I perceive I have not really understood any thing, not a single object,
>   and that no man ever can,
> Nature here in sight of the sea taking advantage of me to dart upon me
>   and sting me,
> Because I have dared to open my mouth.

"As I Ebb'd" is a meditation on impotence and unfulfillment which ends with an image of spent and wasted seed. "Out of the Cradle," on the other hand, is a positive discovery of sexuality and verbal potency. Whitman makes explicit that which is implicit in Milton and Wordsworth: that sexual and poetic power are related, that writing is a kind of mastery with the symbolic power of potency. Milton's success at raising Lycidas's drooping head and Wordsworth's compensatory marital relationship to nature both sexualize poetic achievements. Literary initiation in this displaced elegy, it should come as no surprise, calls for explicitly sexual metaphors.

  Initiation in this poem is mediated by two figures, the "dusky demon and brother" bird and the muselike mother sea. What is in fact imparted to the boy in the form of the death carol is a secret knowledge of sexuality; the bird transfers to him a tension from which he will never be immune again, but which will empower him to create poetry:

> Never more shall I escape, never more the reverberations,
> Never more the cries of unsatisfied love be absent from me,
> Never again leave me to be the peaceful child I was before what there
>   was in the night,
> By the sea under the yellow and sagging moon,
> The messenger there arous'd, the fire, the sweet hell within,
> The unknown want, the destiny of me.
>
>   (ll. 153–58)

The nexus of this complex fusion is the place where eros and thanatos meet: from the bird, the boy-poet learns the "sweet hell" of love; the second part of the mystery is death itself. The sea, the other parent in this poem of birth and generation, is mother to the boy, "an old crone rocking the cradle, swathed in sweet garments." It is she who passes to him, in the form of a lisped "word final, superior to all," the "clew" he needs to make sense of the bird's love song. The word is, of course, "death," love's opposite and dynamic contrary—that which circumscribes life and lends urgency to all our actions. In this confrontation with death, Whitman achieves psychological mastery over his own fear of annihilation: with reiteration, the word "death" begins to give the speaker an illusion of omnipotence and control. To this interpretation of "the low and delicious word death" must be added an additional qualification: the repetition, incantatory and incremental, of this formula becomes for me a linguistic approximation to the act of coitus. The incarnation that takes place in the last section of the poem is a fleshly act in every sense: it is at once an expulsion from amniotic fluids up on to the "sands" where the boy stands for the first time on his own "feet" and a baptismal immersion, "laving me softly all over." In this sense the sea-mother "whisper'd me," literally breathing life into the boy. But this section also makes the sea into a bride with whom sexual consummation must take place: "hissing melodious," an oxymoronic formulation not unlike Spenser's "doolful pleasaunce," conveys something of the tension in this initiation to manhood. "Death, death, death, death, death," signifying the merging of poet and mother-bride, becomes the sexual rhythm itself.

For the act of writing an elegy, as Whitman makes clear, is a sexual accomplishment; in this instant sexual destiny and poetic destiny fuse. "My own songs awaked from that hour" of first sexuality, Whitman ends his poem, "and with them the word up from the waves." In an associative passage on potency and language, messengers and intercession, Norman O. Brown offers a gloss on Whitman's and Milton's initiatory dramas:

> Speech resexualized . . . The tongue made potent again, out of his mouth goeth a sharp sword. The spermatic word, the Word as seed; the sower soweth the word. Annunciations, messages, messengers, angels, having intercourse with the daughters of men, making pregnant through the ear; angels or birds, winged words or doves of the spirit. The flying bird or angel is an erection or winged phallus; "a single word stands for the penis and the sentence for the thrust of the penis in coitus." A supernatural pregnancy: "A being, be it man or woman, who has the Holy Ghost

within him is pregnant or full of semen and in ejaculating words of prophecy the wizard either ejaculates or gives birth to a child."[19]

The similarity of symbols in Milton's elegy and Whitman's ode is tantalizing—potent birds, messengers, angels, intercessors, mediators—but even beyond the association of images their procedures are identical: Milton achieves by resurrection of Lycidas from the waves what Whitman gains by immersion in the sea, imaginative and literary mastery of a situation in which, at the outset, he was a neophyte.

If in fact an elegy lays to rest a former self in the act of articulating the poem and with it the burden of apprenticeship, and if, in that moment, an elegy represents a gesture toward the future (death of the child promises potency to the man, and confrontation with death provides for transcendence), then "Out of the Cradle Endlessly Rocking" is a more powerful imitation of *Lycidas* than Whitman's better-known "When Lilacs Last in the Dooryard Bloom'd."[20] Dirge, mourners, flowers, drooping star, establish in that poem an incontrovertible relationship to Milton's elegy and the shopworn literary conventions of previous pastoral dirges; still "Lilacs" captures none of Milton's tone of orphic success. "Out of the Cradle," on the other hand, is at once farther from and closer to *Lycidas* and the Immortality Ode—poems to which at first reading it bears no visible relation. On the one hand, the elegiac framework is so attenuated and displaced in "Cradle" that the poem appears to be an independent creation, not one in debt to elegy's store of imagery. Yet, on the other, "Out of the Cradle" so accurately taps the energy of Milton's and Wordsworth's incarnational odes, so successfully translates the initiatory drama in a range of ceremonial forms, that it, rather than Whitman's elegy for Lincoln, appears to take its place in an initiatory tradition with them.

III

Like Whitman's "Out of the Cradle," Hart Crane's unlikely "Voyages" is also a more conventional elegy than it seems on the surface. Where his "At Melville's Tomb" roundly denied the possibilities of elegiac self-transformation, "Voyages," like Whitman's ode, strikes a more successful, more insistently careerist, note. In fact Crane's "Voyages," a six-part meditation on the sea, love, death, potency, and poetry, reproduces under guise the same set of characters as Whitman's poem: poet-initiate, ambiguous sea-woman, both mother and bride, and "Prodigal," from whom Crane is imparted the mystery of sexuality.[21] Like Whitman's poem, it is not a formal funeral elegy, but an odd love poem which traces the course of love from consummation to separation and in so doing locates poetic strength in ultimate separation, or death, and the unexpected consolation of a permanent kingdom of poetic immortality. Like that poem, it traces a personal and literary history: from innocent, unseasoned childhood to the knowing adult state preliminary to visionary experience. Like that poem, it is an elegiac initiation, calling, at its close, for the traditional, if somewhat "splintered," "garlands" of poetic accomplishment.

Most important in "Voyages," however, is the refraction of the classical pastoral elegy through important intervening Renaissance and Romantic elegies. Crane not only echoes classical conventions—ruptured state of pastoral bliss, untimely death, flower-strewing, initiatory (especially orphic) motifs, final award of the wreath of poetic achievement—he plainly reads back through Whitman's "Out of the Cradle," Wordsworth's Immortality Ode, and Milton's *Lycidas* to the classical initiation scenario. The first poem in "Voyages," for example, serves as a prologue to the whole and provides an analogue to the birth or childhood section of Whitman's ode. The evocation of an earlier state of pastoral bliss prior to the experiential confrontation with untimely death is the first task of elegy, as the flock-battening passages in Milton's *Lycidas* and the festival verses of Wordsworth's Immortality Ode attest. In fact in "Voyages I" we watch Crane watching Wordsworth's adult exclusion from the May morning festivities: the contrast drawn in the first poem is between "bright striped urchins . . . gaily digging and scattering" upon the beach and the grown man watching the children frisk with their dog. As in Wordsworth's poem, the man sees what the children innocently fail to perceive—"And could they hear me I would tell them"—that the growth process is a perilous journey on treacherous water:

> but there is a line
> You must not cross nor ever trust beyond it
> Spry cordage of your bodies to caresses
> Too lichen-faithful from too wide a breast.
> The bottom of the sea is cruel.
>
> (p. 35)

The children are warned not to trust the sea's "too wide" breast and lichen-like affection; the "spry cordage" of their bodies does not guarantee that they will be seaworthy. The line between their safe beach frolic—in the Immortality Ode too the children "sport upon the shore"—and the harrowing voyage is, of course, the decision to brave the waters. The last line of the warning becomes a prophetic utterance with something of adult recognition of mortality in its tone. Compare Milton's "but O the heavy change" and Wordsworth's elegiac "But now . . ." to the sudden shift in the last line of the first voyage poem. This utterance sounds the bass note of the entire suite of poems; the remaining lyrics climb with difficulty back from that bleak recognition that any risk of self entails loss of self in the enveloping, yet treacherous, waters of maturity. Untimely death prompts once more an elegy, but it is death of the self explicitly that is at stake.

The second and third poems of the sextet explore love and lovemaking in the bed of the sea in a manner that so fuses love and death as to recall the carol of Whitman's bird. The telling thing about these poems is that sexual experience, the erotic metaphor, stands for literary experience—the imagery of consummation is superimposed upon the ritual language of initiation. The sea is at once a seductive lover whose "undinal vast belly moonward bends" and a judge or lawgiver "whose diapason knells / On scrolls of silver snowy sentences"—the "sceptred terror of whose sessions" rends all but those who trust themselves to the death that is love.

> Bequeath to us no earthly shore until
> Is answered in the vortex of our grave
> The seal's wide spindrift gaze toward paradise.
>   (p. 36)

The vortex in which love and death meet is, of course, as in Whitman's poem, orgasm. "Sleep, death, desire" come together in the moment the Elizabethans termed "little death"; the three "close round one instant in one floating flower," Crane's image for post-coital bliss. The sea, in this second poem of the collection, acts as mistress of ceremonies to the occasion: the real consummation, mirrored in her "turning shoulders," takes place between poet and Prodigal, who is called upon, like the bird of Whitman's ode, to "complete the dark confessions her veins spell." Critics note that Crane enjoyed the most passionate affair of his life—with a sailor—at the moment of the poem's conception; no doubt too in Whitman's sexual initiation by a male bird, Crane found inspiration and sanction for his own homosexual portrayal of initiation. The biographical proof of such intent, however, remains less convincing to me than the literary evidence: in pastoral initiation poems from Theocritus to Milton, the presence or absence of attendant nymphs notwithstanding, a man is treated to arcane lore and welcomed to mature poetic stature—that is, actually initiated—by a member of the same sex. The homosexual pair of each poem derives from the Greek initiatory pattern and the father/son rivalry of the Freudian model. Literary genetics, as women poets' notable absence from the traditions of ceremonial poetry attests, is not merely metaphorically dominated by patriarchal custom.[22]

The third poem is the climax of the sequence. In this lyric, in a supreme invocation of pathetic fallacy, sea and sky achieve cosmic intercourse which bears "infinite consanguinity" to the consummation of the poet and his other or Prodigal—"sea plains where the sky / Resigns a breast that every wave enthrones." In these "ribboned water lanes," the poet and his lover have made ritual ablutions (Crane uses Whitman's word "laved" for the baptismal effect of immersion in the sea); in a show of support for their union the sea lifts "reliquary hands." This poem, of the entire suite, is the initiation poem *par excellence*. Note the overlay of conventional symbols of initiation—"gates" recalling those Neoplatonic portals of Blake and Spenser, the "pillars" and "pediments" of Psyche's house in Apuleius's allegory—and sexual merging:

> And so, admitted through black swollen gates
> That must arrest all distance otherwise,—
> Past whirling pillar and lithe pediments,
> Light wrestling there incessantly with light,
> Star kissing star through wave on wave unto
> Your body rocking!
>
> (p. 37)

The moment of passage itself, termed a "death," "presumes no carnage, but this simple change," the metamorphosis undergone in the waves:

> Upon the steep floor flung from dawn to dawn
> The silken skilled transmemberment of song.
>
> (p. 37)

Not only Ariel's lyric evocation of a sea-change, but also Milton's fifth stanza of *Lycidas,* stands beyond these lines: that verse beginning with reference to the "remorseless deep" which "clos'd o'er the head of your lov'd Lycidas" and ending with the "gorie visage" of Orpheus floating down the "swift Hebrus." Crane condenses this passage into two reverberant lines: the initiate is, like the drowned Lycidas, tossed by the relentless waves, but the drowning proves restorative, and "transmemberment," a coinage, supersedes its primary association with the dismemberment of Orpheus. This line, coupled with the prayer "permit me voyage, love, into your hands," marks the midpoint of the poem and sets our "gaze toward" the "paradise" regained at the close of the series in the poet's mythic "Belle Isle." Just as in *Lycidas* the violent death of Orpheus looks forward to Lycidas's retrieval but does not guarantee immortality until the Christian transvaluation at the end of the poem, so in this poem of "Voyages" immersion in the sea and consequent dissolution of self prepare for the consolations of the last.

"Voyages IV" and "V" backtrack in characteristic elegiac fashion and follow upon the orphic climax much as Milton's long meditation on the uses of poetry and the need for fame fills out the reference to ritual dismemberment. Milton likens flirtation with fame to earthly erotics, the pleasurable tangling in Neaera's hair which distracts him from both worldly and heavenly vocation. Crane, in his post-coital speculation on the risks and pleasures of self-expenditure, cries: "No, / In all the argosy of your bright hair I dreamed / Nothing so flagless as this piracy." In fact both reach the same conclusion: Milton resolves to let others "sport with Amaryllis in the shade" while he devotes himself to earning his heavenly "meed" of fame; Crane greets post-coital separation and the inevitable mortality of human love with a resolve to find a principle of permanence in "the signature of the incarnate word," that is, in the sacred, imperishable word of poetry rather than physical union. The entire movement of the poem, toward the permanence of a consoling verbal paradise, is rigorously conventional: it strains, in high elegiac fashion, toward transcendence.

Crane's floral imagery is deserving of further discussion because, as his experiment with the pastoral catalogue in "Cape Hatteras" reveals, he was very much aware of the peculiar eroticism—at once bridal and funereal—of the bouquet. As mentioned previously, the love-death of orgasm is figured in "one floating flower." In "Voyages II," "crocus lustres" of stars and "poinsettia meadows" of the sea's tides are offered to the Prodigal in a gesture of sexual invitation. The fourth poem relies on the language of flowers to evoke that safe harbor, couched in nuptial terms, which would cement their union and confer upon it a permanence, "the chancel port and portion of our June." In a telling chiasmus of elegiac and epithalamic imagery, Crane calls for flower-strewing: bouquets marking the path of wedded lovers are superimposed upon the staves honoring the bier of the one "lost in fatal tides."

> Shall they not stem and close in our own steps
> Bright staves of flowers and quills to-day as I
> Must first be lost in fatal tides to tell?
>
> (p. 38)

He still hopes for transcendental recovery of song through love:

> No stream of greater love advancing now
> Than, singing, this mortality alone
> Through clay aflow immortally to you.
>
> (p. 38)

But if the last lines of "IV" leave the lover still hoping to achieve a wedding with the beloved—"widening noon within your breast for gathering," expecting still to "receive / The secret oar and petals of all love"—the fifth poem of the sequence renounces love and sex in favor of poetry. The lover literally dissolves and falls away as the poet realizes nothing is there for futurity and permanence:

> Knowing I cannot touch your hand and look
> Too, into that godless cleft of sky
> Where nothing turns but dead sands flashing.
> (p. 39)

The ultimate "piracy" has been the betrayal that is mortality—the recognition that human life is as transient and unreliable as "moon light, moon light loved / And changed. . . ."

The last poem of "Voyages" is a nuptial hymn and a benediction, a vision of that Wordsworthian rainbow of covenant which promises resurrection. The poem is, like the close of Whitman's ode, a retrieval of the "word" out of the sea—that poet's secret word "death" and Milton's "unexpressive nuptial song"—which the poet fears to name: "waiting, afire, what name, unspoke, / I cannot claim." Suddenly, as in Whitman's poem, the sea becomes a collaborator rather than an adversary: "ocean rivers, churning, swift green borders" have the power to lift the "lost morning eyes" of "swimmers." In fact the last poem is as much about loss and restoration of vision as it is about failure and recovery of voice. The poet, as "derelict and blinded guest," must, in the terms of the paradox, lose his vision in order to find it; in the "lost morning eyes" of the "swimmers" too we recall that "those are pearls which were his eyes." Supreme poetic vision replaces ordinary sight, and earthly expenditures are transmuted into ideal and enduring values, but not without cost. For example, in this last poem of the series, all the words associated with the purgatorial fire of sex now return transformed; "creation's blithe and petalled word" becomes a consoling substitute for the "floating flower" of orgasm; a goddess rises from her couch, "conceding dialogue with eyes / That smile unsearchable repose," to replace the treacherous sea-muse of the earlier poems. Finally, the sargasso sea of the lover's hair entwines transcendentally with rainbows in the final poem, and rebirth is promised in an image recalling Crashaw's *Epithalamion,* that of the nurturing "phoenix' breast." Paradise is at last achieved in the "fervid covenant" of "Belle Isle," "white echo" of the poet's imaginative Eden.

"Voyages VI," especially in the transvaluations of imagery, has learned its technique from Virgil's twin songs in the fifth bucolic and Milton's apotheosis of Lycidas. In the conventional manner of the pastoral elegy too it calls for recognition of the poet and announces his ascension to mature poetic style. It was this poem which closed *White Buildings* and served as a prelude to *The Bridge,* Crane's version of American epic.[23] No wonder, then, that he begs for the "waves" to "rear" "some splintered garland for the seer." A highly conventional symbol of poetic achievement, the wreath is in this poem self-claimed, even if, at this late date in literary history, somewhat the worse for wear. R. W. B. Lewis's reading of the phrase, by transposition, as a garland for the splintered seer[24] finds in "Voyages" as "dramatic a statement as one can find to say about the nature of the Romantic tradition. . . ."[25] The poem "bespeaks what is probably the key historic event in that tradition: the emergence of the poet—replacing the king or prince—as the hero of poetry; and of the exacting processes of the creative imagination that most absorb the poet's attention." Beyond that "Voyages" restages an initiatory drama with ancestral ties before the Renaissance. Crane's conversion to the "imaged Word" of poetry is not unlike Platonic consecration to the philosophical life, or Mopsus's devotion to the profession of singing *carmina:* it offers the poet of this world an enduring relation to the next—an "unbetrayable" and "anchored" connection to a principle of permanence and rebirth.

> The imaged Word, it is, that holds
> Hushed willows anchored in its glow,
> It is the unbetrayable reply
> Whose accent no farewell can know.
> (p. 41)

In this poem of Crane's, "monody" not only wakes the mariner, it guarantees him transcendence and poetic recognition. The poem's achievement is canonically elegiac: resuscitation of the orphic head "transmembered," laureled and immortally capable of song.

IV

The "Word" Crane and Whitman recover from the waves has sacramental undertones—all ritual borrows a liturgical vocabulary—but its tone is more archetypal than devotional. The same trinity—father, mother, poet—which in "Cradle" and "Voyages" together effected the initiation to stature of the poet dominates the ritual stage in Gerard Manley Hopkins's "The Wreck of *The Deutschland*" and T. S. Eliot's "The Dry Salvages," two Anglo-Catholic responses to the preoccupations and procedures, of Milton's *Lycidas*.²⁶ Eliot even alludes to Whitman's "Lilacs" in his opening stanza, using as point of departure for his own meditation a translation of Whitman's doorstep blooms: "the rank ailanthus of the April dooryard." In these poems, of course, the shaman/initiator is the Father God himself; the intercessor is Mary, who like the Holy Ghost mediates between God and men, spirit and flesh. But both "The Wreck of *The Deutschland*" and "The Dry Salvages" borrow the central occasion, shipwreck, of Milton's poem. Each attempts, during the course of a dirge for worldliness, to recover the voice of "prayer" that might prove a source of permanence, a "ragged rock" in the "restless waters" of our uncertain life. Each attempts to rebuild a foundation for faith in the face of senseless destruction and failure of nerve. Each appeals, for succor and strength, to the "Lady, whose shrine stands on the promontory"—that female muse who might once again teach the stuttering poet to articulate. Finally, each attempts, as did Milton in *Lycidas,* to reverse the course of elegy: Eliot devotes himself, by "selflessness and surrender," "prayer, observance, discipline, thought and action," to an exacting spiritual life in hopes of gaining initiated vision.

> The hint half guessed, the gift half understood, is Incarnation
> Here the impossible union.
> Of spheres of existence is actual,
> Here the past and future
> Are conquered and reconciled.

Hopkins too views himself as an initiate who, from a "pastoral forehead in Wales," attempts to enter the ordeal by water of that martyr shipwrecked on *The Deutschland*. Like the other "elegies" of this chapter, it is a meditation upon linguistic incarnation which the poet figures in the tall nun's relationship to Christ. That pair serve as parents to the poet's birth here much as the sea and Prodigal function to initiate the poet of "Voyages."²⁷ This poem too balances the dirge by recourse to epithalamium. During the course of this piscatorial elegy, shipwreck gives over to "harvest." Hopkins ultimately sings a bridal invitation in the language of Canticles—"Sister, a sister calling"—and makes of his dirge for faithlessness and imaginative bankruptcy a birth announcement. As triumphantly as his Lord is Hopkins—as poet—"new born to the world."

Mourning and Panegyric:
The Poetics of Pastoral Ceremony

It was in October, a favorite season,
He went for his last walk. The covered bridge,
Most natural of all the works of reason,
Received him, let him go. Along the hedge

He rattled his stick; observed the blackening bushes
In his familiar field; thought he espied
Late meadow larks; considered picking rushes
For a dry arrangement; returned home, and died

Of a catarrh caught in the autumn rains
And let go on uncared for. He was too rapt
In contemplation to recall that brains
Like his should not be kept too long uncapped

In the wet and cold weather. While we mourned,
We thought of his imprudence and how Nature,
Whom he'd done so much for, has finally turned
Against her creature.

His gift was daily his delight, he peeled
The landscape back to show it was a story;
An old bird or burning bush revealed
At his hands just another allegory.

Nothing too great, nothing too trivial
For him; from mountain range or humble vermin
He could extract the hidden parable—
If need be, crack the stone to get the sermon.

And now, poor man, he's gone. Without his name
The field reverts to wilderness again.
The rocks are silent, woods don't seem the same
Demoralized small birds will fly insane.

Rude Nature, whom he loved to idealize
And would have wed, pretends she never heard
His voice at all, as, taken by surprise
At last, he goes to her without a word.

   Howard Nemerov, "Elegy for a Nature Poet"

In the first section of *The Dyer's Hand,* W. H. Auden sketches a representative biography of the poetic apprentice, a literary chronology that ends with the creation of a first good poem:

> We must assume that our apprentice does succeed in becoming a poet, that sooner or later, a day arrives when his Censor is able to say truthfully and for the first time: "All the words are right, and all are yours." His thrill at hearing this does not last long, however, for a moment later comes the thought: "Will it ever happen again?" Whatever his future life as a wage-earner, a citizen, a family man may be, to the end of his days his life as a poet will be without anticipation. He will never be able to say: "Tomorrow I will write a poem and, thanks to my training and experience, I already know I shall do a good job." In the eyes of others a man is a poet if he has written one good poem. In his own he is only a poet at the moment when he is making his last revision to a new poem. The moment before, he was still only a potential poet; the moment after, he is a man who has ceased to write poetry, perhaps forever.[1]

The recognition behind these lines is that apprenticeship—that period of psychological and literary adolescence during which a poet struggles to demonstrate mastery of the canon and be recognized in his own right—is not ended with a first poem. In fact a poetic career, as Auden so eloquently understands, involves a constant effort to maintain confidence and authoritative voice: the creation of each work in a writer's life is both a birth pang and an epitaph; the writing of a poem brings him to a crucial junction from which he looks backward upon his own accomplishments through the lens of those of his predecessors and forward to an imagined "Belle Isle" of permanence and enduring value, literary recognition—anchored and unbetrayable. A poetic career, as poets from Plato to Crane have known, is a hazardous course. And initiation to the literary life only entitles a poet to retrace the imagination's emergence from obscurity daily and obsessively for the remainder of his poetic life.

For what is initiation if not a recapitulation of anterior states and an induction into the new? René Guénon writes, in his *Esotérisme de Dante:*

> Since true initiation is a process by which we take conscious possession of superior states, it is easy to understand why it is symbolically described as an ascent or a "celestial journey"; but it might be asked why this ascent must be preceded by a descent into the Underworld . . . We will say only this: on the one hand, this descent is like a recapitulation of states which logically precede the

human state, which have determined its special conditions and which must also share in the "transformation" to come; on the other hand it permits the revelation (according to certain modalities) of possibilities of a lower order which the individual still carries within him in an undeveloped state and which must be exhausted by him before he may arrive at the realization of his higher states.[2]

Initiation in literature is a ritual procedure which allegorizes a soul's voyage toward incarnation, a drama which symbolically reenacts, looking Janus-faced at once backward and forward, the primal fall into consciousness. All the poems in this study, from Plato's allegory "in a figure" of a pair of horses and Spenser's marriage ceremony for which the orphic poet composes an involving hymn of unprecedented resonance, retrace this pattern. Wordsworth's Ode attempts to evolve a compensation for the intense primal joy of childhood he can recover only in thought. Milton's arrival at the marriage feast of the Christian soul comes after his evocation of Orpheus's grisly ritual dismemberment. For the modern poet, in the absence of a reliable surround of initiates, the process of symbolizing the soul's journey becomes more difficult—and this is marked by his use of literary forms. Thus in Blake and Shelley we get failed elegies, poems which assert finally the impossibility of transcendence, valorize the martyrdom of defeat; thus in the poems of Mallarmé and Crane, as in those of their baroque predecessors, we get perverse epithalamia, poems that dramatize the difficulty of achieving communion and recognize the death that marriage as rite of passage entails.

Ceremonial poems like funeral and marriage odes provide poets with structures for staging initiation rituals. Codified, formal, and rigidly conventional, the elegy and epithalamium offer poets a form in which to cast and a language in which to couch literary passage. For this reason I would disagree with Wallace Stevens, in "An Ordinary Evening in New Haven," that "the poem is the cry of its occasion, / part of the *res* itself and not about it."[3] Ceremonial poetry is, to my mind, more often than not about the conditions that call for it, about the literary institutions and traditions, social arrangements, and psychological needs that drive us perennially to repeat ritual forms. As John Peale Bishop puts it, more aptly, I think, than Stevens:

> The ceremony must be found
> that will wed Desdemona to the huge Moor.
> . . . .
> The ceremony must be found

> Traditional, with all its symbols
> ancient as the metaphors in dreams;
> strange, with never before heard music; continuous
> until the torches deaden at the bedroom door.[4]

Even when they offer up resistance to traditional models, elegists and epithalamists seek to find that ceremony which will structure the enactment of significant ritual passages. The elegist epitaphically honors poetic ancestors even as he hastens to seize the pastoral pipes of the barely cold predecessor, gaining in the process a reprieve from mortality for himself, imaginative mastery of death. The singer of epithalamium too celebrates passage from relative obscurity into the public light of recognition, but he does so under guise of the marriage ceremony: the virgin's death has the compensatory consequence of the full cradle, image of potency and literary productivity. Both forms provide, even in their most obscure modern versions, patterns for recapitulation of a past state and structures for transcendence of that state. It is no wonder, then, that the imagery of elegy and epithalamium overlap: that Orpheus appears in both marriage and funeral poems; that nuptial choruses find their way into dirges; that a beheaded saint still arrives to greet his bride on her wedding day. Ceremonial bouquets, liturgical refrains, ritual dress—veils, shrouds—are as at home in Spenser's *Epithalamion* as they are in Milton's *Lycidas*.

Whether elegiac or epithalamic, the ceremonial mode typically marks a shift from one vocational state of mind to another—unless it articulates instead the difficulty or impossibility of passage. "Every poem" is "a step to the block" in the sense Eliot intends: in fact a poet's corpus may be viewed as a series of epitaphs written to master and commemorate crucial moments in his literary career. "Great poems," Thomas McFarland reminds us, "are monuments to our lost selves."[5] At these important junctures, to fall back on Crane's term, a poet's vision is both regressive and progressive: he must both mourn the loss of pastoral or youthful and orphic immediacy, and he must evolve compensation for it. Thematically—and it is important to emphasize that I am speaking of themes and not genres in this instance since certain anti-epithalamia can mourn the loss of a maidenhead as convincingly as traditional elegies can voice consolation in nuptial terms—the ceremonial poem has two main options: either it can elaborate panegyrically, often in vatic registers, the restorative power of language to fill the palpably felt void and, like the fifth bucolic, *Epithalamion, Lycidas,* and the Immortality Ode, celebrate the triumph of consolation over loss, or else, like *Prothalamion, Thel,* and *Alastor,* it can register its doubt that compensation for such losses can be evolved at all; in this case, the poem's task is to mourn the lost confidence of presence, inscribing threats to immortality within the very rhetoric of celebration. The first kind of poem tends to affirm vision by transmitting ceremonial forms relatively intact; in poems of this sort the eternally singing Orphic voice continues to function with all the power of convention as a guarantee of transcendence, and the poem itself becomes both transcript of and consolation for loss. The second kind of poem, usually resorting to parody and inversion, deliberate rupture of ceremonial patterns, results in works which are generically mutant. In this second kind of ceremonial poem, Orpheus is not, in Lear's terms, a "smugge bridegroom." Eurydice can no longer be brought back into the light; only her absence can be described. As Maurice Blanchot writes in *The Gaze of Orpheus:* "Only in the song does Orpheus have power over Eurydice, but in the song Eurydice is already lost and Orpheus himself is the scattered Orpheus, the 'infinitely dead' Orpheus into which the power of song transforms him."[6]

Juxtaposition of Thomas Kinsella's "A Country Walk" and Howard Nemerov's "Elegy for a Nature Poet," by way of conclusion, brings these two thematic directions into relief and clarifies the ceremonial options available to the orphic poet-initiate.[7] Thomas Kinsella, for all his displacement of the elegiac bier-strewing fiction, writes a profoundly conventional and serious poem which fulfills the very purpose of the classical elegy: to generate voice out of the silence left by a predecessor or even a predecessor poem of one's own, to guarantee future poetic production. Nemerov, almost contemporaneously, marshalls all the conventions of the elegy, but ironically, to lament that the elegist has lost his capacity to articulate transcendentally; the contemporary "nature poet" lacks the power to sing even for himself. The first poem ends with the conjuring of words out of the void; the second specifies that the pastoralist goes to his death "without a word," back to a nature prepared to absorb him.

Kinsella's poem, written in 1962, is neither an obsequy nor a formal encomium—it is rather a lyric investigation of loss, landscape, personal and cultural history, and the possibilities therein for orphic song—but it nonetheless follows elegiac convention so closely as to claim for itself almost classical ancestry.[8] The poem is a sunset meditation in a charged *locus*. Like the elegy, it includes a psychic journey read onto a landscape; searching, hesitant rhythms characteristic of the elegiac quest for a principle of permanence; recapitulation of personal and historical past; vision of Orpheus's dismemberment "in threads of foam" under apocalyptic "darkening and clearing heaven"; moment of vision at "failing dusk" in the very words of Virgil's tenth eclogue, *Venit Hesperus*; final rising movement to a consolation like Milton's "fresh woods and pastures new." But the form "sweet trade" or compensation takes in Kinsella's poem is his own radically new, yet intelligible, solution: where Milton might offer the revived head of Lycidas superimposed upon that of the classical Orpheus and the Christian Saviour as adequate compensation for losses sustained, Kinsella puts within quotation marks, at the apocalyptic moment of frankly sexual release, the heretofore repressed first line of a new poem:

> In green and golden light; bringing sweet trade.
> The inert stirred. Heart and tongue were loosed:
> "The waters hurtle through the flooded night . . ."
>   (p. 57)

Whereas Kinsella's elegy ends with a flood of words generated out of the "inert," Nemerov's "Elegy for a Nature Poet," perhaps an ironic self-elegy, illustrates the opposing thematic orientation. More overtly even than Kinsella's poem, it bears the entire range of elegiac conventions: fall season, meditative journey, untimely death of the poet figure, symbolic reading of nature in a version of the pathetic fallacy, that same nature turned threateningly alien in a parodic version of the pastoral *adynata*, animals reduced to muteness by the absence of an ordering human singing voice, wedding hymn of aggregation entertained by the close. But Nemerov marshalls these conventions to very different ends. This nature poet will not sing an "unexpressive nuptial song," will not make a Wordsworthian marriage with nature—in short, will not transcend his mortality by means of pastoral song. In fact, just as the waters close over Daphnis in Theocritus's first idyll, denying him the transcendence he desires, so Nemerov's Nature, "whom he loved to idealize / And would have wed, pretends she never heard / His voice at all" and consigns him to the very mortal fate of remaining unremembered and unsung. This poet, unlike Kinsella's, does not draw poetic strength from a rehearsal of Orpheus's dismemberment; consolation does not take the form of a newly worded beginning. Instead he goes to her [Nature] "without a word," as conclusively silenced as Yeats's Sad Shepherd.

So much for the thematics of ceremonial poems. A word remains to be said about genre. The allied pastoral genres of epithalamium and elegy with which I began this study tend, after all, to manifest different generic histories—alternate conceptions of genre are illustrated by their twin forms. Elegy, from the outset a song of subjective utterance built on rupture and discontinuity, tends to find its way into modern lyrics in what we think of as traditional generic development: the *agon* of form contesting form, first staged in the pastoral singing contest, was ritually enacted by subsequent practitioners of the mode—who demonstrated their own mastery of the form by altering inventively the basic initiation scenario. Theocritus preserves the basic configuration of Plato's primal instruction scene but radically alters the nature and use of *otium*; in this initiatory scenario, an unnamed goatherd, parody of Socrates, counsels the singer of Daphnis's woes to accept a relaxed, sensually sweet enjoyment of that canonical hour. Virgil rewrites the frame of Theocritus's idyll by reversing the roles of the participants. In his ritual fifth eclogue, the elder only appears to grant recognition to the initiate: in fact Mopsus chooses the site, song, and manner of pastoral singing. Spenser parodies the pastoral contest by adding a third singer who emerges from the shadows in time to outshine the others, a master at elaborate, Italianate forms. The elegy remains a compelling form for poets even after the singing contest has given way—after Milton's imitation of the form of Virgil's tenth, narrative eclogue—to a lyric meditation. Poets from Whitman to Crane and beyond remain faithful to elegy's first premise: the recovery of poetic voice from ritual burial of the past. Both Kinsella's and Nemerov's poems, although thematically opposite, are illustrative of elegy's intactness as a literary genre.

The epithalamium undergoes a different, and diametrically opposed, transformation. As a set of literary expectations and conventions, it survives just as persistently as elegy. But imitated straightforwardly, it remains an occasional piece of limited interest, a flat, predictable poem, often of state, evidencing none of the tension with the form that lends power to poems like Mallarmé's *Hérodiade*. It is as negative model that the epithalamium retains its vitality as a literary form: poets return to its formality and enforcement of ceremony, but they bring to it a fierce dialectics in place of Spenserian symmetries, balance, stasis. In the literature of the Renaissance, human nuptials symbolized hierarchies affirmed, social and cultural coherence of belief, Platonic absorption of dualism between this world and the next—in short they stood for cosmic reconciliation of a permanent and dependable sort. After the Renaissance, that set of symbolisms comes more and more to stand for the tense wedding of opposites yoked in eternal combat. If the wedding ceremony imaged for Spenser orphic control of his literary and political circle, it represents at best, for poets like Mallarmé and Crane, a private rite of ascetic self-surrender, devotion to pursuit of an eternally elusive bride, poetry's source or beauty. Nuptial rites continue to be staged in dramatic works when their symbolism is needed to preside over a communal rite of aggregation. But waning confidence in marriage as a central cultural ceremony and a peculiarly modern poetics of tension enforce symbolic inversion of the convention in lyric works and produce a much stronger response to the tradition, the anti-epithalamium.

The alternate histories of these genres reveal—even in their most attenuated modal manifestations and especially at crucial junctions where each invades the territory of the other—the importance of not over-reading those expectations genre licenses us to apply. The fact of their different histories also makes a persuasive argument for opening genre study to investigation of mutant forms: those poems in which genres overlap and conjoin, works that follow a prescribed modal orientation only to reverse its conclusion, poems that invert the meaning of imagery and confound expectation. Such study sacrifices symmetry, the confident establishment of an orderly sequence of texts, the satisfaction of generalization and pattern completed, for a different kind of literary history—one as idiosyncratic in its way as the works it entertains, but one faithful in spirit to the poems upon which it depends.

Notes

INTRODUCTION

1. T. S. Eliot, "Little Gidding," in *The Complete Poems and Plays* (New York: Harcourt, Brace and World, 1971), p. 144.
2. Harold Bloom, *The Map of Misreading* (New York: Oxford, 1975), p. 19.
3. Paul Fry, *The Poet's Calling in the English Ode* (New Haven and London: Yale Univ. Press, 1980), p. 3. Fry's reading of the English ode from Jonson and Drayton to Keats, focusing on the ode as a "vehicle of ontological and vocational doubt," parallels my own interest in the vocational subtext of elegiac and epithalamic ceremonial poetry.
4. William Wordsworth, *Ode: Intimations of Immortality*, in *The Poetical Works of William Wordsworth*, ed. E. de Selincourt and Helen Darbishire (Oxford: Clarendon Press, 1947), IV, 279–85.
5. Stéphane Mallarmé, *Selected Prose Poems, Essays, and Letters*, trans. Bradford Booth (Baltimore: Johns Hopkins Univ. Press, 1956), p. 19; quoted in Fry, p. 10.
6. Hart Crane, *The Complete Poems and Selected Letters and Prose of Hart Crane*, ed. Brom Weber (Garden City, N.Y.: Doubleday, 1966), pp. 37, 116.
7. John Van Sickle, "Theocritus and the Development of the Conception of Bucolic Genre," *Ramus: Critical Studies in Greek and Roman Literature* 5 (1976): 18.
8. Rosalie Colie, *The Resources of Kind: Genre-Theory in the Renaissance* (Berkeley: Univ. of California Press, 1973), p. 76. I follow Colie's lead here in writing on "uncanonical forms, mixed kinds" and apologize similarly for the resulting, though necessary, discontinuities.
9. Heather Dubrow, *Genre* (London: Methuen, 1982), p. 39.
10. Adena Rosmarin, *The Power of Genre* (Minneapolis: Univ. of Minnesota Press, 1985), p. 25.
11. Crane, "Cape Hatteras," *The Bridge*, in *Complete Poems*, pp. 93–95.
12. Frances Ferguson, *Wordsworth: Language as Counter-Spirit* (New Haven: Yale Univ. Press, 1977), p. xvi.
13. Jonathan Culler, *Structuralist Poetics* (Ithaca: Cornell Univ. Press, 1975), p. 178. I paraphrase Culler's description of the biographical convention or expectation governing criticism of the lyric.
14. See Rosalie Colie, " 'All in Peeces': Problems of Interpretation in Donne's Anniversary Poems," in *Just So Much Honor*, ed. Peter Amadeus Fiore (University Park and London: Pennsylvania State Univ. Press, 1972), p. 215, n. 4.
15. Geoffrey Hartman, "Toward Literary History," in *Beyond Formalism: Literary Essays 1958–1970* (New Haven: Yale Univ. Press, 1970), p. 367. See also Paul Fry's double use of vocation in *The Poet's Calling* and Otto Rank, *Art and Artist* (New York: Tudor, 1932), ch. 1. For another approach to initiation scenes in literature, see Bloom, *Map,* ch. 3.

16. See Steele Commager's remarks on the epitaph on Virgil's supposed tomb in his Introduction to *Virgil: A Collection of Critical Essays* (Englewood Cliffs, N.J.: Prentice-Hall, 1966), p. 1.

17. E. A. Barber, "Alexandrian Literature," in *The Hellenistic Age*, ed. J. B. Bury, E. A. Barber, Edwyn Buvan, and W. W. Tarn (1925; rpt. New York: Kraus, 1968). See also in this connection Brooks Otis, *Virgil: A Study in Civilized Poetry* (Oxford: Clarendon, 1964), and David Halperin, *Before Pastoral: Theocritus and the Ancient Tradition of Bucolic Poetry* (New Haven: Yale Univ. Press, 1983).

18. Barber, p. 30.

19. W. J. Bate, *The Burden of the Past and the English Poet* (Cambridge: Harvard Belknap Press, 1970), p. 3.

20. Richard Cody, *The Landscape of the Mind* (Oxford: Clarendon, 1969), p. 171.

21. Recent pastoral criticism has tended to ape the errors of its predecessors by succumbing to the temptation to classify, to delimit, to establish a pure tradition, to exclude all but full participants. W. Leonard Grant's *Neo-Latin Literature and the Latin Middle Ages* (1965) is a species of pastoral birdwatching offering a dizzying catalogue of pastoral forms: art-pastoral, Mary-eclogues, *genethliacon, epinicium*. When Ellen Lambert writes her history of the pastoral elegy, *Placing Sorrow: A Study of the Pastoral Elegy Convention from Theocritus to Milton* (Chapel Hill: Univ. of North Carolina Press, 1976), she feels compelled to exclude even Theocritus himself from the tradition—so narrowly does she define it—because after a herdsman sings of Daphnis's death "the waters close over him. That is all; we are not told anything further about this Daphnis' fate" (p. xii). When T. G. Rosenmeyer publishes an influence study of Theocritus on the European pastoral lyric, he erects a standard of pastoral based on the Theocritean canon so rigorous, so exclusive, and so localized that nothing written after it, save Virgil's *Bucolics,* can be seen as a response to it. Rosenmeyer's analysis of Theocritus against the background of Epicureanism in *The Green Cabinet: Theocritus and the European Pastoral Lyric* (Berkeley and L.A.: Univ. of California Press, 1969) is a substantial contribution to the field of pastoral criticism. But his repressive concern for preserving the purity of Theocritean pastoral precludes the possibility for dialogue between it and later poetry.

The student of pastoral, it seems to me, does better to imitate the methods of William Empson, Harold Toliver, and Renato Poggioli, who—incurring censure for their expansion of the domain of pastoral to include, respectively, Lewis Carroll, Saul Bellow, and Tolstoy—have nonetheless resurrected pastoral as a useful, vital, and intelligent critical category. Taking their cue from Empson's "some versions," these critics have abandoned the summary/anecdotal history of previous criticism in favor of defining "form and attitudes" or "modes of analogy" often in seemingly unpastoral texts. These critics choose, to use Erich Auerbach's term, "key texts" often widely separated in time in order to refract through the lens of pastoral significant patterns of literary history. Philip Damon, in "Modes of Analogy in Ancient and Medieval Verse," *University of California Publications in Classical Philology* 15 (1961): 261–334, studies the transformation of certain pastoral "tropes" in the hands of Theocritus, Virgil, and their Latin imitators. Abbie Findlay Potts in *The Elegiac Mode* (Ithaca: Cornell Univ. Press, 1967), Harold Toliver in *Pastoral Forms and Attitudes* (Berkeley and L.A.: Univ. of California Press, 1971), and Renato Poggioli in *The Oaten Flute* (Cambridge: Harvard Univ. Press, 1975) vastly extend the life of pastoral beyond its conventional demise in the eighteenth century by defining the pastoral idea that survives the form and locating it in any number of texts hitherto not labeled pastoral. Andrew Ettin, too, in his *Literature and the Pastoral,* determines that pastoral as genre is defunct even though the pastoral mode enjoys literary currency in works by authors as disparate as Tasso, Mary Shelley, Morike, Unamuno, Flannery O'Connor, and Marge Piercy (New Haven and London: Yale Univ. Press, 1984).

22. Dubrow, p. 117.

23. Peter Marinelli, *Pastoral: The Critical Idiom* (London: Methuen, 1971), p. 37.

24. Poggioli, p. 65.

25. David Wagenknecht, *Blake's Night: William Blake and the Idea of Pastoral* (Cam-

bridge: Harvard Belknap Press, 1973). I am particularly indebted to Wagenknecht for his remarks on the collision of eros and thanatos in pastoral myth; his suggestive remarks on the community of imagery shared by elegy and epithalamium; his work—with Richard Cody—on the replacement of the pastoral Adonis by a Renaissance Orpheus; and his discernment, beneath the pastoral pretense to ignorance or artlessness, of "the face of ambition and interest" or *negotium,* pastoral *otium's* opposite and seeming enemy.

26. Theocritus, "The Women at the Adonis-Festival," in *The Greek Bucolic Poets,* trans. J. M. Edmonds (Loeb Classical Edition, 1912; London: William Heinemann, 1960), p. 193.

27. Wagenknecht, p. 3.

28. Apuleius, *The Golden Ass,* trans. Robert Graves (New York: Farrar, Straus and Giroux, 1951), p. 100.

29. Claudio Guillén, *Literature as System* (Princeton: Princeton Univ. Press, 1971).

30. Paul Van Tieghem, "La question des genres littéraires," *Helicon* 1 (1938): 95–101.

31. Alastair Fowler, *Kinds of Literature: An Introduction to the Theory of Genres and Modes* (Cambridge: Harvard Univ. Press, 1982), p. 206ff. Fowler's pages on "elegiac modulations" in the nineteenth century (p. 206ff.), "counterstatement" (p. 174), "subgenre," and "modal transformation" (p. 167) are particularly relevant to the chiasmus I am charting here.

32. Paul Hernadi, *Beyond Genre* (Ithaca: Cornell Univ. Press, 1972), pp. 8, 184.

33. Fry says of such modal terms that "they describe orientations but tend not to prescribe a set style, form, or occasion," p. 5.

34. See Virginia Tufte's history of the epithalamium, *The Poetry of Marriage: The Epithalamium in Europe and Its Development in England* (L.A.: Tinnon-Brown, 1970), and her anthology of the genre, *"High Wedlock Then Be Honoured": Wedding Poems from Nineteen Countries and Twenty-Five Centuries* (New York: Viking, 1970). See also James A. S. McPeek, *Catullus in Strange and Distant Britain* (Cambridge: Harvard Univ. Press, 1939).

35. Cody, p. 73.

36. Potts, p. 437.

37. For standard approaches to the elegy and description of its conventions, see George Norlin, "The Conventions of the Pastoral Elegy," *American Journal of Philology* 32 (1911): 294–312; and James Holly Hanford, "The Pastoral Elegy and Milton's *Lycidas,*" *PMLA* 25 (1910): 403–47. See also *The Pastoral Elegy: An Anthology,* ed. T. P. Harrison, trans. H. J. Leon (Austin: Univ. of Texas, 1939). Recent criticism on the elegy as genre includes Eric Smith, *By Mourning Tongues: Studies in English Elegy* (Ipswich: Boydell Press, 1977); Peter Sacks, *The English Elegy: Studies in the Genre from Spenser to Yeats* (Baltimore: Johns Hopkins Univ. Press, 1985); and G. W. Pigman III, *Grief and English Renaissance Elegy* (Cambridge: Cambridge Univ. Press, 1985).

38. J. Huizinga, *The Waning of the Middle Ages,* trans. F. Hopman (St. Martin's Press, 1949; Garden City, N.Y.: Doubleday Anchor, 1954), p. 110. Huizinga notes the split between the Church's use of nuptial symbolism to convey the "mystery of copulation" and erotic poetry's bold enjoyment of "licentious expression and gross symbolism," speculating that the whole comic mode is derived from the epithalamium. "It is as though erotic poetry even in this perverse way strove to recover that primitive connection with sacred matters of which the Christian religion had bereft it."

39. Paul Miller, "The Decline of the English Epithalamion," *Texas Studies in Literature and Language* 12 (1970): 405–16. Heather Dubrow will take issue with Miller's elegy for epithalamium in her forthcoming book on the Stuart epithalamium, *"The Happier Eden": The Epithalamium in Stuart England.* I am particularly grateful to Dubrow for sharing much of this work in progress with me. For full bibliographical references, see my ch. 4, n. 1.

40. Arthur Hoffman catalogues many of the similarities between the two works in "Spenser and *The Rape of the Lock,*" *Philological Quarterly* 49 (1970): 530–46.

41. Clark Emery, *The Marriage of Heaven and Hell* (Coral Gables, Fla.: Univ. of Miami Press, 1969), p. 8.

42. My use of the term epitaph throughout is literal (as when I refer to Daphnis's inset

tombstone in Virgil's fifth eclogue, or when making the leap to Spenser's "endlesse moniment"—more graven evidence of memorializing a past self, or even the eternally weeping statue which Marvell's nymph makes of herself) as well as, broadly understood, modal. I follow Frances Ferguson's work on Wordsworth's *Essay on Epitaphs* and my understanding of Eliot's suggestion in "Little Gidding" that every poem pays tribute to a past artistic self from which one has successfully unsheathed. In the larger, modal sense, the epitaphic is directly relevant to a poetics of ceremony which marks passage from one state to another. Finally, we would do better to preserve a sense of epitaph and elegy along a continuum of poetic pronouncements on death rather than to erect high boundaries between them. The *Princeton Encyclopedia of Poetry and Poetics,* ed. Alex Preminger (Princeton: Princeton Univ. Press, 1965), supports me here, calling epitaph outright "a shortened form of the elegy," since it is in common with that form "a literary production suitable for placing on the grave of someone or something, although this need not actually be done or intended" (p. 249). As to other related terms, threnody is a smaller and more restricted term than elegy, and it means the same thing as dirge—an alternate term for a lamentation which I use when I mean literary mourning without the equal and opposite emphasis on consolation. Elegy differs from these by its simultaneous (or sequential) inclusion of both of those two attitudes. Monody is a term relevant in specific instances, as, for example, when speaking of the expansive, even dramatic, non-monodic voice of the singer in Spenser's *Epithalamion,* or the Miltonic reproduction of the lyric mode of Virgil's tenth eclogue rather than the dialogic mode of the fifth in his *Lycidas.* Distinctions between the abovementioned terms for funeral lamentation are very difficult to make, as any dictionary of literary terminology makes clear, even if taxonomy were the critic's *only* goal: elegy, dirge, threnody, obsequy, in modern usage, can be applied to any lyric of mourning or memorial on the subject of death, even those composed in the absence of a proper corpse. Elegy, for its suggesting pairing with epithalamium, shall be used throughout this study to describe funeral pronouncements ranging from the briefly and graphically epitaphic to the diffusely and modally elegiac.

CHAPTER 1

A version of this chapter has appeared in *Mosaic: A Journal for the Interdisciplinary Study of Literature* (March 1988): 93–113. I am grateful to *Mosaic*'s anonymous reviewer for making many valuable suggestions for revision during my preparation of the final draft.

1. I allude here to David Halperin's distinction in his *Before Pastoral: Theocritus and the Ancient Tradition of Bucolic Poetry* (New Haven: Yale Univ. Press, 1983) between what we have come to call pastoral and ancient bucolic. Although Halperin maintains that Theocritus is the undisputed inventor of bucolic poetry, he adumbrates an even earlier tradition of pastoral, coherently accessible in peasant culture as well as in art. But writes Halperin, "no sophisticated, erudite, and widely informed Alexandrian *littérateur,* such as Callimachus . . . , could possibly have thought that the originality of bucolic poetry as it had been invented lay in its rustic or pastoral qualities" (p. 117). It is precisely in the sophistication of intellectual and literary material juxtaposed to rustic setting and pretense that I find important points of intersection between Plato and Theocritus, both of whom may have drawn, as Halperin suggests, upon the pre-existing and pervasive Mesopotamian influence on early Western thought.

2. For discussions of Platonism and pastoralism, see Bruno Snell, *The Discovery of a Spiritual Landscape: The Greek Origins of European Thought,* trans. T. G. Rosenmeyer (Oxford: Basil Blackwell, 1953), esp. "Arcadia: Discovery of a Spiritual Landscape." For a few critics, Plato's *Phaedrus* provides earliest evidence of awareness of landscape as symbol in Greek literature: Ernst Curtius places Theocritus directly after Plato in a discussion of the *locus amoenus* in his *European Literature and the Latin Middle Ages,* trans. Willard Trask (Princeton: Princeton Bollingen, 1953), p. 187. For Adam Parry, pastoral originates "in the period when disillusion with society became a marked feature of literature . . . in the works

of a man who most clearly expressed that disillusion, Plato"; see his "Landscape in Greek Poetry," *Yale Classical Studies* 15 (1957): 3–29. Rosenmeyer suggests that there is much in the *Phaedrus* to "put us in the mind of Theocritus," citing a resemblance between lines of the Dialogue and an image in Idyll X, pp. 41, 42. A few critics, following the lead of Edgar Wind in his *Pagan Mysteries in the Renaissance* (London: Faber and Faber, 1958; rpt. New York: Norton, 1968), insist upon the dependence of Christian pastoral upon Platonic theory read by the commentators. In his *The Landscape of the Mind*, Richard Cody stresses the "mutual concerns" of the two traditions in their "Renaissance phase," pp. 6–7. Wagenknecht, too, believes that "educative eroticism" is at the heart of the *Phaedrus*: "The ambition of which I have been speaking has its erotic manifestation in the attachment of a young man to an older, wiser mentor, and Plato expresses the meaning of this attachment in terms of the emancipation of the soul and the achievement of a harmonious, inward-looking life," pp. 19, 20. See also, for brief juxtaposition of the texts, Clyde Murley's "Plato's *Phaedrus* and Theocritean Pastoral," *Transactions of the American Philological Association* 71 (1940): 281–95; Charles Segal, " 'Since Daphnis Dies': The Meaning of the First Idyll," *Museum Helveticum* 3 (1974): 1–22; and "Death by Water," *Hermes* 102 (1974): 20–38.

3. Mircea Eliade, *Rites and Symbols of Initiation*, trans. Willard Trask (*Birth and Rebirth*, 1958; rpt. New York: Harper and Row, 1975), p. 114.

4. Eliade, p. 114.

5. Eliade, p. 114.

6. E. R. Dodds, *The Greeks and the Irrational* (Berkeley and L.A.: Univ. of California Press, 1964), p. 147.

7. Wagenknecht, p. 24.

8. Cody, p. 14.

9. W. K. C. Guthrie, *The Greeks and Their Gods* (Boston: Beacon, 1950), pp. 307, 317, 311, 289.

10. Pico, *De Hominis dignate* (Garin, p. 161); quoted in Wind, p. 18.

11. Plato, *The Dialogues of Plato*, trans. B. Jowett (New York: Macmillan, 1892; rpt. New York: Random House, 1937), II, 215. Stephanus numbers follow in the text.

12. Wind, p. 189.

13. J. Huizinga, *Homo Ludens: A Study of the Play Element in Culture* (Boston: Beacon, 1966), p. 180. Citations follow in the text.

14. Professor Helen Bacon of Barnard College has suggested to me in conversation that this Dialogue represents Plato's invention of a dramatic literary mode in which to convey his cherished philosophy, a kind of literature which would be suitable for the youth of the Republic. The *Phaedrus*, exploring enthusiasm and mantic possession, does the same for lyric.

15. Parry, p. 3.

16. Michael Putnam, *Virgil's Pastoral Art: Studies in the Eclogues* (Princeton: Princeton Univ. Press, 1970), p. 10.

17. Werner Jaeger, *Paideia: The Ideals of Greek Culture*, trans. Gilbert Highet (Oxford: Basil Blackwell, 1970), p. 10; quoted in Wagenknecht, p. 19.

18. Cody, p. 23.

19. Curtius, pp. 185–87; André Motte, *Prairies et jardins de la Grèce antique de la réligion à la philosophie* (Brussels: Academie Royale de Belgique, 1971), p. 426.

20. Paul Friedländer, *Plato: The Dialogues*, trans. Hans Meyerhoff (London: Routledge and Kegan Paul, 1969), III, 220.

21. Motte, p. 409.

22. Rosenmeyer, p. 89.

23. I allude here to Eric Havelock's thesis in *Preface to Plato* (Oxford: Basil Blackwell, 1963), esp. "Poetry as Preserved Communication," pp. 36–49.

24. Jacques Derrida, *La Pharmacie de Platon*, in *La Dissémination* (Paris: Editions de Seuil, 1972), pp. 69–180.

25. Culler, *Structuralist Poetics*, p. 19.

26. See Barbara Johnson's introduction to her English translation of Derrida's *Dissemination* (Chicago: Univ. of Chicago Press, 1981), p. xxiv. Derrida will argue, of course, that "only a blind and insensitive reading could indeed have spread the rumor that Plato was *simply* condemning the writer's activity. Nothing here is of a single piece and the *Phaedrus* also, in its own writing, plays at saving writing—which also means causing it to be lost—as the best, the noblest game," p. 67. See also John Van Sickle, "Theocritus and the Development of the Conception of the Bucolic Genre," p. 40, n. 39.

27. Anne Lebeck, "The Central Myth of Plato's *Phaedrus*," *Greek, Roman and Byzantine Studies* 13, 3 (1972): 267–90.

28. Wind, p. 3.

29. This and the following quotations are from Harold Bloom, *Poetry and Repression* (New Haven and London: Yale Univ. Press, 1976), p. 27.

30. Philip Damon pays close attention to revisions of landscape imagery in his monograph on "Echoes and Other Noises in the Later Pastoral," but he does not link these challenges to an overtly careerist program.

31. John Fowles, *The French Lieutenant's Woman* (Boston: Little, Brown, and Co., 1969), pp. 67–69; quoted to very different ends by Eleanor Winsor Leach in her *Virgil's Eclogues: Landscapes of Experience* (Ithaca: Cornell Univ. Press, 1974), pp. 25–26, in order to illustrate the "essential conflict of emotions in the pastoral experience."

32. See David Quint's reading of the story of Virgil's (Fourth Georgic) Orpheus as a model of the poetic act in his *Origin and Originality in Renaissance Literature: Versions of the Source* (New Haven: Yale Univ. Press, 1983), pp. 38–42. See also Sacks's discussion of orphic ritual and vegetation deities, pp. 29–32. Although Sacks's book on the English elegy appeared after I had completed this manuscript, I have nonetheless included reference to his work where it intersects with my own. Although a psychoanalytic orientation and terminology govern Sacks's approach—"castrative submission" (p. 309), "the work of mourning" (p. 319), for example—our readings of elegy as genre overlap on the important point of viewing its essential drama as that of the coming-to-succession of the poetic heir. As Sacks phrases it, "the elegist's own transaction of loss and gain must, as we have seen, also work toward a trope for sexual power" (p. 32). With the exception of Spenser's "November" and Milton's *Lycidas*, however, we do not cite the same texts. For a theory of elegy as "The Poet's Quest for the Father," see Stanley Kunitz, *The New York Times Book Review*, February 22, 1987, pp. 1, 36–37. Kunitz quotes from a "tortuous elegy written in my 23rd year, opened with the apostrophe, 'O ruined father dead,' and concluded with the lines, 'Let sons learn from their lipless fathers how / Man enters hell without a golden bough,' " p. 1.

CHAPTER 2

A version of this chapter has appeared in *Mosaic: A Journal for the Interdisciplinary Study of Literature* (March 1988): 93–113. I am grateful to *Mosaic*'s anonymous reviewer for making many valuable suggestions for revision during my preparation of the final draft.

1. William Empson, "Ignorance of Death," in *Collected Poems* (New York: Harcourt Brace Jovanovich, 1935), pp. 58–59.

2. The misunderstanding of elegy which I attribute to Lambert—her failure to understand poetic genres as verbal constructs which mediate rather than merely represent experience—is not limited to her. Eric Smith and G. W. Pigman are equally quick to judge the efficacy of elegy by its power to assuage real, felt grief. Even Peter Sacks's otherwise exemplary analysis of English elegy begins with an attempt to match up the "traditional forms and figures of elegy" with "the experience of loss and search for consolation" (p. 1). See my review of Pigman's book for a fuller discussion of the problem, *The Sixteenth Century Journal* 17 (Winter 1986): 528–29.

3. Northrop Frye, "Literature as Context: Milton's *Lycidas*," in *Milton's 'Lycidas':*

The Tradition and the Poem, ed. C. A. Patrides (1961; rpt. Columbia: Univ. of Missouri Press, 1984), p. 209.

4. Geoffrey Hartman, "Toward Literary History," in *Beyond Formalism,* p. 369. Hartman uses the term to describe the struggle for "self-objectification" enacted in Keats's *Hyperion.*

5. Virginia Woolf, *A Writer's Diary,* ed. Leonard Woolf (New York: Harvest, 1953), pp. 78, 135.

6. Cody, p. 23. See also Eduard Norden, *Die Antike Kunstprosa* (Leipzig: B. G. Teubner, 1915), I, 105.

7. The conventional post-Virgilian designation of funeral elegy would be, strictly speaking, inapplicable in the Theocritean context, both because the contemporary generic definition of elegy was metrical rather than occasional ("the classical elegy was a poem in elegiac distichs [alternating hexameters and pentameters]," Fowler, p. 136) and because Daphnis was disconcertingly present to receive his cortège of mourners.

8. Many other elegies, necessarily beyond the scope of this chapter, display a similar strain of ambition. Moschus's *Lament for Bion,* for example, in its dirge for the loss of Bion, that mentor and Doric Orpheus, ends with Moschus's self-presentation as a new Orpheus who might sing the dead Bion-Eurydice figure back up from the shades. See the Loeb Classical Edition, *The Greek Bucolic Poets,* trans. J. M. Edmonds (1912; rpt. London: William Heinemann, 1960), p. 455.

9. Bate, p. 134.

10. John Van Sickle, p. 19; see also Gianfranco Fabiano, "Fluctuation in Theocritus' Style," *Greek, Roman and Byzantine Studies* 12 (1971): 517–83.

11. Van Sickle, p. 40, n. 39.

12. Van Sickle, for example, speaks of a "goatherd who equals natural music and a shepherd who excells it" (p. 21).

13. My text for Theocritus's first idyll is that of A. S. F. Gow, *Theocritus: Edited with a Translation and Commentary* (Cambridge: Cambridge Univ. Press, 1965), I, 4–15. Hereafter page numbers follow in the text.

14. Rosenmeyer, p. 89.

15. Rosenmeyer, pp. 112, 111.

16. This is Gow's thesis, II, 19.

17. Rosenmeyer, p. 112.

18. For a theory of the Sumerian "forebears" of Daphnis, and a different reading of his "obscure erotic predicament," see William Berg, "Daphnis and Prometheus," *Transactions of the American Philological Association* 96 (1965): 11–23, and David Halperin, "The Forebears of Daphnis," *Transactions of the American Philological Association* 113 (1983): 183–200.

19. Harriet Edquist, "Aspects of Theocritean Otium," in *Ancient Pastoral: Essays on Greek and Roman Pastoral Poetry,* ed. A. J. Boyle (Melbourne: Hawthorn, 1975), pp. 19–32. In a fine essay on Theocritus, Edquist is one of the few critics to accord the unnamed goatherd his due, although she reads the goatherd's and Thyrsis's songs together as implicit criticism of Daphnis's stance.

20. Rosenmeyer, p. 81.

21. Barriss Mills, "The Poetry of Theokritos," Introduction to his translation of *The Idylls of Theokritos* (West Lafayette: Purdue Univ. Studies, 1963), p. xii.

22. Mills, p. xii.

23. Rosenmeyer, p. 176.

24. Edquist, p. 19.

25. Charles Segal discusses the archetypal significance of water imagery in the idylls in his "Death by Water," pp. 20–24, 38. But in a note to his " 'Since Daphnis Dies,' " he states, commenting on an article by G. Wojaczek, that Daphnis is not an orphic initiate in the first idyll. Whereas Segal's remarks on sacred water in the first article suggest perhaps more of an afterlife than I read in the poem, I agree with him in the second article that

Daphnis's death is not "eine mystiche Unterweisung." There is no promise of rebirth in Daphnis's drowning.

26. Virgil, *Opera* (Oxford: Clarendon, 1969), pp. 12–14, ll. 4–7. Hereafter line numbers follow in the text.

27. English translation by C. Day Lewis, *The Eclogues and Georgics of Virgil* (Garden City, N.Y.: Doubleday Anchor, 1964), p. 37. Hereafter page numbers follow in the text.

28. Putnam, p. 167.

29. See Erwin Panofsky's well-known article, "*Et in Arcadia Ego: Poussin and the Elegiac Tradition*," in *Meaning in the Visual Arts* (Garden City, N.Y.: Doubleday Anchor, 1955), pp. 295–320.

30. Paul Alpers, "The Eclogue Tradition and the Nature of Pastoral," *College English* 34 (1972): 360.

31. Putnam, p. 191. I do not agree, however, that Mopsus "disappoints Menalcas' hopes" (p. 169).

32. See Marie Desport, *Incantation virgilienne: Virgile et Orphée* (Bordeaux: Imprimeries Delmas, 1952), p. 14.

33. Pierre Grimal, "La Ve Eglogue et la culte de Cesar," in *Mélanges d'archéologie et d'histoire Charles Picard, Rev. Arch.* 30 (1948): 406–19.

34. Cicero, *De Legibus,* trans. C. W. Keyes (Loeb Classical Edition; London: William Heinemann, 1966), pp. 414–15. Eleanor Winsor Leach refers to this passage in Cicero with reservations because she wants to link the rites to historical phenomena, *Virgil's Eclogues,* p. 190.

35. Putnam, p. 192.

36. Putnam, p. 194.

37. Poggioli, p. 76.

38. Harrison, p. 263.

39. George Mylonas, *Eleusis and the Eleusinian Mysteries* (Princeton: Princeton Univ. Press, 1961), p. 270.

40. Cody finds the first important Renaissance model of this chiasmus in the *canzoniere* of Petrarch, p. 37.

41. Spenser's publication of the *Shepheardes Calender,* perhaps the most original contribution to English pastoral, was a decidedly literary event. Introduced and glossed by the famous "E.K.," it was preceded by no fewer than four documents: 1) a dedication to his friend Sir Philip Sidney; 2) an address "To His Booke" promising to send "more after thee"; 3) an epistle to his mentor declaring his debt to "the best and most aunciont Poetes" and his simultaneous devotion to the "mother Tongue," announcing himself as a rival of Chaucer, Theocritus, and Virgil: "So finally flyeth this our new Poete, as a bird, whose principals be scarce grown out, but yet as that in time shall be hable to keep wing with the best"; and 4) a "generall argument" in which Spenser/E.K. hints at "special purpose and meaning I am not privie to." My text of Spenser's *Shepheardes Calender* throughout is that of Edwin Greenlaw, *The Works of Edmund Spenser: A Variorium Edition. The Minor Poems* (Baltimore: Johns Hopkins Univ. Press), I, 1–120. Hereafter line numbers follow in the text for April and November poems.

42. See A. C. Hamilton, "The Argument of Spenser's *Shepheardes Calender*," *English Literary History* 23 (1956): 171–82; Harry Berger, "The Prospect of Imagination: Spenser and the Limits of Poetry," *Studies in English Literature* 1 (1961): 93–120, and "Mode and Diction in *The Shepheardes Calender,*" *Modern Philology* 67 (1969): 140–49; Louis Montrose, " 'The perfecte paterne of a Poete': The Poetics of Courtship in *The Shepheardes Calender*," *Texas Studies in Literature and Language* 21 (1979): 34–67, and "Of Gentlemen and Shepherds: The Politics of Elizabethan Pastoral Form," *ELH* 50 (Fall 1983): 415–59; and L. Staley Johnson's reading of the eclogue as a biblical epithalamium reflecting the ideals of English Protestantism, "Elizabeth, Bride and Queen: A Study of Spenser's April Eclogue and the Metaphors of English Protestantism," *Spenser Studies* 2 (1981): 75–91.

43. Paul McLane, *Spenser's Shepheardes Calender: A Study in Elizabethan Allegory* (South Bend: Univ. of Notre Dame Press, 1961), pp. 47–60. In his reading of the thematics

of inheritance in the *Shepheardes Calender,* Sacks concentrates on the complex of attitudes he attributes to mourning and by extension elegy, but thereby fails to read the April blazon as contributory to Spenser's poetics of ambition (pp. 40–51).

44. Isabel MacCaffrey, "Allegory and Pastoral in the *Shepheardes Calender,*" in *Essential Articles for the Study of Edmund Spenser,* ed. A. C. Hamilton (Hamden, Conn.: Archon, 1972), p. 553.

45. Nancy Jo Hoffman, *Spenser's Pastorals* (Baltimore: Johns Hopkins Univ. Press, 1977), p. 88.

46. See Hoffman, p. 53ff., and Anne Lake Prescott, *French Poets and the English Renaissance* (New Haven: Yale Univ. Press, 1978), p. 11, for readings of the poem next to Marot's elegy for Loyse.

47. For a reading of the *Calender* as the emergence of a modern counterpart to Orpheus, see Thomas Cain, "Spenser and Renaissance Orpheus," *UTQ* 41 (1971): 28–30; see also Thomas Berger's critique of Cain's position in his "Orpheus, Pan, and the Poetics of Misogyny: Spenser's Critique of Pastoral Love and Art," *ELH* 50 (Spring 1983): 27–60. Berger argues that most critics fail to see the "functional interdependence between poetic power and erotic failure" (p. 28) and views the "Orphean paradigm" as "more admonitory than exemplary" (p. 29).

48. T. P. Harrison, p. 284, n. 16.

49. In contrast to my view of the elegy as a vocational poem, Poggioli speaks for the majority of critics when he states that the "real function of the pagan funeral elegy" is to "sublimate one's coming death through compassion for the recent death of a dear one," p. 78.

50. Calpurnius, *Minor Latin Poets,* trans. J. Wight and Arnold Duff (Loeb Classical Edition, 1934; rpt. London: William Heinemann, 1961), pp. 245–59.

51. Nemesianus, *Minor Latin Poets,* pp. 457–64.

52. *Daphnaïda,* in *The Minor Poems,* I, 125–42, ll. 267–71.

CHAPTER 3

1. Richard Helgerson, *Self-Crowned Laureates: Spenser, Jonson, Milton and the Literary System* (Berkeley and L.A.: Univ. of California Press, 1984), p. 97.

2. My text for Spenser's *Epithalamion* throughout is Edwin Greenlaw's *The Works of Edmund Spenser: A Variorium Edition, The Minor Poems,* II, 241–52. Hereafter line numbers follow in the text.

3. Louis Adrian Montrose, " 'Eliza, Queene of shepheardes,' and the Pastoral of Power," *English Literary Renaissance* 10 (Spring 1980): 153, 155.

4. See John Mulryan, "The Function of Ritual in the Marriage Poems of Catullus, Spenser and Ronsard," *Illinois Quarterly* 35 (1972): 50–64, for an alternate reading of the ritual function of propitiation, celebration, and efficacy.

5. I allude here to the ground covered by Virginia Tufte in her *The Poetry of Marriage.* See also Thomas Greene, "Spenser and Epithalamic Convention," *Comparative Literature* 9 (1957): 215–16.

6. See Thomas Greene, pp. 215–28, for suggestive commentary on the "bourgeois milieu" of the poem.

7. Leonard Forster, "Conventional Safety Valves: Alba, Pastourelle and Epithalamium," in *Lebende Antike* (Berlin: Erich Schmidt Verlag, 1967), p. 120.

8. Hallett Smith, in "The Use of Convention in Spenser's Minor Poems," in *Form and Convention in the Poetry of Edmund Spenser,* ed. William Nelson (New York: Columbia Univ. Press, 1961), p. 136, notes a number of "preliminary sketches" for the *Epithalamion: The Faerie Queene,* I.i.48 and the marriage of Redcross and Una, and Sonnets 15 and 70 of *Amoretti.*

9. E. Faye Wilson, "Pastoral and Epithalamium in Latin Literature," *Speculum* 23 (1948): 40–41.

10. See Greene for a reading of Spenser's technical modifications of the convention, pp. 215–18, and Paul Miller for praise of Spenser's "delicate balance between mythic and personal expression" in the poem, p. 413. See also Wolfgang Clemen, "The Uniqueness of Spenser's *Epithalamion*," in *Essential Articles for the Study of Edmund Spenser*, pp. 569–84.

11. See Richard Helgerson's "The New Poete Presents Himself: Spenser and the Idea of a Literary Career," *PMLA* 93 (1978): 893. Helgerson demonstrates Spenser's struggle to define his own career against prevailing notions of literary vocation. See also David Shore, *Spenser and the Poetics of Pastoral: A Study of the World of Colin Clout* (Montreal: McGill-Queens Univ. Press, 1985).

12. See Walter Strauss, *Descent and Return: The Orphic Theme in Modern Literature* (Cambridge: Harvard Univ. Press, 1971); Hermine Riffaterre, *L'Orphisme dans la poésie romantique* (Paris: Nizet, 1970); Gwendolyn Bays, *The Orphic Vision: Seer Poets from Novalis to Rimbaud* (Lincoln: Univ. of Nebraska Press, 1964); and Elizabeth Sewall, *Orphic Voice: Poetry and Natural History* (New Haven: Yale Univ. Press, 1960).

13. For information in this section I am indebted to Ivan Linforth, *The Arts of Orpheus* (Berkeley and L.A.: Univ. of California Press, 1941; rpt. New York: Arno, 1973), and Strauss, ch. 1, "Introduction: The Metamorphosis of Orpheus."

14. E. R. Dodds calls it an "edifice reared by ingenious scholarship" in *The Greeks and the Irrational*, p. 148.

15. Strauss, p. 5.
16. Wind, p. 14.
17. Wind, p. 15.
18. Wind, p. 173.
19. Wagenknecht, p. 24.
20. Moschus, "Lament for Bion," in *The Greek Bucolic Poets*, p. 455.
21. Virgil, *Opera*, p. 99, l. 516. English translation by C. Day Lewis, *The Georgics of Virgil* (New York: Oxford, 1947), pp. 81–82.

22. The information in this section is summarized from John Black Friedman's *Orpheus in the Middle Ages* (Cambridge: Harvard Univ. Press, 1970).

23. Pierre Bersuire, *Metamorphosis Ovidiana, moraliter explanata* (Paris, 1509), fol. LXXIIIV; quoted by Friedman, pp. 127–28.

24. Friedman, p. 158.
25. Greene, pp. 221, 219.
26. For support of my reading of "Aprill" as epithalamium, see Johnson, "Elizabeth, Bride and Queen: A Study of Spenser's April Eclogue and the Metaphors of English Protestantism," pp. 75–91, and Tufte, pp. 167–78.

27. I am indebted to Hoffman, pp. 100–101, for pointing me to the *Helicon* version of the poem. See *Englands Helicon, Scolar Press Facsimile* (London: Scolar Press, 1973), n. pag.

28. Wagenknecht, p. 30, notes that "not the least success of the *Epithalamion* is its translation of erotic wish-fulfillment into Orphic terms."

29. Greene, p. 218.
30. *Variorium Spenser, The Minor Poems*, II, 193.
31. A. Kent Hieatt, "The Daughters of Horus: Order in the Stanzas of the *Epithalamion*," in *Form and Convention*, ed. Nelson, pp. 113–14.

32. Virgil, *Opera*, p. 26, l. 8. Translation—"Not to deaf ears I sing, for the woods echo my singing"—C. Day Lewis, p. 41. See also Jacopo Sannazaro, Eclogue 9, ll. 40–42, in *Arcadia and Piscatorial Eclogues*, trans. Ralph Nash (Detroit: Wayne State Press, 1966), p. 97. Natural echo of the human singing voice, and even repetition of the formula, occur in Pierre Poupo's epithalamia before Spenser's own, but not in the refrain.

33. Theocritus, "The Epithalamy of Helen," in *The Greek Bucolic Poets*, pp. 230–31. See also Catullus 61 and 62 in *Catullus, Tibullus and Pervigilium Veneris*, trans. F. W. Cornish (Loeb Classical Library); London: William Heinemann, 1931, pp. 68–69, 84–85.

34. Rosenmeyer, pp. 93–95, 118. See as well the thrice-varied, invocational refrain in

Theocritus's first idyll. For more on the poetic function of the refrain, as well as reference to the Theocritean example, see John Hollander, "Breaking into Song: Some Notes on Refrain," in *Lyric Poetry: Beyond New Criticism,* ed. Chaviva Hošek and Patricia Parker (Ithaca: Cornell Univ. Press, 1985), pp. 73–89.

35. See Wagenknecht, p. 62, for a discussion of the English flower-strewing tradition and for suggestive remarks on the shared imagery of elegy and epithalamium in the context of Blake's *Songs.*

36. Israel Baroway, "Imagery of Spenser and the Song of Songs," *Journal of English and Germanic Philology* 33 (1934): 23–45.

37. Richard Neuse, "The Triumph Over Hasty Accidents: A Note on the Symbolic Mode of the *Epithalamion,"* in *Essential Articles,* p. 542. Neuse's thesis, based on his reading of the envoy, is that a deliberate progression can be charted from the sonnets to the marriage song.

38. Jowett, pp. 333–34.

39. Otto Rank reminds us in *Art and Artist* of the history of the notion of genius—that figure which presides over the conclusion of Spenser's poem. "The idea of genius is, in its mythical origin, a representation of the immortal soul, that part of the personality which can beget *(gignere)* what is immortal, be it a child or a work" (pp. 19–20). Geoffrey Hartman works these notions of genius into an archetypal confrontation in the life of an artist between tradition and individual talent, what he calls "genius and Genius: the struggle of art with natural religion or the dominant myth of its age revealed mainly at crucial historical or self-conscious junctures," "Toward Literary History" (pp. 373–74).

40. See Hieatt, Neuse, and Max Wickert, "Structure and Ceremony in Spenser's *Epithalamion,"* *ELH* 35 (1968): 135–57.

41. Wagenknecht, p. 30. See Neuse's opposite view that Spenser approaches a "realm before which his art finally abdicates," p. 535.

42. For alternate readings of the envoy, highly unusual in a marriage poem, see Enid Welsford, *Spenser: Fowre Hymnes and Epithalamion* (New York: Barnes and Noble, 1967), p. 175n.; also Neuse, pp. 534–35. Both see it as a fulfillment of the *Amoretti* sequence.

43. See Hartman's essay on this poem, " 'The Nymph Complaining for the Death of her Faun': A Brief Allegory," in *Beyond Formalism,* pp. 173–92.

44. My text of *Prothalamion* throughout is that of the *Variorum,* II, 255–62. Hereafter line numbers follow in the text.

45. Harry Berger, "Spenser's *Prothalamion*: An Interpretation," in *Essential Articles,* p. 509.

46. Jay Halio, " 'Prothalamion,' 'Ulysses,' and Intention in Poetry," *College English* 22 (1961): 302. See also Dan Norton, "The Bibliography of Spenser's *Prothalamion," Journal of English and Germanic Philology* 43 (1944): 349–53, and J. Norton Smith, "Spenser's *Prothalamion:* A New Genre," *Review of English Studies* 10 (1959): 173–78.

47. Quoted in *Variorium Spenser, The Minor Poems,* II, 495–96.

48. See Alastair Fowler, *Conceitful Thought* (Edinburgh: Univ. of Scotland Press, 1975), p. 60, for the view that the poem was in fact commissioned by Essex as a gift to the brides. Jay Halio argues that the poem courts Essex by means of implied comparison with Spenser's former patron Leicester, p. 392.

49. Halio, p. 392. He draws here upon Alexander Judson's *The Life of Edmund Spenser* (Baltimore, 1945), p. 142.

50. Berger, p. 509.

51. Dubrow emphasizes the simultaneous presence of anti-nuptial and nuptial conventions in seventeenth-century epithalamia: "the norms of the genre permit, even enjoin, an exploration not only of the joys of marriage but also of the cultural tensions that threaten those joys," " 'The Happier Eden'?: Discord and Violence in the Stuart Epithalamium," paper given at 1986 MLA, New York, p. 2.

52. Berger, p. 513, hears a similar tension in these lines.

53. Berger, p. 523.

54. Stéphane Mallarmé, *L'Après-midi d'un faune,* in *Oeuvres complètes,* ed. Henri Mondor and G. Jean-Aubry (Paris: Gallimard, 1945), pp. 50–53.
55. Steven F. Walker, "Mallarmé's Symbolist Eclogue: The 'Faune' as Pastoral," *PMLA* 93 (1978): 116.

CHAPTER 4

1. See Paul Miller, "The Decline of the English Epithalamion," pp. 405–16. Dubrow, who counters Miller's argument in her forthcoming reading of the Stuart epithalamium, is particularly concerned with the rich commerce between epithalamium as genre during the seventeenth century and prevailing social tensions surrounding marriage and patronage as institution. Portions of *"The Happier Eden": The Epithalamium in Stuart England,* forthcoming, have appeared as follows: Heather Ousby, "Donne's 'Epithalamion Made at Lincolnes Inne': An Alternate Interpretation," *Studies in English Literature* 16 (1976): 131–44; "Love's Labour's Legitimated: The Popularity of the Epithalamium in Stuart England," paper given at MLA, 1983; " 'The Happier Eden'?: Discord and Violence in the Stuart Epithalamium," paper given at MLA, 1986; "Tradition and the Individualistic Talent: Donne's 'An Epithalamion, Or mariage Song on the Lady Elizabeth . . . ,' " in *The Eagle and the Dove: Reassessing John Donne,* ed. Claude Summers and Ted-Larry Pebworth (Columbia: Univ. of Missouri Press, 1986); " 'The Sun in Water': Donne's Somerset Epithalamium and the Poetics of Patronage," in *The Historical Renaissance: New Essays on Tudor and Stuart Literature and Culture,* ed. Heather Dubrow and Richard Strier (Chicago: Univ. of Chicago Press, 1988).
2. Tufte, p. 37.
3. Bion, "Lament for Adonis," in *The Greek Bucolic Poets,* pp. 392–93.
4. Apuleius, *The Golden Ass,* pp. 100–101.
5. Apuleius, p. 100.
6. See Kathleen Raine's discussion of the Cupid and Psyche story in relation to Blake's "The Sick Rose" in *Blake and Tradition* (Princeton: Bollingen, 1968), I, 200ff.
7. William Blake, "London," in *The Complete Poetry and Prose of William Blake,* ed. David Erdman (1965; rpt. Berkeley and L.A.: Univ. of California Press, 1982), p. 26. Hereafter citations will refer to the Erdman edition and will follow in the text. See Raine, I, 201.
8. My texts for these two epithalamia are as follows: John Donne, "Epithalamion Made at Lincolnes Inne," in *John Donne: The Epithalamions, Anniversaries and Epicedes,* ed. W. Milgate (Oxford: Clarendon, 1978), pp. 3–6; and Richard Crashaw, "Epithalamion," in *The Poems of Richard Crashaw,* ed. L. C. Martin (1956; rpt. Oxford: Clarendon, 1966), pp. 406–9. Hereafter line numbers follow in the text.
9. William Blake, *Visions of the Daughters of Albion,* pp. 45–50. Hereafter plate and line numbers follow in the text.
10. Heather Dubrow notes in her article on Donne's Palatine epithalamium that in the Lincolnes Inne poem "his ambivalence about Spenser's 'Epithalamion' produces an uneven and inconsistent poem," "Tradition and the Individualistic Talent," p. 115.
11. Clay Hunt, *Donne's Poetry: Essays in Literary Analysis* (New Haven: Yale Univ. Press, 1954; rpt. New York: Archon, 1969), p. 166. The chapter "Some Conclusions" offers a particularly thorough reading of Donne's poetics against the conventions of his age and attempts a psychological sketch of the poet.
12. David Novarr, "Donne's 'Epithalamion Made at Lincoln's Inn': Context and Date," *Review of English Studies* 7 (1956): 252, 253. See also Heather Ousby's (Dubrow's) response to Novarr in "Donne's 'Epithalamion Made at Lincolnes Inne': An Alternate Interpretation," pp. 131–44.
13. Jay Halio, *"Perfection* and Elizabethan Ideas of Conception," *English Language Notes* 1 (1964): 179.
14. The ritual purification—washing and decking of the bride—which Tufte cites seems

to me unrelated to the sacrificial imagery which closes the poem, p. 303, n. 65. See also Novarr, p. 252.

15. See Raine, I, 196, for a reproduction of the plate.

16. See Hunt's analysis of "Elegy 19: To His Mistress Going To Bed," in *Donne's Poetry*, p. 24ff., for an elaboration of the theological and philosophical implications of the analogy.

17. "Sheet," *OED*, compact edition.

18. John Donne, *The Sermons of John Donne*, ed. Evelyn M. Simpson and George R. Potter (Berkeley: Univ. of California Press, 1953), VI, 316.

19. See Paul Miller's brief reading of the poem in "The Decline of the English Epithalamion," p. 414. Miller notes the conversion of epithalamic into elegiac imagery but attributes it to "diminishing value of the marriage myth." See also R. V. LeClerq's "Crashaw's *Epithalamium*: Pattern and Vision," *Literary Monographs: Medieval and Renaissance Literature* 6 (Madison: Univ. of Wisconsin Press, 1975): 73–108, for an account of generic modulation very different from my own. LeClerq is interested in the way various "readings" of marriage "work in harmony to engage the reader vicariously in an artistic enactment of that experience," p. 73.

20. L. C. Martin, Commentary, *The Poems of Richard Crashaw*, p. 462, n. 1.

21. Ruth Wallerstein, *Richard Crashaw: A Study in Style and Poetic Development* (Madison: Univ. of Wisconsin Press, 1935; 3rd ed., 1962), p. 137.

22. Marc Bertonasco, *Crashaw and the Baroque* (University: Univ. of Alabama Press, 1971), p. 25.

23. Northrop Frye sees *Visions* as the complement of *Thel* and views the poem as an attack on deistic concepts of the universe in *Fearful Symmetry: A Study of William Blake* (Princeton: Princeton Univ. Press, 1947; 4th ed., 1974), p. 337. David Wagenknecht notes appropriately that *Thel* is an "aborted elegy," *Visions* an "aborted epithalamium," discusses the conflation of imagery shared by both, and places the poems in the context of Blake's other works. His approach is only incidentally comparative; I hope to amplify his suggestive commentary by closer comparison with *Epithalamion* and *Lycidas*. Kathleen Raine's discussion of the poem against the background of Blake's late-eighteenth-century Neoplatonism has been equally helpful, *Blake and Tradition*, I, 166ff. See also Wagenknecht's reading of the poem, p. 199ff. He calls Oothoon a "sort of female Orpheus."

24. David Erdman, *Blake: Prophet Against Empire*, 2nd ed. (Princeton: Princeton Univ. Press, 1969).

25. Foster Damon, *William Blake: His Philosophy and Symbols* (Gloucester, Mass.: Peter Smith, 1958), pp. 105–6.

26. Raine, I, 166–68.

27. Wagenknecht, p. 205; Frye, p. 205.

28. "A Song of Liberty," Erdman ed., p. 44.

29. "To Spring," Erdman ed., p. 400.

30. Tufte's anthology, "*High Wedlock Then Be Honoured*," p. 255.

31. Heinrich Heine, *Lyric Poems and Ballads*, trans Ernst Feise, bilingual ed. (Pittsburgh: Univ. of Pittsburgh Press, 1961; rpt. 1968), pp. 26–31.

32. Salvador Díaz Miron, "Nox," *Antología Poética*, ed. Antonio Castro Leal (Mexico City: Ediciones de la Universidad Nacional, 1953), pp. 116–19. English translation by Samuel Beckett in Tufte, p. 249.

CHAPTER 5

1. See Flavia Alaya, "The Imagination Is a Square Wheel: Towards a Poetics of Place," paper given at Ramapo College Colloquium, Spring 1976.

2. Rainer Maria Rilke, *Duino Elegies*, trans. J. B. Leishman (London: Hogarth, 1939), pp. 82–89.

3. William Madsen, *From Shadowy Types to Truth: Studies in Milton's Symbolism* (New Haven: Yale Univ. Press, 1968), pp. 9–10.

4. My text of *Lycidas* throughout is that of Douglas Bush, ed., *Milton: Poetical Works* (London and Oxford: Oxford Univ. Press, 1969), pp. 141–47. Hereafter citations and line numbers follow in the text. Milton's "unexpressive," of course, means "inexpressible" or "unutterable." J. B. Leishman notes in his *Milton's Minor Poems* (London: Hutchinson, 1969), p. 343, that the word appears three times in the whole course of English literature, once in Shakespeare's *As You Like It*, once in Milton's own Nativity Ode, and once in *Lycidas*.

5. John Crowe Ransom, "A Poem Nearly Anonymous," in *Milton's 'Lycidas': The Tradition and the Poem*, ed. C. A. Patrides (1961; rpt. Columbia: Univ. of Missouri Press, 1983), p. 72. See also Leishman, who notes the poem's "affinities" with the Italian *canzone* and with Spenser's nuptial poems, p. 271.

6. Michael Lieb's "Milton's 'Unexpressive Nuptial Song': A Reading of *Lycidas*," in *Renaissance Papers*, ed. A. Leigh Deneef and M. Thomas Hester, The Southeastern Renaissance Conference (Raleigh: North Carolina State Univ. Press, 1983), pp. 15–26, is the only exception. Lieb links the poem's epithalamic subtext to "the amatory tradition of classical bucolic verse" and attributes the poem's interest in nuptial imagery to its "recasting of that tradition to accord with a Christian perspective," p. 15. See also his "Scriptural Formula and Prophetic Utterance in *Lycidas*," in *Milton and Scriptural Tradition: The Bible Into Poetry*, ed. James Sims and Leland Ryken (Columbia: Univ. of Missouri Press, 1984), pp. 31–42.

7. Edward Tayler alludes to the proliferation of scholarship on the poem in the title of his "*Lycidas* Yet Once More," *The Huntington Library Quarterly* 41 (1978): 103–17. Stanley Fish's "*Lycidas*: A Poem Finally Anonymous," *Glyph* 8 (1981): 1–18, discusses the replacement of an individualist voice by a communal force that challenges it, and Paul Alpers's "*Lycidas* and Modern Criticism," *ELH* 49 (Summer 1982): 468–96, discusses recent scholarship gathered in the Patrides collection, including the Fish article, and focuses on generic issues. For readings stressing the poem's theological criticism and ecclesiastical satire, see Sacks, pp. 90–117, and John W. Erwin, "Lycidas and the Sweet Societies," in *Lyric Apocalypse: Reconstruction in Ancient and Modern Poetry* (Chico, Ca.: Scholars Press, 1984), pp. 57–66.

8. Milton uses the term in self-description in a letter "to a friend" reprinted in *Milton's 'Lycidas,'* ed. Scott Elledge (New York: Harper and Row, 1966), p. 172. Milton's term has been used by Bloom and Hartman to describe the revisionist poetics of latecomers beginning with Milton.

9. E. M. W. Tillyard, *Milton* (New York: Macmillan, 1930); in Patrides, pp. 61–66.

10. Lambert, ch. 9 and Epilogue, excludes even Arnold's *Thyrsis* and Shelley's *Adonais* from the pastoral elegy tradition because of their "night-time" setting. My quarrel with Lambert's first premise is described in more detail at the outset of my second chapter.

11. Arthur Barker, quoted by Wayne Shumaker, "Flowerets and Sounding Seas: A Study in the Affective Structure of *Lycidas*," in Patrides, p. 130.

12. M. H. Abrams, "Five Types of *Lycidas*," in Patrides, pp. 216–35, and Madsen, pp. 9–10.

13. See Geoffrey Harman's "placement" of *Lycidas* in his article on "Romantic Poetry and the *Genius Loci*," in *Beyond Formalism*, pp. 316–17.

14. The imagery of *L'Allegro* is overtly epithalamic:

> There let Hymen oft appear
> In saffron robe, with taper clear,
> And pomp, and feast, and revelry,
> With masque and antique pageantry:
> Such sights as youthful poets dream.
> (*Poetical Works*, pp. 88–92)

15. See Sacks on the complex occasion of the poem, pp. 90–94.

16. See Moschus, p. 40; Petrarch, p. 68; Boccaccio, p. 83; Alamanni, p. 123, in Harri-

son's anthology of the elegy. See also Jacopo Sannazaro, *Arcadia and Piscatorial Eclogues,* trans. Ralph Nash (Detroit: Wayne State Univ. Press, 1966), pp. 54, 130, 136.

17. *L'Allegro,* pp. 88–92; *Il Penseroso,* pp. 92–96, in *Poetical Works.* Hereafter citations follow in the text.

18. See Carolyn Mayerson, "The Orpheus Myth in Milton's *Lycidas,*" *PMLA* 64 (1949): 189–207. For all the erudition in this article—Mayerson explores Orpheus's role as a theologian, patron of the arts, husband to Eurydice; she traces his relationship to Druids, early Christianity, and Christian symbolism generally—little mention is made of the dismemberment theme as an initiatory motif. I do agree with Mayerson in principle, of course, that the allusion to Orpheus is central to the poem's meaning. For another reading of Orpheus's role in the work, see Gretchen Finney, "A Musical Background for *Lycidas,*" *The Huntington Library Quarterly* 15 (1951–52): 325–50. Finney finds the musical and operatic Orpheus of the Italian musical drama a likely source for the poem's reference.

19. Louis Sigmund Friedland, "Milton's *Lycidas* and Spenser's *The Ruines of Time,*" *MLN* 27 (1912): 246–50.

20. John Milton, "from a Letter to Charles Diodati," November 1637, in *John Milton: Complete Prose Works,* ed. Douglas Bush (New Haven: Yale Univ. Press, 1953), I (1624–42), 327. In the Cambridge Ms., according to Bush's introduction to *Lycidas* in *Poetical Works,* Milton dated *Lycidas* the same month and year as the Diodati letter.

21. See Erwin, p. 59, and Sacks, p. 99, for alternate readings of this passage.

22. Daniel 10:7–17 in the Bible. Authorized King James Version, Oxford Crown Edition, p. 749.

23. George Steiner, quoted by Leslie Brisman, *Milton's Poetry of Choice and Its Romantic Heirs* (Ithaca: Cornell Univ. Press, 1973), p. 85.

24. Lieb also notes the amatory emphasis of the flower passage in its earliest version, linking this earlier constellation of images to the pastoral Venus-Adonis context, p. 24.

25. The following citations are from "Corrigenda," reprinted from the Trinity Manuscript, Patrides, pp. 12–13.

26. Mayerson, p. 204.

27. Leishman, p. 310.

28. G. S. Fraser, "Approaches to *Lycidas,*" in *The Living Milton,* ed. Frank Kermode (London: Routledge and Kegan Paul, 1960; New York: Barnes and Noble, 1968), p. 34.

29. Here is the blazon catalogue in the *Variorium* text, VII, 40:

>Bring hether the Pincke and purple Cullambine,
>>With Gelliflowres:
>
>Bring Coronations, and Sops in Wine,
>>worne of Paramoures.
>
>Strowe me the ground with Daffadowndillies,
>And Cowslips, and Kingcups, and loued Lillies:
>>The pretie Pawnce,
>>And the Cheuisaunce,
>Shall match with the fayre flowre Delice.
>>>(ll. 136–44)

Additionally, Leishman finds two other flower catalogues in Spenser's translations of Virgil, pp. 302–3. See for contrast Brisman's reading of the drafts of the Orpheus and the flower passages from the point of view of time and the arrest of time that is death, p. 246ff.

30. "Corrigenda," pp. 12–13.

31. Shakespeare, *The Winter's Tale* (IV.iv.113–34).

32. See Henry Hitch Adams, "The Development of the Flower Passage in *Lycidas,*" *MLN* 65 (1950): 469. Adams cites the "long-recognized" source of the flower passage as *The Winter's Tale* and notes the two kinds of flower symbolism at play.

33. See Wayne Shumaker in Patrides, pp. 129–39, for a discussion of the archetypal water imagery in the poem. See also David Shelley Berkeley, *Inwrought With Figures Dim* (The Hague: Mouton, 1974), esp. chapters 1 and 5, for a typological approach to the poem. Abrams, in "Five Types," p. 233, describes the transvaluations thus: "even that last infir-

mity of noble mind, the desire for fame," has been purged "in the blest Kingdoms meek of joy and love," the earthly inclination to Amaryllis and Neaera has been sublimated into the "unexpressive nuptial Song" of the marriage of the Lamb, and "the pastoral properties of grove, stream and song serve only to shadow forth a Kingdom outside of space and beyond the vicissitude of the seasons."

34. See, for comparison, Boccaccio's "Olympia," in Harrison, p. 89.
35. Roy Daniells, *Milton, Mannerism and Baroque* (Toronto: Univ. of Toronto Press, 1963), p. 46.
36. Hartman, "Romantic Poetry and the *Genius Loci*," in *Beyond Formalism*, p. 322.
37. Hartman, "Toward Literary History," in *Beyond Formalism*, p. 381. Hartman finds the end of *Lycidas* inconclusive, suggesting that Milton "vacillates" and returns to "swainishness" at the close.
38. Poggioli, p. 103.
39. Lambert, p. 180.
40. *Epitaphium Damonis*, in *Poetical Works*, pp. 157–67. Hereafter citations follow in the text.
41. English translation by Helen Waddell, in Patrides, pp. 19–26. Hereafter citations follow in the text.
42. E. K. Rand, "Milton in Rustication," *Speculum* 19 (1922): 109–35.
43. Leishman, p. 334.
44. Sir Philip Sidney, *A Defence of Poetry*, in *Miscellaneous Prose of Sir Philip Sidney*, ed. Katherine Duncan-Jones and Jan Van Dorsten (Oxford: Clarendon Press, 1973), p. 121.
45. Alaya, Ramapo College Colloquium.
46. W. B. Yeats, "The Song of the Happy Shepherd" and "The Sad Shepherd," in *The Collected Poems of W. B. Yeats* (New York: Macmillan, 1933; 19th ed., 1973), pp. 7–9. Hereafter page numbers follow in the text.

CHAPTER 6

1. Harrison, ed., introduction to *The Pastoral Elegy*, p. 19.
2. Sacks's reading of the English elegy, although it notes the "general powerlessness of the pastoral elegy" between 1637 and the publication of Shelley's *Adonais* in 1821, nonetheless discusses the distinctive features of seventeenth-century mortuary poetry. His "tradition" after that includes the obvious contributions of Shelley and Tennyson, and ends with a provocative reading of Hardy's "A Singer Asleep" and *Poems of 1912–13* and Yeats's "In Memory of Major Robert Gregory," but these are not read as responses to *Lycidas*. His epilogue on the English elegy after Yeats and his note on the American elegy extend the genre's vital history into modern and contemporary poetry.
3. A. Reeve Parker, "Wordsworth's Whelming Tide: Coleridge and the Art of Analogy," in *Forms of Lyric: Selected Papers from the English Institute*, ed. Ruben Brower (New York: Columbia Univ. Press, 1970), pp. 75–102.
4. Geoffrey Hartman, " 'The Nymph Complaining for the Death of her Faun': A Brief Allegory," in *Beyond Formalism*, p. 189.
5. The texts of the poems are as follows: William Blake, *The Book of Thel*, in *The Complete Poetry and Prose of William Blake*, ed. David Erdman (1965; Berkeley and L.A.: Univ. of California Press, 1982), pp. 3–6; and Percy Bysshe Shelley, *Alastor: Or The Spirit of Solitude*, in *The Complete Poetical Works of Percy Bysshe Shelley*, ed. Neville Rogers (Oxford: Clarendon Press, 1975), II, 43–65. Line numbers follow in the text.
6. John Keats, "Sleep and Poetry," in *The Poetical Works of John Keats*, ed. H. W. Garrod (Oxford: Clarendon, 1939; 2nd ed., 1958), p. 53.
7. In his Commentary in the Erdman edition of Blake, Harold Bloom suggests that the "river of Adona" is "probably derived from *Paradise Lost*, I, 450–452, and may be an allusion to Spenser's Garden of Adonis, an excellent analogue to the unborn world of the vales of Har," p. 895.

8. See Raine's reading of *Thel*, I, 99–125; water imagery, I, 108; alchemical versus Platonist philosophy, I, 118.
9. Northrop Frye, "Blake's Treatment of the Archetype," in *Discussions of William Blake*, ed. John Grant (Boston: D. C. Heath, 1961), p. 9.
10. Wagenknecht, p. 29ff.
11. Frye, *Anatomy of Criticism*, pp. 36–37.
12. Robert Gleckner, *The Piper and the Bard* (Detroit: Wayne State Univ. Press, 1959), pp. 157–74. See also his *Blake and Spenser* (Baltimore: Johns Hopkins Univ. Press, 1985), a reading of the epics.
13. Although a more conservative reader may prefer to view the imagery of Lilly's speech as more generally pastoral than epithalamic, or to read the passage as assuming a function comparable to that of the epithalamic elements in other works, it seems to me that the imagery of Blake's state of childlike Innocence of *Poetical Sketches* and the *Songs* (and used here in the context of generation) is largely that of nuptial celebration, nourishment, and anointing; thus, as in Canticles, nurturing postures accompany the more conventional epithalamic symbolism of courtship and marriage. Even if Lilly's images are only suggestive of nuptial revelry, however, Cloud's and Clay's speeches allude unequivocally to "partners," "golden bands," etc.
14. Harold Bloom, *The Visionary Company* (Ithaca: Cornell Univ. Press, 1970), p. 51.
15. See Raine's exegesis of the gates in terms of Porphyry's *The Cave of the Nymphs*, itself a Neoplatonic allegory of Homer's *Cave of Nymphs*, I, 93–100; and Bloom's Commentary, p. 895.
16. Wagenknecht, p. 153.
17. Bloom, *Visionary Company*, p. 53.
18. Gleckner, p. 164.
19. I am indebted here to Northrop Frye's outline of the fourfold vision in *Fables of Identity*, pp. 48–50.
20. Donald Reiman, *Percy Bysshe Shelley* (Boston: Twayne, 1969), p. 35. See also Neil Freistat, "Poetic Quests and Questioning in Shelley's *Alastor* Collection," *Keats-Shelley Journal* 33 (1984): 148–60.
21. Harold Hoffman, *An Odyssey of the Soul: Shelley's Alastor* (New York: Columbia Univ. Press, 1933; New York: AMS, 1966). Hoffman's essay is a catalogue of Shelley's reading: it explores the content of the poem against the backdrop of eighteenth-century philosophical debates, setting the poem, in the mode of Lowes's *The Road to Xanadu*, against a host of journal entries, gothic romances, travel accounts, nature poems.
22. Kenneth Cameron, "*Rasselas* and *Alastor*: A Study in Transmutation," *Studies in Philology* 60 (1943): 58–78.
23. See Paul Mueschke and Earl Griggs, "Wordsworth as Prototype of the Poet in Shelley's *Alastor*," *PMLA* 69 (1934): 229–45. Their article responds to John Harrington Smith's contention that *Alastor* is a self-portrait, *PMLA* 54 (1939): 785–815. See also Marcel Kessel's response to Mueschke and Griggs in *PMLA* 51 (1936): 302–12. More recent readings continue and correct the same debate: Earl Wasserman, in *Shelley: A Critical Reading* (Baltimore: Johns Hopkins Univ. Press, 1971), pp. 11–42, finds a tension between the Wordsworthian narrator of opening and close and the Shelleyan quester's anti-Wordsworthian program; and Yvonne Carothers, in "*Alastor*: Shelley Corrects Wordsworth," *MLQ* 42 (March 1981): 21–47, contends that *Alastor* re-creates Wordsworth's "two consciousnesses." See also Lisa Steinman, "Shelley's Skepticism: Allegory in *Alastor*," *ELH* 45 (1978): 225–69.
24. Bloom, *Visionary Company*, p. 290.
25. Potts, *The Elegiac Mode*, p. 244.
26. Carothers, who reads *Alastor* next to *The Excursion*, hears an echo of Wordsworth in the opening lines.
27. Potts, p. 244.
28. Edward Strickland, in his "Transfigured Night: The Visionary Inversions of *Alastor*," *Keats-Shelley Journal* 33 (1984): 148–60, revises the poem's axis of influence from

Wordsworth upon Shelley to Coleridge upon Shelley and notes overlapping imagery in *The Rime of the Ancient Mariner* and *Alastor*.

29. In contrast to the "almost abstracted generic purity" of Shelley's *Adonais, Alastor* is a "pastoral that retreats to the mind, dislocating itself from the garden as a place." See Stuart Curran's brief discussion of the poem in his chapter on pastoral in *Poetic Form and British Romanticism* (New York: Oxford Univ. Press, 1986), pp. 124–27.

CHAPTER 7

1. The most important recent work on the poem's genre is that of Joseph C. Sitterson, Jr., "The Genre and Place of the Immortality Ode," *PMLA* 101 (1986): 24–37. Sitterson calls the poem an ode, and notes its allusion to other poetic forms, but ultimately finds "generic comprehensiveness" characteristic of the ode itself as genre. I do not wish to refute the general view, reinforced by its title, that the poem is an ode, but merely to explore the opposite modal registers of elegy and epithalamium in the poem.

2. Wordsworth valorizes those "obstinate questionings" or mental processes by which we attain a philosophical relation to the perceptions of childhood. Shelley misreads him in line 26 of *Alastor* when he hopes "to still those obstinate questionings" arising from fear of "black Death," although we can presume that apprehension about the imagination's adequacy is at the heart of each. In the Immortality Ode, Wordsworth mourns the loss of childhood immediacy; Shelley borrows that language to mourn the poet's ebbing power. A recent comparison of the Immortality Ode and *Alastor* is that of William Keach, "Obstinate Questionings: The Immortality Ode and *Alastor*," *Wordsworth Circle* 12 (Winter 1981): 36–44.

3. My text of the poem is that of *The Poetical Works of William Wordsworth*, ed. E. de Selincourt and Helen Darbishire (Oxford: Clarendon Press, 1947), IV, 279–85. Hereafter line numbers follow in the text.

4. Sitterson, for example, finds the birdsong of the third stanza to be "in the service of epithalamium," p. 26, but I will argue that more than merely scattered conventions of epithalamium will be marshalled to panegyrical ends.

5. Important readings of the poem include: Cleanth Brooks, "Wordsworth and the Paradox of the Imagination," in *The Well Wrought Urn* (New York: Harcourt, Brace and World, 1947), pp. 124–50; Herbert Hartman, "The Intimations of Wordsworth's *Ode*," *Review of English Studies* 6 (1930): 129–46; Lionel Trilling, "The Immortality Ode," in *The Liberal Imagination: Essays on Literature and Society* (New York: Viking, 1950); Geoffrey Hartman, *Wordsworth's Poetry* (New Haven: Yale Univ. Press, 1964), pp. 273–77; Jared Curtis, *Wordsworth's Experiments With Tradition* (Ithaca: Cornell Univ. Press, 1971), pp. 114–44; Harold Bloom, *The Map of Misreading* (New York: Oxford, 1975), pp. 144–59; Frances Ferguson, *Wordsworth: Language as Counter-Spirit* (New Haven: Yale Univ. Press, 1977), pp. 96–125; Paul Fry, "Wordsworth's Severe Intimations," in *The Poet's Calling*, pp. 133–61.

6. Wordsworth, Preface to the Second Edition of *Lyrical Ballads*, in *Poetical Works*, II, 390. My allusion is to the distinction Wordsworth makes in the Preface between poems written in the language of man speaking to men and those self-consciously literary artifacts founded upon "poetic diction," generic imitations, styled speech, etc.

7. Ferguson, p. 103. See also Peter J. Manning, "Wordsworth's Intimations Ode and Its Epigraphs," *Journal of English and Germanic Philology* 82 (1983): 526–40, for a reading of the Ode's internal contradictions based upon the two epigraphs of the poem.

8. Hartman, *Wordsworth's Poetry*, p. 273.

9. Abbie Findlay Potts, "The Spenserian and Miltonic Influence in Wordsworth's *Ode* and *Rainbow*," *Studies in Philology* 29 (1932): 606. Potts notes in particular that most of Wordsworth's end-rhymes are from *Prothalamion*.

10. Prospectus to *The Excursion*, in *Poetical Works*, V, 3–6.

11. I use Cody's notion that "all pastoral aspires to the condition of epithalamium" to explore the boundary between them here: the child's experience of the harmony of his world is analogous to the satisfactions offered by epithalamia at their close. Additionally, and more concretely, the birds, coronals, bouquets, and choruses are in my view explicitly allusive to Spenser's *Epithalamion*.

12. To my knowledge, no critic has as yet noted the elegiac similarities between the two poems. See Geoffrey Hartman's brief mention of the Immortality Ode and *Prothalamion* as dream visions in his *Wordsworth's Poetry*, p. 267. Samuel Schulman's very different comparison of the two poems, "The Spenser of the Intimations Ode," may be found in *Wordsworth Circle* 12 (Winter 1981): 31–35. Schulman reads the *Prothalamion* much more positively epithalamically than I do, and hence his reading of Spenser's influence upon Wordsworth is that of celebratory professionalism.

13. John Erwin notes the dependence of the Ode upon the double association of marriage and athletic contest in solar cycles derived from Psalm 19 and Pindar's third Pythian ode, *Lyric Apocalypse*, pp. 67–82. Erwin notes in an earlier chapter that Wordsworth approximates the "conjugal community" of *Lycidas*'s "unexpressive nuptial song" in his Great Ode, p. 65.

14. Bloom sets these two passages next to each other in *Map*, p. 148. See his alternate comparison on p. 149.

15. Bloom, *Map*, p. 144.

16. Manning, pp. 526–27.

17. Ferguson, p. 155.

18. Ferguson, p. xvi.

19. Ferguson, p. 125.

20. See Jared Curtis for an alternate structural division in his "Design in the 'Immortality Ode,'" in *Wordsworth's Experiments With Tradition*, pp. 114–42. Most critics support the poem's division into the following groups of stanzas: I–IV, V–VIII, and IX–XI. See Bloom, *Map*, p. 145.

21. See Ferguson's discussion of this counter-image, p. 112.

22. Manning believes that "the Ode proceeds from pastoral elegy in 1802 to an elegy for pastoral in 1804" and hears in the second epigraph and close an attempt at a more confident tone than the poem actually musters, pp. 539–40. For a view of the Ode's failure to achieve Spenserian registers, see Schulman, p. 35.

23. The "little actor" of course apes the speech on the seven ages of man in *As You Like It*, but the effect here is hurried and parodic.

24. Hartman, *Wordsworth's Poetry*, pp. 275–76.

25. Bloom, *Map*, p. 249.

26. Compare Wordsworth's compensatory "another race" with the initiatory course of Spenser's bride in *Epithalamion*, ll. 150–51: "Arysing forth to run her mighty race / Clad all in white, that seemes a virgin best."

CHAPTER 8

1. Miller, "Decline of the English Epithalamion," p. 405.

2. T. S. Eliot, "East Coker," in *The Complete Poems and Plays*, pp. 124, 126. See in this connection the following passage from Spenser's *Epithalamion* (ll. 276–77):
   And bone fiers make all day,
   And daunce about them, and about them sing.

3. Mallarmé's *Hérodiade* was never published as a trilogy during his lifetime, but editors have determined that the poems constitute a logical progression. "Ouverture" was not published in France until 1926 even though Mallarmé first wrote of the work as a trilogy—"Ouverture," "Scène," "Finale"—in 1896. See the publication history of this poem in the introduction to Gardner Davies's *Les Noces d'Hérodiade* (Paris: Gallimard,

1959). Similarly the three parts of Crane's poem were both written and submitted for publication separately. As in the case of *Hérodiade*, "Faustus and Helen" is printed as a triptych in the *Complete Poems* and calls for commentary as a complete entity.

4. My texts of the poems are as follows: Stéphane Mallarmé, *Hérodiade*, in *Oeuvres complètes* (Bibliothèque de la Pléiade; Paris: Gallimard, 1945), pp. 41–49. English translation supplied for longer passages is that of Keith Bosley, *Mallarmé: The Poems* (London: Penguin, 1977), pp. 96–117. Hart Crane, "For the Marriage of Faustus and Helen," in *The Complete Poems*, ed. Brom Weber, pp. 27–33. Hereafter page numbers follow in the text.

5. Mallarmé, letter to Henri Cazalis, 30 October 1864, *Documents Stéphane Mallarmé: Correspondance avec Henri Cazalis 1862–1897*, ed. Lawrence A. Joseph (Paris: Nizet, 1977), p. 238.

6. Robert Cohn, *Toward the Poems of Mallarmé* (Berkeley and L.A.: Univ. of California Press, 1965), p. 82; p. 88, n. 9.

7. Thomas Williams, *Mallarmé and the Language of Mysticism* (Athens: Univ. of Georgia Press, 1970), p. 60.

8. Charles Mauron, *Introduction to the Psychoanalysis of Mallarmé*, trans. Archibald Henderson, Jr., and Will McLendon (Berkeley and L.A.: Univ. of California Press, 1963), p. 111ff.

9. Erwin reads the poem as a development of "ancient choral poets' strategy of dramatizing the complex dynamics of poetic genesis and performance in order to project a community animated by continual exchanges of self-criticism," *Lyric Apocalypse*, pp. 105–15.

10. Mallarmé, letter to Villiers de L'Isle-Adam, 31 December 1865; quoted by Gardner Davies, Introduction, p. 16.

11. Mallarmé, *Crayonné au Théâtre*, in *Oeuvres*, p. 295.

12. Crane, "General Aims and Theories," in *Complete Poems*, p. 217.

13. See Katherine C. Kurk, "The Lily, the Rose, and the Lotus: An Erotic Bouquet in Mallarmé's *Hérodiade*," *Publications of the Missouri Philological Association* 6 (1981): 23–29, for a different reading of the flower motif.

14. See Mauron, "Anxiety This Midnight," p. 111ff., for an alternate reading of the beheading.

15. Cohn, p. 71.

16. Mauron, pp. 125–26.

17. See Erwin's alternate reading of the beheading, p. 114ff.

18. Song of Solomon, *The New Oxford Annotated Bible*, 5:8.

19. Mallarmé, letter to Henri Cazalis, 30 October 1864, *Documents*, p. 238.

20. Strauss, *Descent and Return*, p. 81. See also Mauron's interpretation of Mallarmé's orphism as a psychoanalytic descent into the depths of the unconscious, p. 206ff. "Orpheus can descend to the Underworld and charm the monsters who otherwise would keep him captive. So in the realm of the mind, this superior self can pass the barriers of those cerberi, superego, repression and censorship in order to penetrate the dungeon of our unconscious night," p. 209. Erwin wonders if Mallarmé was thinking of the Orpheus passage in *Lycidas* directly, pp. 111–12.

21. Strauss, p. 110.

22. Mallarmé, letter to Verlaine, 16 November 1865, *Correspondance*, ed. Henri Mondor and Lloyd James Austin (Paris: Gallimard, 1965), II, 301. English translation of the passage, Strauss, p. 83: "I'll even go further and say: the Book, since I am convinced there is after all only one, striven for unknowingly by anyone who has ever written, even the Geniuses. The Orphic explanation of the Earth, which is the only duty of the poet and the literary game *par excellence:* for the very rhythm of the book, impersonal and yet alive, even in its pagination, juxtaposes itself to the equations of this dream, this Ode."

23. Hart Crane, letter to Allen Tate, 16 May 1922, *The Letters of Hart Crane 1916–1932*, ed. Brom Weber (Berkeley and L.A.: Univ. of California Press, 1965), p. 89.

24. See esp. M. D. Uroff, *Hart Crane: The Patterns of His Poetry* (Urbana: Univ. of Illinois Press, 1968).

25. Alfred Hanley calls the poem "a paradigm for *The Bridge*" and a "summary of

White Buildings," Hart Crane's Holy Vision: "White Buildings" (Pittsburgh: Duquesne Univ. Press, 1981), p. 112. See also David Clark's explication of the poem in his essay "For the Marriage of Faustus and Helen," in *Critical Essays on Hart Crane*, ed. David R. Clark (Boston: G. K. Hall, 1982), pp. 56–67.

26. Herbert Leibowitz, *Hart Crane: An Introduction to the Poetry* (New York: Columbia Univ. Press, 1968), p. 59. He calls the poem Crane's "Ode to Psyche," "his dedication to service and homage of the muse." See also R. W. B. Lewis, *The Poetry of Hart Crane* (Princeton: Princeton Univ. Press, 1967), p. 80ff., for a very Christian reading of the poem. Lewis reads the invitation to fall down the stairs (and into bed) in Part II as an analogue of the Fall.

27. Crane's description of "For the Marriage," quoted by Uroff, p. 3.

28. Crane uses this phrase to describe the culminating section of *The Bridge*; it seems apt in this connection too. Letter to Otto K. Kahn, 18 March 1926, *Letters*, p. 240.

29. Hanley also reads the poem as a reconciliation or marriage of body and soul, p. 117ff.

30. Crane, "General Aims and Theories," p. 217.

31. Rilke, *Sonnets to Orpheus*, trans. J. B. Leishman (London: Hogarth, 1949), pp. 112–13.

32. Strauss, p. 197.

CHAPTER 9

This chapter first appeared as " 'Every Poem an Epitaph': Sea-Changes in Whitman's 'Out of the Cradle . . .' and Crane's 'Voyages,' " *Ariel* (January 1985): 3–25.

1. Crane, *Complete Poems*, p. 34.
2. Bloom, *Map*, p. 13.
3. Bloom, *Map*, p. 15.
4. Paul Fussell, Jr., "Whitman's Curious Warble: Reminiscence and Reconciliation," in *The Presence of Walt Whitman: Papers from the English Institute*, ed. R. W. B. Lewis (New York: Columbia Univ. Press, 1962), p. 31.
5. Leo Spitzer, "Explication de Texte Applied to Walt Whitman's Poem 'Out of the Cradle Endlessly Rocking,' " in *A Century of Whitman Criticism*, ed. Edwin H. Miller (Bloomington: Indiana Univ. Press, 1969), p. 273.
6. Paul Valéry, *Oeuvres complètes* (Paris: Pléiade, 1957–60), I, 1503–4.
7. Paul Valéry, *Le Cimetière marin*, trans. Graham Dunstan Martin, bilingual edition (Edinburgh: University Press, 1971), n. pag.
8. St.-Jean Perse, quoted in Introduction to *Sea-Marks*, trans. Wallace Fowlie, bilingual edition (New York: Pantheon, 1958), p. 16.
9. Pierre Emmanuel, *Saint-John Perse: Praise and Presence* (Washington: Library of Congress, 1971), p. 17.
10. R. W. B. Lewis, *The Poetry of Hart Crane*, p. 105, n. 16. The following quotations from Keats and Whitman are cited by Lewis.
11. My text for "Out of the Cradle Endlessly Rocking" is that of *The Collected Writings of Walt Whitman*, ed. Harold Blodgett and Sculley Bradley (New York: New York Univ. Press, 1965), pp. 246–53. Line numbers follow in the text.
12. Geoffrey Hartman, in "Toward Literary History," in *Beyond Formalism*, p. 381, finds the end of *Lycidas* inconclusive, suggesting that Milton "vacillates" and returns to "swainishness" at the close.
13. Stephen Whicher quite rightly notes the "brief May idyll of Two Together" which the poet evokes in "flashback," in his "Whitman's Awakening to Death—Toward a Biographical Reading of 'Out of the Cradle Endlessly Rocking,' " in *The Presence of Walt Whitman*, p. 21.
14. See Erwin's comparison of this passage to *Lycidas*, *Lyric Apocalypse*, p. 123. Erwin

is interested in poetic dialogue and the projection of "uncommonly vital communities" within the poem.

15. Whitman, quoted by Edgar Lee Masters, *Whitman* (New York: Charles Scribner's, 1937), pp. 250–51.

16. Bloom, *Map*, p. 15.

17. Bloom, *Agon: Towards a Theory of Revisionism* (New York: Oxford Press, 1982), p. 259. Bloom writes that "the assumption of that daemon, or what the poets of Sensibility called 'the incarnation of Poetical Character,' is the inner plot of many of the lyrics in *White Buildings*. The kenosis or ebbing away of the daemon is the plot of the *Voyages* sequence, where the other Orphic deities reduce Crane to a 'derelict and blinded guest' of his own vision," p. 255. He writes on the more fully orphic poems, "Repose of Rivers" and "Passage," in his chapter on Crane.

18. "As I Ebb'd . . . ," in *Collected Writings*, p. 253ff.

19. Norman O. Brown, *Love's Body* (New York: Random House, 1966), pp. 250–51.

20. For a reading of "Lilacs" as a crisis poem, see Mutlu Konuk Blasing's "Whitman's 'Lilacs' and the Grammars of Time," *PMLA* 97 (1982): 31–39.

21. My text of "Voyages" is that of *Complete Poems*, pp. 35–41.

22. See my article on women's elegies and the masculine elegiac tradition, "Feminism and Deconstruction: Re-Constructing the Elegy," in *Tulsa Studies in Women's Literature* 5 (Spring 1986): 13–28.

23. An interesting reading of Crane's epic revision of Blake, centering upon *The Bridge* as a rewriting of Milton, is that of Donald Pease, "Blake, Crane, Whitman and Modernism: A Poetics of Pure Possibility," *PMLA* 96 (1981): 64–85.

24. Lewis, p. 175.

25. For a reading of the poem against "an age old tradition of romance," see Lewis, pp. 150–51.

26. My texts of these poems are as follows: "The Wreck of *The Deutschland*," in *Chief Modern Poets of Britain and America,* ed. Gerald Sanders, John Nelson, and M. L. Rosenthal (New York: Macmillan, 1970), I, 52–60; "The Dry Salvages," in *The Complete Poems and Plays,* pp. 130–37.

27. See in this context Michael Sprinker's "The Elegiac Sublime and the Birth of the Poet: 'The Wreck of *The Deutschland,*' " in *"A Counterpoint of Dissonance": The Aesthetics and Poetry of Gerard Manley Hopkins* (Baltimore and London: Johns Hopkins Univ. Press, 1980), pp. 96–119.

CONCLUSION

A version of this chapter first appeared as "When the Moderns Write Elegy: Crane, Kinsella, Nemerov," in *Classical and Modern Literature: A Quarterly,* 6 (1986): 97–108.

1. W. H. Auden, *The Dyer's Hand and Other Essays* (New York: Random House, 1948; rpt. 1962), p. 41.

2. René Guénon, *Esotérisme de Dante* (Paris: Les Editions Traditionelles, 1939); quoted in Mauron, p. 207.

3. Wallace Stevens, "An Ordinary Evening in New Haven," in *Collected Poems* (New York: Knopf, 1954), p. 473.

4. John Peale Bishop, "Speaking of Poetry," in *Selected Poems* (London: Chatto and Windus, 1960), pp. 15–16.

5. Thomas MacFarland, "Poetry and the Poem: The Structure of Poetic Content," in *Literary Theory and Structure,* ed. Frank Brady, John Palmer, and Martin Price (New Haven: Yale Univ. Press, 1973), p. 104.

6. Maurice Blanchot, *The Gaze of Orpheus,* trans. Lydia Davis (Barrytown, N.Y.: Station Hill Press, 1981), p. 101. Blanchot's account, for all its denial of orphic transcendence or immortality, remains squarely within what I have established throughout as the orphic paradigm, imitated and revised by subsequent male poets. In an article in *New*

German Critique 36 (Fall 1985): 133–56, called "The Politics of Orpheus Between Women, Hades, Political Power and the Media: Some Thoughts on the Configuration of the European Artist, Starting with the Figure of Gottfried Benn, Or: What Happens to Eurydice?", Klaus Theweleit analyzes what he calls alternatively the "Orphic mode of production." Noting the "deep ambivalence everybody feels in the enjoyment of poetry—where does this beauty come from, [this beauty] . . . so closely connected with the dead?", he points to "the absence of the sacrificed body of the beloved woman which the poet manages to transform into the beauty of the poem; to reshape it there; to make loving words of great intensity out of the flesh of the vanished," p. 156. It is precisely this orphic paradigm from which Eurydice is omitted and the absence more generally of women poets in this book which I attempt to account for in *Corinna Sings: Women Poets and the Politics of Genre* (forthcoming, Cornell Univ. Press). The book includes chapters on elegy, epithalamium, aubade, sonnet, body-and-soul debates, as well as a critique of genre theory from the vantage point of gender.

7. My texts of the poems are as follows: Thomas Kinsella, "A Country Walk," in *Poems 1956–1973* (Winston-Salem, N.C.: Wake Forest Univ. Press, 1979), pp. 53–57; Howard Nemerov, "Elegy for a Nature Poet," in *The Next Room of the Dream* (Chicago: Univ. of Chicago Press, 1962), pp. 41–42.

8. Robert Lowell's "The Quaker Graveyard in Nantucket," in *Lord Weary's Castle* (New York: Harcourt, Brace and Company, 1944), pp. 8–14, may similarly be said to manifest its Miltonic (elegiac) heritage. Like *Lycidas*, it has a piscatorial setting, untimely death, victim of death by drowning, concern for issues beyond the dirge (such as contemporary patriotic capitalism), social commentary, homage to mentors, emphasis on place names, etc. But the poem, in a different register from Nemerov's, eschews consolation and refuses the panegyrical close in what amounts to commentary upon the elegiac tradition: "ask for no Orphean lute / To pluck life back."

List of Works Cited

Adams, Henry Hitch. "The Development of the Flower Passage in *Lycidas*." *MLN* 65 (1950): 469–72.
Alaya, Flavia. "The Imagination Is a Square Wheel: Toward a Poetics of Place." Ramapo College Colloquium. Spring 1976.
Alpers, Paul. "The Eclogue Tradition and the Nature of Pastoral." *College English* 34 (1972): 352–71.
———. "*Lycidas* and Modern Criticism." *ELH* 49 (Summer 1982): 468–96.
Apuleius. *The Golden Ass*. Translated by Robert Graves. New York: Farrar, Straus and Giroux, 1951.
Auden, W. H. *The Dyer's Hand and Other Essays*. 1948; rpt. New York: Random House, 1962.
Barber, E. A. "Alexandrian Literature." In *The Hellenistic Age,* edited by J. B. Bury, E. A. Barber, Edwyn Buvan, and W. W. Tarn. 1925; rpt. New York: Kraus, 1968.
Baroway, Israel. "Imagery of Spenser and the Song of Songs." *Journal of English and Germanic Philology* 33 (1934): 23–45.
Bate, W. J. *The Burden of the Past and the English Poet*. Cambridge: Harvard Belknap Press, 1970.
Bays, Gwendolyn. *The Orphic Vision: Seer Poets from Novalis to Rimbaud*. Lincoln: Univ. of Nebraska Press, 1964.
Berg, William. "Daphnis and Prometheus." *Transactions of the American Philological Association* 96 (1965): 11–23.
Berger, Thomas, Jr. "Orpheus, Pan, and the Poetics of Misogyny: Spenser's Critique of Pastoral Love and Art." *ELH* 50 (Spring 1983): 27–60.
Berkeley, David Shelley. *Inwrought With Figures Dim*. The Hague: Mouton, 1974.
Bertonasco, Marc. *Crashaw and the Baroque*. University: Univ. of Alabama Press, 1971.
The Bible. Authorized King James Version. Oxford Crown Edition.
Bishop, John Peale. *Selected Poems*. London: Chatto and Windus, 1960.
Blake, William. *The Complete Poetry and Prose of William Blake*. Newly Revised Edition. Edited by David Erdman. Berkeley and L.A.: Univ. of California Press, 1982.

Blanchot, Maurice. *The Gaze of Orpheus.* Translated by Lydia Davis. Barrytown, N.Y.: Station Hill Press, 1981.
Blasing, Mutlu Konuk. "Whitman's 'Lilacs' and the Grammars of Time." *PMLA* 97 (1982): 31–39.
Bloom, Harold. *Agon: Towards a Theory of Revisionism.* New York: Oxford Press, 1982.
―――. *The Map of Misreading.* New York: Oxford, 1975.
―――. *Poetry and Repression.* New Haven: Yale Univ. Press, 1969.
―――. *The Visionary Company.* Ithaca: Cornell Univ. Press, 1970.
Brisman, Leslie. *Milton's Poetry of Choice and Its Romantic Heirs.* Ithaca: Cornell Univ. Press, 1973.
Brooks, Cleanth. "Wordsworth and the Paradox of the Imagination." *The Well Wrought Urn.* New York: Harcourt, Brace and World, 1947.
Brower, Ruben, ed. *Forms of Lyric: Selected Papers from the English Institute.* New York: Columbia Univ. Press, 1970.
Brown, Norman O. *Love's Body.* New York: Random House, 1966.
Burke, Kenneth. *Philosophy of Literary Form.* New York: Vintage, 1957.
Cain, Thomas. "Spenser and Renaissance Orpheus." *UTQ* 41 (1971): 28–30.
Cameron, Kenneth. "*Rasselas* and *Alastor*: A Study in Transmutation." *Studies in Philology* 60 (1943): 58–78.
Carlisle, E. Fred. *The Uncertain Self: Whitman's Drama of Identity.* East Lansing: Michigan State Univ. Press, 1973.
Carothers, Yvonne. "*Alastor*: Shelley Corrects Wordsworth." *MLQ* 42 (March 1981): 21–47.
Catullus, Tibullus and Pervigilium Veneris. Translated by F. W. Cornish. Loeb Classical Library. London: William Heinemann, 1931.
Chief Modern Poets of Britain and America. 5th Ed. Edited by Gerald Sanders, John Nelson, and M. L. Rosenthal. Vol. I. London: Macmillan, 1970.
Cicero. *De Legibus.* Translated by C. W. Keyes. Loeb Classical Library. London: William Heinemann, 1966.
Clark, David, ed. *Critical Essays on Hart Crane.* Boston: G. K. Hall, 1982.
Coburn, Kathleen, ed. *Coleridge: A Collection of Critical Essays.* Englewood Cliffs, N.J.: Prentice-Hall, 1967.
Cody, Richard. *The Landscape of the Mind.* Oxford: Clarendon Press, 1969.
Cohn, Robert. *Toward the Poems of Mallarmé.* Berkeley and L.A.: Univ. of California Press, 1965.
Colie, Rosalie. *The Resources of Kind: Genre-Theory in the Renaissance.* Berkeley and L.A.: Univ. of California Press, 1973.
Commager, Steele, ed. *Virgil: A Collection of Critical Essays.* Englewood Cliffs, N.J.: Prentice-Hall, 1966.
Crane, Hart. *The Complete Poems and Selected Letters and Prose of Hart Crane.* Edited by Brom Weber. Garden City, N.Y.: Doubleday, 1966.
―――. *The Letters of Hart Crane 1916–1932.* Edited by Brom Weber. Berkeley and L.A.: Univ. of California Press, 1965.
Crashaw, Richard. *The Poems of Richard Crashaw.* Edited by L. C. Martin. 1956; rpt. Oxford: Clarendon, 1966.
Culler, Jonathan. *Structuralist Poetics.* Ithaca: Cornell Univ. Press, 1975.
Curran, Stuart. *Poetic Form and British Romanticism.* New York: Oxford, 1986.
Curtis, Jared. *Wordsworth's Experiments With Tradition.* Ithaca: Cornell Univ. Press, 1971.

Curtius, Ernst. *European Literature and the Latin Middle Ages.* Translated by Willard Trask. Princeton: Princeton Bollingen, 1953.
Damon, Foster. *William Blake: His Philosophy and Symbols.* Gloucester, Mass.: Peter Smith, 1958.
Damon, Philip. "Modes of Analogy in Ancient and Medieval Verse." *Univ. of California Publications in Classical Philology* 15 (1961): 261–334.
Daniells, Roy. *Milton, Mannerism and Baroque.* Toronto: Univ. of Toronto Press, 1963.
Davies, Gardner, ed. *Les Noces d'Hérodiade.* Paris: Gallimard, 1959.
Derrida, Jacques. *Dissemination.* Translated by Barbara Johnson. Chicago: Univ. of Chicago Press, 1981.
———. *La Dissémination.* Paris: Editions du Seuil, 1972.
Desport, Marie. *Incantation virgilienne: Virgile et Orphée.* Bordeaux: Imprimeries Delmas, 1952.
Dodds, E. R. *The Greeks and the Irrational.* Berkeley and L.A.: Univ. of California Press, 1964.
Donne, John. *John Donne: Epithalamions, Anniversaries and Epicedes.* Edited by W. Milgate. Oxford: Clarendon, 1978.
———. *The Sermons of John Donne.* Edited by Evelyn M. Simpson and George R. Potter. Berkeley and L.A.: Univ. of California Press, 1953.
Dubrow, Heather. *Genre.* London: Methuen, 1982.
———. " 'The Happier Eden': Discord and Violence in the Stuart Epithalamium." Paper given at 1986 MLA.
———. *"The Happier Eden": The Epithalamium in Stuart England.* Forthcoming.
———. "Love's Labour's Legitimated: The Popularity of the Epithalamium in Stuart England." Paper given at 1983 MLA.
———. " 'The Sun in Water': Donne's Somerset Epithalamium and the Poetics of Patronage." In *The Historical Renaissance: New Essays on Tudor and Stuart Literature and Culture,* edited by Heather Dubrow and Richard Strier. Chicago: Univ. of Chicago Press, 1988.
———. "Tradition and the Individualistic Talent: Donne's 'An Epithalamion, Or mariage Song on the Lady Elizabeth. . . .' " In *The Eagle and the Dove: Reassessing John Donne,* edited by Claude Summers and Ted-Larry Pebworth. Columbia: Univ. of Missouri Press, 1986.
Edquist, Harriet. "Aspects of Theocritean Otium." In *Ancient Pastoral: Ramus Essays on Greek and Roman Pastoral Poetry,* edited by A. J. Boyle. Melbourne: Hawthorn, 1975.
Eliade, Mircea. *Rites and Symbols of Initiation.* Translated by Willard Trask. 1958; rpt. New York: Harper and Row, 1975.
Eliot, T. S. *The Complete Poems and Plays of T. S. Eliot.* New York: Harcourt, Brace and World, 1971.
Elledge, Scott, ed. *Milton's "Lycidas."* New York: Harper and Row, 1966.
Emery, Clark. *The Marriage of Heaven and Hell.* Coral Gables, Fla.: Univ. of Miami Press, 1969.
Emmanuel, Pierre. *Saint-Jean Perse: Praise and Presence.* Washington: Library of Congress, 1971.
Empson, William. *Some Versions of Pastoral.* 1935; rpt. New York: New Directions, 1950.
Englands Helicon. London: Scolar Press, 1973.

Erdman, David. *Blake: Prophet Against Empire.* 2nd Ed. Princeton: Princeton Univ. Press, 1969.
Erwin, John. *Lyric Apocalypse: Reconstruction in Ancient and Modern Poetry.* Chico, Ca.: Scholars Press, 1984.
Ettin, Andrew. *Literature and the Pastoral.* New Haven: Yale Univ. Press, 1984.
Fabiano, Gianfranco. "Fluctuation in Theocritus' Style." *Greek, Roman and Byzantine Studies* 12 (1971): 517–38.
Ferguson, Frances. *Wordsworth: Language as Counter-Spirit.* New Haven: Yale Univ. Press, 1977.
Finney, Gretchen. "A Musical Background for *Lycidas*." *The Huntington Library Quarterly* 15 (1951–52): 325–50.
Fiore, Peter Amadeus, ed. *Just So Much Honor.* University Park and London: Pennsylvania State Univ. Press, 1972.
Fish, Stanley. "*Lycidas*: A Poem Finally Anonymous." *Glyph* 8 (1981): 1–18.
Forster, Leonard. "Conventional Safety Valves: Alba, Pastourelle and Epithalamium." In *Lebende Antike.* Berlin: Erich Schmidt Verlag, 1967.
Fowler, Alastair. *Conceitful Thought.* Edinburgh: Univ. of Scotland Press, 1975.
———. *Kinds of Literature: An Introduction to the Theory of Genres and Modes.* Cambridge: Harvard Univ. Press, 1982.
Fowles, John. *The French Lieutenant's Woman.* Boston: Little, Brown, and Co., 1969.
Freistat, Neil. "Poetic Quests and Questioning in Shelley's *Alastor* Collection." *Keats-Shelley Journal* 33 (1984): 148–60.
Friedland, Louis Sigmund. "Milton's *Lycidas* and Spenser's *The Ruines of Time.*" *MLN* 27 (1912): 246–50.
Friedländer, Paul. *Plato: The Dialogues.* Translated by Hans Meyerhoff. London: Routledge and Kegan Paul, 1969.
Friedman, John Black. *Orpheus in the Middle Ages.* Cambridge: Harvard Univ. Press, 1970.
Fry, Paul. *The Poet's Calling in the English Ode.* New Haven: Yale Univ. Press, 1980.
Frye, Northrop. *Anatomy of Criticism: Four Essays.* Princeton: Princeton Univ. Press, 1957.
———. *Fables of Identity: Studies in Poetic Mythology.* New York: Harcourt, Brace and World, 1963.
———. *Fearful Symmetry: A Study of William Blake.* 1947; rpt. Princeton: Princeton Univ. Press, 1969.
Gleckner, Robert. *Blake and Spenser.* Baltimore: Johns Hopkins Univ. Press, 1985.
———. *The Piper and the Bard.* Detroit: Wayne State Univ. Press, 1959.
Grant, John, ed. *Discussions of William Blake.* Boston: D. C. Heath, 1961.
The Greek Bucolic Poets. Translated by J. M. Edmonds. Loeb Classical Library. 1912; London: William Heinemann, 1960.
Greene, Thomas. "Spenser and Epithalamic Convention." *Comparative Literature* 9, No. 3 (1957): 215–28.
Greg, Walter. *Pastoral Poetry and Pastoral Drama.* London, 1906.
Grimal, Walter. "La Ve Eglogue et la culte de César." *Mélanges d'archéologie et d'histoire Charles Picard, Rev. Arch.* 30 (1948): 406–19.
Guénon, René. *Esotérisme de Dante.* Paris: Les Editions Traditionelles, 1939.

Guillén, Claudio. *Literature as System*. Princeton: Princeton Univ. Press, 1971.
Guthrie, W. K. C. *The Greeks and Their Gods*. Boston: Beacon, 1950.
Halio, Jay. "*Perfection* and Elizabethan Ideas of Conception." *English Language Notes* 1, No. 3 (1964): 179–82.
———. " 'Prothalamion,' 'Ulysses,' and Intention in Poetry." *College English* 22 (1961): 390–93.
Halperin, David. *Before Pastoral: Theocritus and the Ancient Tradition of Bucolic Poetry*. New Haven: Yale Univ. Press, 1983.
———. "The Forebears of Daphnis." *Transactions of the American Philological Association* 113 (1983): 183–200.
Hamilton, A. C. "The Argument of Spenser's *Shepheardes Calender*." *ELH* 13 (1956): 171–82.
———, ed. *Essential Articles for the Study of Edmund Spenser*. Hamden, Conn.: Archon, 1972.
Hanford, James Holly. "The Pastoral Elegy and Milton's *Lycidas*." *PMLA* 25 (1910): 403–47.
Hanley, Alfred. *Hart Crane's Holy Vision: "White Buildings."* Pittsburgh: Duquesne Univ. Press, 1981.
Harrison, T. P., ed. *The Pastoral Elegy: An Anthology*. Translated by H. J. Leon. Austin: Univ. of Texas, 1939.
Hartman, Geoffrey. *Beyond Formalism: Literary Essays 1958–1970*. New Haven: Yale Univ. Press, 1970.
———. *Wordsworth's Poetry*. New Haven: Yale Univ. Press, 1964.
Hartman, Herbert. "The Intimations of Wordsworth's Ode." *Review of English Studies* 6 (1930): 129–46.
Havelock, Eric. *Preface to Plato*. Oxford: Basil Blackwell, 1963.
Heine, Heinrich. *Lyric Poems and Ballads*. Translated by Ernst Feise. Pittsburgh: Univ. of Pittsburgh Press, 1968.
Helgerson, Richard. "The New Poet Presents Himself: Spenser and the Idea of a Literary Career." *PMLA* 93 (1978): 893–911.
———. *Self-Crowned Laureates: Spenser, Jonson, Milton and the Literary System*. Berkeley and L.A.: Univ. of California Press, 1984.
Hernadi, Paul. *Beyond Genre*. Ithaca: Cornell Univ. Press, 1972.
Hoffman, Arthur. "Spenser and the Rape of the Lock." *Philological Quarterly* 49 (1970): 530–46.
Hoffman, Harold. *An Odyssey of the Soul: Shelley's Alastor*. New York: Columbia Univ. Press, 1933; rpt. New York: AMS, 1966.
Hoffman, Nancy Jo. *Spenser's Pastorals*. Baltimore: Johns Hopkins Univ. Press, 1977.
Hošek, Chaviva, and Patricia Parker. *Lyric Poetry: Beyond New Criticism*. Ithaca: Cornell Univ. Press, 1985.
Huizinga, Johan. *Homo Ludens: A Study of the Play Element in Culture*. Boston: Beacon, 1966.
———. *The Waning of the Middle Ages*. Translated by F. Hopman. 1949; rpt. Garden City, N.Y.: Doubleday Anchor, 1954.
Hunt, Clay. *Donne's Poetry: Essays in Literary Analysis*. New Haven: Yale Univ. Press, 1954; rpt. New York: Archon, 1969.
Jaeger, Werner. *Paideia: The Ideals of Greek Culture*. Translated by G. Highet. Oxford: Basil Blackwell, 1939–45.

Johnson, L. Staley. "Elizabeth, Bride and Queen: A Study of Spenser's April Eclogue and the Metaphors of English Protestantism." *Spenser Studies* 2 (1981): 75–91.
Keach, William. "Obstinate Questionings: The Immortality Ode and *Alastor*." *Wordsworth Circle* 12 (Winter 1981): 36–44.
Keats, John. *The Poetical Works of John Keats*. Edited by H. W. Garrod. Oxford: Clarendon, 1939; 2nd Ed., 1958.
Kermode, Frank, ed. *The Living Milton*. 1960; rpt. New York: Barnes and Noble, 1968.
Kinsella, Thomas. *Poems 1956–1973*. Winston-Salem, N.C.: Wake Forest Univ. Press, 1979.
Kunitz, Stanley. "The Poet's Quest for the Father." *The New York Times Book Review*, February 22, 1987.
Kurk, Katherine C. "The Lily, the Rose, and the Lotus: An Erotic Bouquet in Mallarmé's *Hérodiade*." *Publications of the Missouri Philological Association* 6 (1981): 23–29.
Lambert, Ellen. *Placing Sorrow: A Study of the Pastoral Elegy Convention from Theocritus to Milton*. Chapel Hill: Univ. of North Carolina Press, 1976.
Leach, Eleanor Winsor. *Virgil's Eclogues: Landscapes of Experience*. Ithaca: Cornell Univ. Press, 1974.
Lebeck, Anne. "The Central Myth of Plato's *Phaedrus*." *Greek, Roman and Byzantine Studies* 13 (1972): 267–90.
LeClerq, R. V. "Crashaw's *Epithalamium*: Pattern and Vision." In *Literary Monographs: Medieval and Renaissance Literature*. Vol. 6. Madison: Univ. of Wisconsin Press, 1975.
Leibowitz, Herbert. *Hart Crane: An Introduction to the Poetry*. New York: Columbia Univ. Press, 1968.
Leishman, J. B. *Milton's Minor Poems*. London: Hutchinson, 1969.
Lewis, C. S. *Poems*. Edited by Walter Hooper. New York: Harcourt, Brace and World, 1964.
Lewis, R. W. B. *The Poetry of Hart Crane*. Princeton: Princeton Univ. Press, 1968.
——, ed. *The Presence of Walt Whitman: Papers from the English Institute*. New York: Columbia Univ. Press, 1962.
Lieb, Michael. "Milton's 'Unexpressive Nuptial Song': A Reading of *Lycidas*." In *Renaissance Papers*, edited by A. Leigh Deneef and M. Thomas Hester. Raleigh: North Carolina State Univ. Press, 1983.
——. "Scriptural Formula and Prophetic Utterance in *Lycidas*." In *Milton and Scriptural Tradition: The Bible into Poetry*, edited by James Sims and Leland Ryken. Columbia: Univ. of Missouri Press, 1984.
Linforth, Ivan. *The Arts of Orpheus*. 1941; rpt. New York: Arno, 1973.
Lowell, Robert. *Lord Weary's Castle*. New York: Harcourt, Brace and Co., 1944.
MacFarland, Thomas. "Poetry and the Poem: The Structure of Poetic Content." In *Literary Theory and Structure*, edited by Frank Brady, John Palmer, and Martin Price. New Haven: Yale Univ. Press, 1973.
Madsen, William. *From Shadowy Types to Truth: Studies in Milton's Symbolism*. New Haven: Yale Univ. Press, 1968.
Mallarmé, Stéphane. *Correspondance*. Edited by Henri Mondor and Lloyd James Austin. Paris: Gallimard, 1965.

———. *Documents Stéphane Mallarmé: Correspondance avec Henri Cazalis 1862–1897.* Edited by Lawrence A. Joseph. Paris: Nizet, 1977.
———. *Oeuvres complètes.* Paris: Gallimard, 1945.
———. *The Poems.* Bilingual Edition. Translated by Keith Bosley. New York: Penguin, 1977.
———. *Selected Prose Poems, Essays and Letters.* Translated by Bradford Booth. Baltimore: Johns Hopkins Univ. Press, 1956.
Manning, Peter J. "Wordsworth's Intimations Ode and Its Epigraphs." *Journal of English and Germanic Philology* 82 (1983): 526–40.
Marinelli, Peter. *Pastoral: The Critical Idiom.* London: Methuen, 1971.
Masters, Edgar Lee. *Whitman.* New York: Charles Scribner, 1939.
Mauron, Charles. *Introduction to the Psychoanalysis of Mallarmé.* Translated by Archibald Henderson, Jr., and Will McLendon. Berkeley and L.A.: Univ. of California Press, 1963.
Mayerson, Carolyn. "The Orpheus Myth in Milton's *Lycidas*." *PMLA* 64 (1949): 189–207.
McLane, Paul. *Spenser's Shepheardes Calender: A Study in Elizabethan Allegory.* South Bend: Univ. of Notre Dame Press, 1961.
McPeek, James A. S. *Catullus in Strange and Distant Britain.* Cambridge: Harvard Univ. Press, 1939.
Miller, Edwin, ed. *A Century of Whitman Criticism.* Bloomington: Indiana Univ. Press, 1969.
Miller, Paul. "The Decline of the English Epithalamion." *Texas Studies in Literature and Language* 12 (1970): 405–16.
Milton, John. *John Milton: Complete Prose Works.* Edited by Douglas Bush. New Haven: Yale Univ. Press, 1953.
———. *Milton: Poetical Works.* Edited by Douglas Bush. London and Oxford: Oxford Univ. Press, 1969.
Miron, Salvador Díaz. "Nox." In *Antología Poética,* edited by Antonio Castro Leal. Mexico City: Ediciones de la Universidad Nacional, 1953.
Montrose, Louis Adrian. " 'Eliza, Queene of Shepheardes,' and the Pastoral of Power." *English Literature Review* 10 (1980): 153–62.
———. " 'The perfecte paterne of a Poete': The Poetics of Courtship in *The Shepheardes Calender*." *Texas Studies in Literature and Language* 21 (1979): 34–67.
Motte, André. *Prairies et jardins de la Grèce antique de la réligion à la philosophie.* Brussels: Academie Royale de Belgique, 1971.
Mueschke, Paul, and Earl Griggs. "Wordsworth as Prototype of the Poet in Shelley's *Alastor*." *PMLA* 69 (1934): 229–45.
Mulryan, John. "The Function of Ritual in the Marriage Poems of Catullus, Spenser, and Ronsard." *Illinois Quarterly* 35 (1972): 50–64.
Murley, Clyde. "Plato's *Phaedrus* and Theocritean Pastoral." *Transactions of the American Philological Association* 71 (1940): 281–95.
Mylonas, George. *Eleusis and the Eleusinian Mysteries.* Princeton: Princeton Univ. Press, 1961.
Nelson, William, ed. *Form and Convention in the Poetry of Edmund Spenser.* New York: Columbia Univ. Press, 1961.
Nemerov, Howard. *The Next Room of the Dream.* Chicago: Univ. of Chicago Press, 1962.

Norden, Eduard. *Die Antike Kunstprosa*. Leipzig: B. G. Teubner, 1915.
Norlin, George. "The Conventions of the Pastoral Elegy." *American Journal of Philology* 32 (1911): 294–312.
Norton, Dan. "The Bibliography of Spenser's *Prothalamion*." *Journal of English and Germanic Philology* 43 (1944): 349–53.
Novarr, David. "Donne's 'Epithalamion Made at Lincoln's Inn': Context and Date." *Review of English Studies* 7 (1956): 250–63.
Otis, Brooks. *Virgil: A Study in Civilized Poetry*. Oxford: Clarendon, 1964.
Ousby (Dubrow), Heather. "Donne's 'Epithalamion Made at Lincolnes Inne': An Alternative Interpretation." *Studies in English Literature* 16 (1976): 131–44.
The Oxford English Dictionary. Compact Edition.
Panofsky, Erwin. "*Et in Arcadia Ego*: Poussin and the Elegiac Tradition." In *Meaning in the Visual Arts*. Garden City, N.Y.: Doubleday Anchor, 1955.
Parry, Adam. "Landscape in Greek Poetry." *Yale Classical Studies* 15 (1957): 3–29.
Patrides, C. A., ed. *Milton's "Lycidas": The Tradition and the Poem*. 1961; rpt. Columbia: Univ. of Missouri Press, 1983.
Pease, Donald. "Blake, Crane, Whitman and Modernism: A Poetics of Pure Possibility." *PMLA* 96 (1981): 64–85.
Perse, Saint-Jean. *Sea-Marks*. Translated by Wallace Fowlie. New York: Pantheon, 1958.
Pigman, G. W., III. *Grief and English Renaissance Elegy*. Cambridge: Cambridge Univ. Press, 1985.
Plato. *The Dialogues of Plato*. Translated by B. Jowett. 1892; rpt. New York: Random House, 1937.
Poggioli, Renato. *The Oaten Flute*. Edited by A. Bartlett Giamatti. Cambridge: Harvard Univ. Press, 1975.
Potts, Abbie Findlay. *The Elegiac Mode*. Ithaca: Cornell Univ. Press, 1967.
———. "The Spenserian and Miltonic Influence in Wordsworth's *Ode* and *Rainbow*." *Studies in Philology* 29 (1932): 607–16.
Prescott, Anne Lake. *French Poets and the English Renaissance*. New Haven: Yale Univ. Press, 1978.
The Princeton Encyclopedia of Poetry and Poetics. Edited by Alex Preminger. Princeton: Princeton Univ. Press, 1965.
Putnam, Michael. *Virgil's Pastoral Art: Studies in the Eclogues*. Princeton: Princeton Univ. Press, 1970.
Quint, David. *Origin and Originality in Renaissance Literature: Versions of the Source*. New Haven: Yale Univ. Press, 1983.
Raine, Kathleen. *Blake and Tradition*. 2 vols. Princeton: Princeton Bollingen, 1968.
Rand, E. K. "Milton in Rustication." *Speculum* 19 (1922): 109–35.
Rank, Otto. *Art and Artist*. New York: Tudor, 1932.
Reiman, Donald. *Percy Bysshe Shelley,* Boston: Twayne, 1969.
Riffaterre, Hermine. *L'Orphisme dans la poésie romantique*. Paris: Nizet, 1970.
Rilke, Rainer Maria. *Duino Elegies*. Translated by J. B. Leishman. London: Hogarth, 1939.
———. *Sonnets to Orpheus*. Translated by J. B. Leishman. London: Hogarth, 1949.

Rosenmeyer, T. G. *The Green Cabinet: Theocritus and the European Pastoral Lyric*. Berkeley and L.A.: Univ. of California Press, 1969.
Rosmarin, Adena. *The Power of Genre*. Minneapolis: Univ. of Minnesota Press, 1985.
Sacks, Peter. *The English Elegy: Studies in the Genre from Spenser to Yeats*. Baltimore: Johns Hopkins Univ. Press, 1985.
Sannazaro, Jacopo. *Arcadia and Piscatorial Eclogues*. Translated by Ralph Nash. Detroit: Wayne State Univ. Press, 1966.
Schenck, Celeste. "Birdes and Brides, *Couple et Cygnes:* Pastoral Erotics in Spenser and Mallarmé." Forthcoming in *Proceedings of the XII Congress of the International Comparative Literature Association*.
———. " 'Every Poem an Epitaph': Sea-Changes in Whitman's 'Out of the Cradle . . .' and Crane's 'Voyages.' " *Ariel* (January 1985): 3–25.
———. "Feminism and Deconstruction: Re-Constructing the Elegy." *Tulsa Studies in Women's Literature* 5 (Spring 1986): 13–28.
———. "The Funeral Elegy as Pastoral Initiation: Plato, Theocritus, Virgil." *Mosaic: A Journal for the Interdisciplinary Study of Literature* (March 1988): 93–113.
———. Review of G. W. Pigman III, *Grief and English Renaissance Elegy*. *The Sixteenth Century Journal* 17 (Winter 1986): 528–29.
———. "When the Moderns Write Elegy: Crane, Kinsella, Nemerov." *Classical and Modern Literature: A Quarterly* 6 (1986): 97–108.
Schulman, Samuel. "The Spenser of the Intimations Ode." *Wordsworth Circle* 12 (Winter 1981): 31–35.
Segal, Charles. "Death By Water." *Hermes* 102 (1974): 20–38.
———. " 'Since Daphnis Dies': The Meaning of the First Idyll." *Museum Helveticum* 3 (1974): 1–22.
Sewall, Elizabeth. *Orphic Voice: Poetry and Natural History*. New Haven: Yale Univ. Press, 1960.
Shakespeare, William. *The Complete Works of Shakespeare*. Garden City, N.Y.: Garden City Books, n.d.
Shelley, Percy Bysshe. *The Complete Poetical Works of Percy Bysshe Shelley*. Edited by Neville Rogers. 2 vols. Oxford: Clarendon, 1975.
Shore, David. *Spenser and the Poetics of Pastoral: A Study of the World of Colin Clout*. Montreal: McGill-Queens Univ. Press, 1985.
Sidney, Sir Philip. *A Defence of Poetry*. In *Miscellaneous Prose of Sir Philip Sidney*, edited by Katherine Duncan-Jones and Jan Van Dorsten. Oxford: Clarendon, 1973.
Sitterson, Joseph C., Jr. "The Genre and Place of the Immortality Ode." *PMLA* 101 (1986): 24–37.
Smith, Eric. *By Mourning Tongues: Studies in English Elegy*. Ipswich: Boydell Press, 1977.
Smith, J. Norton. "Spenser's *Prothalamion*: A New Genre." *Review of English Studies* 10 (1959): 173–78.
Snell, Bruno. *The Discovery of a Spiritual Landscape: The Greek Origins of European Thought*. Translated by T. G. Rosenmeyer. Oxford: Basil Blackwell, 1953.
Spenser, Edmund. *The Works of Edmund Spenser: A Variorium Edition. Minor Poems*. Edited by Edwin Greenlaw. 2 vols. Baltimore: Johns Hopkins Univ. Press, 1947.

Sprinker, Michael. *"A Counterpoint of Dissonance"*: *The Aesthetics and Poetry of Gerard Manley Hopkins*. Baltimore: Johns Hopkins Univ. Press, 1980.
Steinman, Lisa. "Shelley's Skepticism: Allegory in *Alastor*." *ELH* 45 (1978): 225–69.
Stevens, Wallace. *Complete Poems*. New York: Knopf, 1954.
———. *The Palm at the End of the Mind*. Edited by Holly Stevens. New York: Random House, 1967.
Strauss, Walter. *Descent and Return: The Orphic Theme in Modern Literature*. Cambridge: Harvard Univ. Press, 1971.
Strickland, Edward. "Transfigured Night: The Visionary Inversions of *Alastor*." *Keats-Shelley Journal* 33 (1984): 148–60.
Tayler, Edward. "*Lycidas* Yet Once More." *The Huntington Library Quarterly* 41 (1978): 103–17.
Theocritus. *The Idylls of Theokritos*. Translated by Barriss Mills. West Lafayette, Ind.: Purdue Univ. Studies, 1963.
———. *Theocritus: Edited with a Translation and Commentary*. Edited by A. S. F. Gow. 2 vols. Cambridge: Cambridge Univ. Press, 1965.
Theweleit, Klaus. "The Politics of Orpheus Between Women, Hades, Political Power and the Media: Some Thoughts on the Configuration of the European Artist, Starting with the Figure of Gottfried Benn, Or: What Happens to Eurydice?" *New German Critique* 36 (Fall 1985): 133–56.
Toliver, Harold. *Pastoral Forms and Attitudes*. Berkeley and L.A.: Univ. of California Press, 1971.
Trilling, Lionel. *The Liberal Imagination: Essays on Literature and Society*. New York: Viking, 1950.
Tufte, Virginia. *"High Wedlock Then Be Honoured": Wedding Poems from Nineteen Countries and Twenty-Five Centuries*. New York: Viking, 1970.
———. *The Poetry of Marriage: The Epithalamium in Europe and Its Development in England*. L.A.: Tinnon-Brown, 1970.
Uroff, M. D. *Hart Crane: The Patterns of His Poetry*. Urbana: Univ. of Illinois Press, 1968.
Valéry, Paul. *Le Cimetière marin*. Bilingual Edition. Translated by Graham Dunstan Martin. Edinburgh: University Press, 1971.
———. *Oeuvres complètes*. Paris: Pléiade, 1957–60.
Van Sickle, John. "Theocritus and the Development of the Conception of the Bucolic Genre." *Ramus: Critical Studies in Greek and Roman Literature* 5 (1976): 18–44.
Van Tieghem, Paul. "La Question des genres littéraires." *Helicon* 1 (1938): 95–101.
Virgil. *The Eclogues and Georgics of Virgil*. Translated by C. Day Lewis. Garden City, N.Y.: Doubleday Anchor, 1964.
———. *The Georgics of Virgil*. Translated by C. Day Lewis. New York: Oxford, 1947.
———. *Opera*. Oxford: Clarendon, 1969.
Wagenknecht, David. *Blake's Night: William Blake and the Idea of Pastoral*. Cambridge: Harvard Univ. Press, 1973.
Walker, Steven F. "Mallarmé's Symbolist Eclogue: The 'Faune' as Pastoral." *PMLA* 93 (1978): 116.
Wallerstein, Ruth. *Richard Crashaw: A Study in Style and Poetic Development*. Madison: Univ. of Wisconsin Press, 1935; 3rd Ed., 1962.

Wasserman, Earl. *Shelley: A Critical Reading*. Baltimore: Johns Hopkins Univ. Press, 1971.
Welsford, Enid. *Spenser: Fowre Hymnes and Epithalamion*. New York: Barnes and Noble, 1967.
Whitman, Walt. *The Collected Writings of Walt Whitman*. Edited by Harold Blodgett and Sculley Bradley. New York: New York Univ. Press, 1965.
Wickert, Max. "Structure and Ceremony in Spenser's *Epithalamion*." *ELH* 35 (1968): 135–37.
Williams, Raymond. *The Country and the City*. New York: Oxford, 1973.
Williams, Thomas. *Mallarmé and the Language of Mysticism*. Athens: Univ. of Georgia Press, 1970.
Wilson, E. Faye. "Pastoral and Epithalamium in Latin Literature." *Speculum* 23 (1948): 40–41.
Wind, Edgar. *Pagan Mysteries in the Renaissance*. London: Faber and Faber, 1958; rpt. New York: Norton, 1968.
Wine, M. L. "Spenser's 'Sweete *Themmes*': Of Time and the River." *Studies in English Literature* 2 (1962): 11–17.
Woolf, Virginia. *A Writer's Diary*. Edited by Leonard Woolf. New York: Harvest, 1953.
Wordsworth, William. *The Poetical Works of William Wordsworth*. Edited by E. de Selincourt and Helen Darbishire. Oxford: Clarendon, 1947.
Yeats, W. B. *The Collected Poems of W. B. Yeats*. New York: Macmillan, 1933; 19th Ed., 1973.

Index

Abrams, M. H., 92, 197 n 33
Adams, Henry Hitch, 197 n 32
Adonis, 11, 20, 58, 109
aggregation, 13, 87, 159, 177, 180–81
Alaya, Flavia, 104
allegory. *See also* marriage
  of human mind, 117
  Neoplatonic, 199 n 15
  parody of spiritual, 77
  of the soul, 14, 25, 74, 82, 84, 86–87, 89, 108, 110, 127, 132, 152, 177
  spiritual, 56–57, 101
Alpers, Paul, 43, 196 n 7
Alvarez, A., 83
Amor, 11
anti-epithalamium, 17, 73–90
  conventions of, 67, 141–42
  in elegy, 17
  history of, 73–74, 137, 181
  and social conventions, 75–76
Aphrodite, 38, 40
Apollo, 44, 57, 74, 96, 163
apprenticeship. *See also* careerism
  epitaphs of, 2
  pastoral as, 6–9, 16, 23, 34, 41, 50, 52, 95, 97, 102–3, 108–9, 115–16, 128–30, 161, 167
  representative poetic, 176
Apuleius, *The Golden Ass,* 11, 74, 170
Aristophanes, 14–15, 55, 73
Arnold, Matthew, *Thyrsis,* 12, 107, 196 n 10
Auden, W. H., *The Dyer's Hand,* 176
audience:
  absence of, 177
  of anti-epithalamium, 75, 88
  choir, 53, 97–98, 100, 113, 115, 127, 163

  in epithalamium, 60–61, 64, 66
  illusion of, 93
  initiated, 34, 53
  mourners, 96, 111
  reader as, 150
Auerbach, Erich, 184 n 21
Austen, Jane, 15

Bacchic religion, 58, 62–63, 98
Bacchus, 44, 94
Bacon, Helen, 186 n 2
baptism, 101, 160, 170
Barber, E. A., 8
Barker, Arthur, 92
Bate, W. J., 9
Baudelaire, Charles, 148
Bellow, Saul, 184 n 21
Berger, Harry, 68
Berger, Thomas, 191 n 48
Bersuire, Pierre, 60
Bertonasco, Marc, 83
Betjeman, John, 12
Bible:
  Daniel, 97
  Genesis, 131
  Psalms, 73, 201 n 13
  Revelation, 97–98, 140
  Song of Songs (Canticles), 56–57, 60–61, 63, 69, 73–74, 86, 88, 101, 146, 156, 174, 199 n 13
Bion, 6, 58
  "Lament for Adonis," 11, 73–74
Bishop, John Peale, "Speaking of Poetry," 177–78
Blake, William, 8, 10, 12, 14, 17, 134, 137, 139, 152, 162, 170, 177
  The Book of Thel, 17, 78, 84, 108–17,

121–22, 123, 127, 129, 132, 142, 178, 195 n 23, 199 n 13
  "London," 74
  Marriage of Heaven and Hell, 15, 83, 89, 109
  Poetical Sketches, 88, 109, 146, 198 n 13
  "A Song of Liberty," 86
  Songs of Experience, 105, 109, 198 n 13
  Songs of Innocence, 105, 109, 131, 198 n 13
  Vala, 78
  Visions of the Daughters of Albion, 75, 83–89, 109, 195 n 23
Blanchot, Maurice, 179, 204 n 6
Bloom, Harold, 1, 28–29, 112, 114, 122, 128, 157, 164, 196 n 8, 198 n 7, 204 n 17
Boreas, 26
bridegrooms, 77, 85, 87–88, 101
brides, 49–50, 56, 61, 63, 66–71, 74–75, 77, 80, 83–85, 88, 93, 101, 111, 195 n 14
Brisman, Leslie, 197 n 29
Brown, Norman O., 166
Bush, Douglas, 197 n 20
Byron, Lord (George Gordon):
  Childe Harold, 109, 117
  Manfred, 117

Callimachus, 8, 186 n 1
Calliope, 57–58, 99
Calpurnius, Siculus, Titus, 34, 51–52
  Elegy for Nero, 51
Camus, Albert, 97, 111
canon, pastoral, 3, 12–13, 16
canzone, 83, 92, 196 n 5
careerism. *See also* apprenticeship
  in anti-epithalamium, 79
  contests, 22–23, 36, 45, 51, 180–81
  in elegy, 33–53, 63, 70, 93, 96, 102, 124, 167–68, 173
  in epithalamium, 7, 55–56, 63, 66–68, 93, 98, 124, 139, 146–48, 178, 181
  and eroticism, 28, 55–56, 62, 65, 67, 69, 71, 165–66, 171
  and incarnation, 164
  and literary predecessors, 5–6, 34, 41, 80, 162–63, 176, 178–81, 190 n 41
  and orphism, 94–95, 148, 157–58, 202 n 22
  and patronage, 2, 55–56, 61, 65–68, 71, 126, 194 n 1
  and Plato, 27–28
Carothers, Yvonne, 199 nn 23, 26

Carroll, Lewis, 184 n 21
Castiglione Baldassar, *Alcon,* 103
Catullus, 13, 15, 55, 63
  LXI, 62
  carmina, 73
Cazalis, Henri, 140
Celan, Paul, 74
  Todesfuge, 156
Ceres, 44
Chaucer, *Parlement,* 81
childhood:
  in Blake, 109–11, 114, 199 n 13
  in Crane, 168
  and epithalamium, 201 n 11
  in Whitman, 161–62
  in Wordsworth, 2, 123–28, 130–31, 133, 200 n 2
Christ, 57, 59–60, 66, 77, 101, 145, 147–48, 174, 180
Christianity. *See also* consolation, mysticism
  and initiation, 151, 155, 173–74
  Mariolatry, 82
  and Orpheus, 56–57, 59–60, 100–101, 177, 180
  and paganism, 100–101
  and Platonism, 186 n 2
  and revelation, 91
  and the Word, 160
Cicero, *De Legibus,* 44–45
Claudian, 63, 73
coda, 102
Cody, Richard, 14, 20, 23, 46, 122, 184 n 25, 186 n 2, 210 n 11
Cohn, Robert, 145
Coleridge, Samuel Taylor, 15, 74, 115, 121
  Dejection, 122
  The Rime of the Ancient Mariner, 109, 118, 122, 156, 200 n 28
  "To William Wordsworth," 107
consolation:
  anagnorisis, 108
  and careerism, 33
  Christian, 52–53, 79, 91, 115, 121, 123, 129, 170, 174, 177, 180
  denial of, 40, 68, 178–79
  elegiac, 52, 97, 102, 130
  and Eros, 16
  failed, 107–8, 114, 121, 157
  nuptial, 7, 46–47, 49–50, 53, 81–82, 92, 97, 113, 126, 128, 178
  orphic, 2–3, 18, 31, 46–47, 66, 179
  panegyric, 2, 7, 43–44, 46, 49–50, 52, 56, 115, 178
  pastoral, 66, 105–6

"philosophic mind," 123, 127, 129, 133–34
poetic, 168, 171–72, 179–80
refusal of, 3, 12, 111, 113–15, 120, 122, 129, 157–59, 164–65, 205 n 8
"unexpressive," 97
Crane, Hart, 2, 12–13, 141, 149, 162
  The Bridge, 161, 173, 202 n 25, 203 n 28
  "Cape Hatteras," 3, 5–6, 15, 161–62, 171, 178
  "The Broken Tower," 149
  "For the Marriage of Faustus and Helen," 17, 137–41, 150–53, 155–56, 177, 201 n 3, 203 n 26
  "At Melville's Tomb," 157, 167
  "Passages," 204 n 17
  "Repose of Rivers," 204 n 17
  "Voyages," 18, 106, 158, 160–61, 168–74, 204 n 17
  White Buildings, 161, 173, 202 n 25, 204 n 17
  "The Wine Menagerie," 149–50
Crashaw, Richard, 17, 74, 78
  "Epithalamion," 75, 80–83, 137, 172, 195 n 19
  "Phaenicis Genethliacon & Epicedion," 81
criticism:
  of Blake, 83–84, 114–15, 195 n 23
  boundaries of pastoral, 3, 9–12, 92
  of Crane, 5, 169
  of Donne, 78
  of elegy, 33, 37–38, 188 n 2, 191 n 48
  elegy as literary, 39, 105
  and genre, 4–5, 184 n 21
  of Mallarmé, 140, 144–45, 202 n 9
  of Milton, 92, 98–99, 102, 196 nn 6, 7, 197 n 18
  of Plato, 186 n 2
  of Shelley, 115–16, 121, 199 nn 21, 23
  of Spenser, 67, 71, 201 n 12
  of Theocritus, 184 n 21, 186 n 1, 189 nn 19, 25
  of Virgil, 184 n 21
  of Wordsworth, 124, 128, 200 n 5, 201 n 12
Cupid, 74, 81
Curtis, Ernst, 186 n 2

Damon, Philip, 184 n 21, 188 n 30
Danger, 78, 81
Daniell, Roy, 101
Dante, 13

Daphnis, 25, 36–44, 46–47, 52, 56, 62, 65–66, 96, 157, 180–81, 184 n 21, 185 n 42, 189 nn 7, 19, 25
death. *See also* eros, love
  and apotheosis, 5–6, 11–12, 34, 46–48, 50
  of art and imagination, 93, 108, 120–22, 129–30, 132–33, 135, 157–58, 174, 200 n 2
  and careerism, 33, 129–30, 162
  finality of (non-orphic), 94, 113–14, 120, 172, 177, 189 n 25
  of "golden age," 25, 30–31, 122, 131–32
  and generation, 84, 118
  imaginative transcendence of, 178
  of innocence, 25, 107
  loss of virginity as, 2, 7, 78, 80–81, 83, 142, 156
  and nature, 14, 96, 127
  and marriage, 75, 78, 80, 89, 138–39, 141, 145–7
  and orgasm, 81–82, 169, 171
  orphic, 1–2, 7, 58–59, 65, 82, 93–94, 98, 101, 103, 155, 170
  of poet, 14, 18
  of "primal joy," 127
  and rebirth, 1–2, 18, 40, 58–59, 82, 109, 160, 174, 176
  sacrificial, 75, 78
  as secret word, 118, 172
  of self, 169
  transcendence of, 1–2, 11
  untimely, 37, 168–69, 180
  by water, 40, 101, 157–58, 170, 189 n 25
  as the Word, 159, 161, 166, 173
de l'Isle-Adam, Villiers, 140
Derrida, Jacques, 26–27, 188 n 26
Díaz Miron, Salvador, "Nox," 89
Dido, 7, 49–50, 97, 99, 133
Diodati, Charles, 95, 102–3
Dionysian mystery, 57–58
Dodds, E. R., 192 n 14, 194 nn 10, 11
Donne, John, 17
  "Epithalamion Made at Lincolnes Inne," 75–80, 83, 137, 139
dualism:
  Blake's rejection of, 84–87
  body-soul, 57, 78, 84–87, 111–12, 114–15, 146, 148, 152, 174, 181
  female-male, 85–87
Dubrow, Heather, 4, 10, 12, 185 n 39, 193 n 51, 194 nn 1, 10
Duke, Richard, 137

Edquist, Harriet, 40, 189 n 19
elegy. *See also* careerism, death
  Christian, 53, 174
  confessional, 102–3
  conventions of, 6–7, 11, 14, 30, 34, 37, 41, 49, 62–63, 68–69, 96, 158–59, 173, 177, 179–80, 205 n 8
  definitions of, 7, 15, 110, 180, 185 n 42
  epithalamic interplay in, 6–7, 10–17, 47–50, 52–53, 73, 79, 92–93, 97–101, 104–5, 111–15, 123–35, 167, 171, 178, 182, 196 n 6, 199 n 13
  "failed," 115–16, 121, 129, 177, 179
  and generation, 110
  history of, 15–16, 107, 180–81, 198 n 2
  modern, 138–39
  for pastoral, 105–6, 157, 201 n 22
  Phaedrus as pretext of, 16, 19–30
  piscatorial, 158–74
  revision of conventions of, 6, 12–13, 96, 108, 116–17, 157–58, 160, 162, 168, 178–80
  "unexpressive nuptial song" in, 91–92, 97–98, 104, 196 n 4
Eleusinian Mysteries, 19–21, 27, 44–46, 84, 97
Eleusis, 74
Eliade, Mircea, 20, 34
Eliot, T. S.:
  "Death of St. Narcissus," 156
  "The Dry Salvages," 106, 158, 173–74
  "East Coker," 138–39
  Four Quartets, 160
  "Little Gidding," 1–2, 18, 178, 185 n 42
Elysian Fields, 97
Emmanuel, Pierre, 159
Empson, William, 33, 184 n 21
envoy, 65, 80, 83, 102, 193 n 37
epic, 8, 15, 52, 103
Epicureanism, 38–40, 184 n 21
epitaph:
  definition of, 185 n 42
  "every poem" as an, 1–2, 13, 18, 176, 178
  on former selves, 129
epithalamium. *See also,* anti-, careerism, marriage
  anti-nuptial, 69, 75, 193 n 51
  and comedy, 14–15, 185 n 38
  conventions of, 6–7, 11, 13–14, 92, 111, 177, 200 n 4
  decline of, 15, 73, 80, 90
  definitions of, 7, 13
  elegiac interplay in, 6–7, 10–17, 47–50, 52–53, 55–56, 62–71, 73–75, 79–80, 89–90, 93, 98–101, 105, 123–35, 140–41, 163, 171, 178, 182, 195 n 19
  history of, 14–16, 55, 73, 137
  modern, 138–40
  as negative model, 15, 87–88, 90, 181
  parodic, 74–78, 137–56
  revision of conventions of, 2, 6–7, 73–74, 85, 87–89, 115, 137–40, 142, 150–51, 156, 177–78, 181
eros. *See also* love
  and ambition, 27–28
  and social and cosmic harmony, 13–14, 16
  and thanatos, 11, 161, 166
Eros, 16
eroticism:
  and initiation, 28, 150–51, 156, 161, 163–64, 169–70, 186 n 2
  of love-death association, 100, 163, 171
  and mysticism, 78, 144–46
  in *Phaedrus*, 23, 27–28
  and poetic power, 56, 167, 191 n 49
  and spiritual transcendence, 146
  in Theocritus, 38
Erwin, John W., 196 n 7, 202 nn 9, 20, 203 n 14
Essex, 2nd Earl of (Robert Devereux), 67–68, 70, 193 n 48
Ettin, Andrew, 184 n 21
Euripides, 15
  Phaethon, 73
  Trojan Women, 73
Eurydice, 3, 12, 18, 31, 59–60, 74, 85, 93, 95, 97–99, 139, 141, 148, 155, 179, 189 n 8, 204 n 6
Experience, 84, 87, 89, 152

Ferguson, Frances, 124, 129–30, 185 n 42
Ficino, Marsilio, 20, 58
Finney, Gretchen, 197 n 18
Fish, Stanley, 196 n 7
Fletcher, Phineas, 92
flower(s), 171, 174
  catalogue, 5–6, 30, 49, 61, 63, 96–100, 126–27, 197 nn 24, 29, 32
Forster, Leonard, 56
Fowler, Alastair, 12–13, 185 n 31, 193 n 48
Fowles, John, *The French Lieutenant's Woman,* 19, 29–31
Fowlie, Wallace, 159
Freud, Sigmund, 1, 13, 159
Freudianism, 10, 128, 169
Friedländer, Paul, 24
Frosch, Thomas, 29

INDEX

Frost, Robert, 25
Fry, Paul, 183 n 3, 185 n 33
Frye, Northrop, 33, 110, 195 n 23
Fussell, Paul, Jr., 158

Galileo, 105
Gay, John, "Friday," 107
generation, 74, 78–79, 84–87, 108, 110–15, 118, 121, 132, 161
genius, 101, 193 n 39
genre:
  anti-epithalamium's challenge to, 89
  contrasted with mode, 8, 12–13, 182, 185 nn 33, 42, 200 n 1
  contrasted with theme, 2, 5, 178
  and "counter-genre," 11
  and elegy, 107, 167, 189 n 7, 196 n 10
  history of elegiac and epithalamic, 180–82
  opening boundaries of pastoral, 9–10, 15–16, 55–56, 167, 182, 184 n 21
  problematics of, 3–5
  revision of theory, 12
georgic, 52. *See also under* Virgil
Gleckner, Robert, 114
God, 83, 174
Goethe, *Faust,* 139
Graces, 49, 60, 64
Grant, W. Leonard, 184 n 21
Greene, Thomas, 56, 61
Griggs, Earl, 199 n 23
Guénon, René, 176–77
Guillén, Claudio, 11–12
Guthrie, W. K. C., 20

Halio, Jay, 67, 77, 193 n 48
Halperin, David, 186 n 1
Hanley, Alfred, 202 n 25, 203 n 29
Hardy, Thomas, 198 n 2
Harrison, T. P., 50, 107
Hartman, Geoffrey, 8, 101, 108, 124, 134, 193 n 39, 196 n 8, 198 n 37, 203 n 12
Heine, Heinrich, "Ritter Olaf," 89
Helen, 141, 153. *See also under* Crane
Helgerson, Richard, 55, 192 n 11
Hermes, 37–38
Hernardi, Paul, 12
Herod Antipas, 139
Herodias, 139
Hessey, James, 159
Hoffman, Harold, 199 n 21
Homer, *Cave of the Nymphs,* 199 n 15
Hopkins, Gerard Manley, "Wreck of *The Deutschland,*" 106, 160, 173–74

Horace, *Art of Poetry,* 58
Housman, A. E., "Epithalamium," 12
Hughes, Ted, 12
Huizinga, Johan, 185 n 38
Hunt, Clay, 194 n 11
Hymen, 59, 64

incarnation:
  as birth, 161, 163–64
  dis-, 164–65
  linguistic, 174
  odes of, 158–74
  of Poetical Character, 204 n 17
  of soul, 177
initiation scenes:
  "American," 158
  and audience, 22, 34, 53
  Bacchic, 62–63
  and death, 119–20
  definition of, 177
  descensus, 161
  descent and ascent of, 176–78
  in elegy, 15–16, 34–53, 95–97, 99, 104, 168
  and eroticism, 28, 150–51, 156, 169–70, 186 n 2
  function of, 20
  marriage as, 66, 85, 88, 92–93, 142, 145
  mentors in, 28, 35, 41, 43, 51, 91–92, 95, 97–98, 100–101, 110–11, 117, 160–67, 169, 172, 174, 186 n 2
  mystic, 101
  orphic, 2, 93, 99, 103, 128, 135, 148, 154, 160–61, 168, 179
  Orphic, 58, 95, 101
  pastoral, 1, 19–31, 34–47, 50–52
  in *Phaedrus,* 19–20, 23–25, 92, 95
  piscatorial, 13, 106, 157–74
  and Pythagoreanism, 20
  refusal of, 108, 110–15
  restagings of, 6–7, 16–17, 40–43, 45, 47–48, 50–52, 95, 115, 119, 157, 170, 173, 180–81
  Scene of Instruction, 1, 22–25, 28–29, 130, 181
  and sexuality, 165–67
  as solitary, 115, 117–18, 122
  and water, 118–19, 122, 134, 157, 159–61, 165–67, 170
  in Wordsworth, 123–25, 128–29, 132, 135
innocence, 7, 25, 86, 110
Innocence, 84, 113, 123, 162, 198 n 13

issue:
    immortality through, 7, 11
    human and literary, 2, 64–65, 147, 178

Jaeger, Werner, 23
John the Baptist, 139, 150. *See also* Mallarmé, *Hérodiade*
Johnson, Samuel, *Rasselas*, 115
Jove, 69

katábasis, 141, 151
Keats, John, 159–60
    Endymion, 109
    Ode to a Nightingale, 122
    "Sleep and Poetry," 108–9
Kinsella, Thomas, 2, 18
    "A Country Walk," 179–81
Kunitz, Stanley, 188 n 32

Lambert, Ellen, 15, 33, 36, 40, 102, 107, 184 n 21, 188 n 2, 196 n 10
landscape:
    allegorical, 131, 179
    barren, 14, 141
    functions of pastoral, 22–25, 29–31
    literary, 36–37
    locus amoenus, 1, 6, 16, 19, 24, 28–29, 97, 118–20, 132, 186 n 2
    triadic composition, 24, 30, 36–37, 118, 131
language, oral to written, 25–27, 43, 51, 188 n 26
Leach, Eleanor Winsor, 188 n 31, 190 n 34
LeClerq, R. V., 195 n 19
Leda, 69
Lee, Sidney, 67
Leicester, 67, 70, 193 n 48
Leishman, J. B., 197 n 29
Lewis, C. S., "Prelude to Space: An Epithalamium," 156
Lewis, R. W. B., 173
Lieb, Michael, 196 n 6, 197 n 24
Liebowitz, Herbert, 150, 203 n 26
Longus, *Daphnis and Chlöe*, 14
love. *See also* eros, eroticism
    in anti-nuptial poetry, 75, 87
    and death, 10–11, 47, 100, 161, 166–69, 171
    Divine Love, 81–82, 84
    of nature and man, 134
    and rhetoric, 27
    transcendence through, 16
    vs. poetry, 171–72
Lowell, Robert, "The Quaker Graveyard in Nantucket," 205 n 8

McCaffrey, Isabel, 48
McFarland, Thomas, 178
Madsen, William, 91–92
Mallarmé, Stéphane, 2, 12, 74
    Crayonné au Théâtre, 141
    Hérodiade, 1, 17, 137–42, 149–56, 177, 181, 201 n 3, 202 n 9; "Ouverture d'Hérodiade," 140–41, 145; "Scène," 140–45; "Cantique de Saint Jean," 140, 145–48
    L'Après-midi d'un faune, 71, 140, 145
    Livre, 148
    Poésies, 140
    swan sonnet, 148–49
    "yx," 148
Manning, Peter J., 201 n 22
Marinelli, Peter, 10
Marot, Clément, 56
    elegy for Loyse, 49, 63
marriage. *See also* brides, careerism, death, epithalamium
    allegorical, 7, 14, 56–57, 65–66, 68–69, 98, 125, 139–41
    Beulah, 87, 114
    conventional, vs. feminine soul, 85–87
    disillusionment with, 68–69, 181
    in elegy, 99, 101, 103–4
    and generation, 112
    as initiation, 66, 85, 88, 92–93, 142, 145
    and issue, 2, 7, 11, 64–65, 147, 178
    and *katábasis*, 151
    of "Mind" and "World," 14, 125
    of oppositional principles, 85, 89, 137, 139–40, 146–47, 150–51, 153–56, 181
    orphic, 50
    of poetic imagination and female beauty, 140–41, 146–51, 153–55, 181
    and rape, 69, 85, 89, 150, 153, 156
    rejection of, 75, 111–13, 115, 117, 122
    repression of, vs. sexuality, 85–88
    in Revelation, 98
    sacred (*hieros gamos*), 46, 56–57, 60, 91–92, 97–98, 101, 104, 140, 197 n 33
    and sacrifice, 138, 145, 156
    social context of, 56, 61, 64, 77–78, 181, 194 n 1
    and social and cosmic harmony, 7, 13–15, 88
    and violence, 139, 146–47, 151, 153, 156
    wedding feast, 56, 63, 97, 111, 122
Marsyas, 58, 94

INDEX

Marvell, Andrew, 17, 24
  "The Nymph Complaining for the Death of her Faun," 14, 66, 107, 185 n 42
Masefield, John, 89
masque, 73, 80
Masters, Edgar Lee, 163
Mauron, Charles, 140, 145, 202 n 20
Mayerson, Carol, 197 n 18
Metaphysicals, 83
Michael (archangel), 91–92, 95, 97–98, 100–101, 111, 163
Milton, John, 8, 28, 30–31, 115, 196 n 8
  L'Allegro, 93, 196 n 14
  Epitaphium Damonis, 46, 92, 102–4
  Lycidas, 5–7, 10, 12, 14–17, 33, 46, 50, 52–53, 59, 63, 79, 82, 84, 91–106, 107–11, 113, 116–17, 120, 122–24, 127–30, 132–35, 139, 157–63, 165–68, 170–74, 177–80, 196 nn 4, 5, 6, 7, 13, 197 nn 18, 33, 198 nn 37, 2, 201 n 13, 202 n 20, 203 nn 12, 13, 205 n 8
  On the Morning of Christ's Nativity, 124, 196 n 4
  Paradise Lost, 59, 94, 109, 198 n 7
  Il Penseroso, 93
Miller, Paul, 15, 195 n 19
mimesis, 5, 33
mode, 13, 124, 130
monody, 92, 157, 159, 173, 185 n 42
Moschus, 115
  "Lament for Bion," 6, 33, 58, 93, 189 n 8
Moses, 59
mourning. *See also* consolation
  localized, 103
  and orphism, 2–3, 18, 31
  and panegyric, 5, 98, 124, 130–32, 149
Mueschke, Paul, 199 n 23
muses, 174, 203 n 26
Muses, 24, 37, 57, 60–61, 64, 94, 96, 99, 111, 150
Mysteries. *See* Eleusinian, Dionysian
mysticism, 14, 78–79, 81–84, 104, 134, 144–46, 149, 152, 154

Narcissus, 117, 119, 144
nature:
  adynata, 44, 180
  and death, 14, 96, 127
  disjunction with, 14, 44–45, 61–62, 98, 179
  and imagination, 133
  invocation to, 116
  and orphism, 9, 17, 42–46, 48, 50, 61–62, 64, 93, 96, 98

  rape of, 96–98
  vs. city, 22–25
Nature, 123, 127, 133–34
Nemerov, Howard, 18
  "Elegy for a Nature Poet," 175, 179–81, 205 n 8
Nemesianus, Marcus Aurelius Olympius, 34, 51–52
Neoplatonism:
  in Apuleius, 74
  in Blake, 84, 110, 170, 195 n 23
  in Shelley, 117–18
  in Spenser, 46, 56, 59–60, 62, 64, 66, 78, 170
  in Wordsworth, 123, 131–33
Neptune, 111
Neuse, Richard, 64, 193 n 37
Novarr, David, 76, 78
nymphs, 5, 60, 63–64, 67, 70, 80, 96, 107, 116–17, 126

Origen, 56
Orithyia, 26
Orpheus, 2–3, 12, 20–21, 53, 57–60, 76, 85, 95, 97–99, 106, 109, 135, 139, 141, 148, 178–80, 189 n 8, 195 n 23, 197 n 18
orphism:
  in Blake, 85, 88
  and Christianity, 59–60, 148, 155
  in Crane, 18, 141, 149–54, 173, 204 n 17
  definition of, 2
  denial of, 120, 204 n 6
  diminished, 105–6
  elegiac, 173
  in elegy, 56, 181
  in epithalamium, 65–66
  failed, 70–71, 94, 157, 179–80
  history of, 58–60
  in Mallarmé, 141–42, 145, 148, 202 nn 20, 22
  medieval, 59
  in Milton, 93–95, 97–99, 101–4, 197 n 18
  and mourning, 2–3, 18, 31
  and nature, 17, 44, 48, 50, 133–35
  "orphic ontology," 155
  paradigm of, 2–3, 18, 31, 204 n 6
  in Spenser, 47, 50, 53, 57, 60–62, 66, 95–96
  and women, 204 n 6
Orphism:
  in Blake, 84
  history of, 7, 20, 57–59

and Platonism, 20–22, 28
  in Spenser, 63
Ovid, 57, 59–60, 98
  tale of Tereus and Procne, 73

Pan, 23–24, 36–38
panegyric, 2, 40, 61, 126
  and careerism, 67–68
  and elegy, 56, 92
  in epithalamium, 50, 67, 125
  in masque, 73, 80
  orphic, 154
  refusal of, 205 n 8
Parker, A. Reeve, 107
parody, 77, 124, 179
  of elegy, 18, 115
  of epithalamium, 15, 17–18, 74–78, 80, 88–89, 137–56
  of initiation scene, 38–39, 132, 181
  of pastoral, 9
Parry, Adam, 22, 186 n 2
pastoral. *See also under* apprenticeship
  and ancient bucolic, 186 n 1
  Arcadia, 10, 103, 105
  binary opposition in, 10–11, 105
  Blake's use of, 109–10
  contests in, 22–23, 36, 45, 51, 180–81
  conventions of, 5, 8–9, 30–31, 60–61, 99, 102–3, 125–26, 162
  history of, 8–10
  and the inexpressible, 91
  love and death paired in, 10–11
  and mystery, 21–22
  revision of conventions of, 9, 18, 35, 96, 120, 122
perfection, 77
peripeteia, 7, 127, 133
Perse, Saint John, *Amers,* 158–59
Peter, Saint, 97
Phaedrus. *See under* Plato
Phoebus, 64, 77, 96–97, 111
phoenix, 81–82
Pico della Mirandola, Count Giovanni, 20–21, 58
Pigman, G. W., 188 n 2
Pindar, 201 n 13
Plato, 13, 16, 173, 186 n 1
  Phaedrus, 1, 3, 16, 19–30, 34–38, 40, 42–43, 58, 92, 94–95, 118, 124, 177, 181, 186 n 2, 187 n 14, 188 n 26
  Symposium, 21–22, 26–28, 58, 65
Platonism, 19–30, 35–41, 173, 186 n 2.
  See also Neoplatonism
Pléiade, 56, 60
Pluto, 93

poet:
  alienation of, 14, 61, 68–70, 126, 130
  centrality of, 14, 53, 56–57, 60–61, 64, 66, 75–76, 105
  death of, 14, 18
  as hero, 173
poetics, 3, 51, 139, 194 n 11, 196 n 8
poetry:
  autobiographical, 2, 92, 129
  ceremonial, 177
  contests, 22–23, 36, 45, 51, 180–81
  Elizabethan, 75
  Metaphysical, 83
  modern, 3, 9, 22, 150, 157–74
  mystic, 78–79, 81–84, 104
  "of negation," 145, 149, 181
  occasional, 2, 12, 15
  odes, 161, 183 n 3, 200 n 1
  as *pharmakon,* 26, 35
  piscatorial, 92, 106, 157–74
  "poetic diction," 124, 200 n 6
  and politics, 46, 57, 181
  Plato's criticism of, 26–28
  public/private aspects of, 93
  Renaissance, 3, 13, 20–21, 73, 83, 168, 181, 186 n 2
  Romantic, 3, 7, 9, 93, 108, 121–22, 168, 173
  and *serio ludens,* 22
Poggioli, Renato, 10, 45–46, 184 n 21, 191 n 48
Pope, Alexander, 8, 107
  "The Rape of the Lock," 15, 81
Porphyry (Malchus), *The Cave of the Nymphs,* 199 n 15
Potts, Abbie Findlay, 15, 121, 184 n 21, 200 n 9
Poupo, Pierre, 192 n 32
Priapus, 37–38, 40
Proserpine, 74
Psyche, 11, 74, 170
Putnam, Michael, 23, 45–46
Puttenham, George, 55
Pythagoreanism, 20

Rabelais, François: *Gargantua and Pantagruel,* 75
Raine, Kathleen, 84, 195 n 23, 199 n 15
Rand, E. K., 103
Rank, Otto, 193 n 39
Ransom, John Crowe, 92
Rapin, Nicolas, 39
refrain:
  anti-orphic, 69
  in elegy, 62, 96

epithalamic, 126
monotonous, 103
orphic, 62, 71, 75, 88, 98, 133
panegyric, 126
revision of orphic, 76, 84–85, 89
Rilke, Rainer Maria, 17, 156
  Dunio Elegies, IX, 91, 154
  Sonnets to Orpheus, 135
Ronsard, Pierre, 12, 30, 49
Rosenmeyer, T. G., 37, 39–40, 184 n 21, 186 n 2
Rosmarin, Adena, 4–5, 12

Sacks, Peter, 188 nn 32, 2, 190 n 43, 196 n 7, 198 n 2
Salomé, 139. *See also* Mallarmé, Hérodiade
Sannazaro, Jacopo, 14, 106, 159
  Eclogue XI, 93
Sappho, 15, 55, 73
Scaliger, Julius Caesar, 55
Schulman, Samuel, 201 n 12
seasons:
  winter, 70, 77, 146
  spring, 13, 88, 138, 146, 162
  summer, 13, 70, 77, 111, 138, 146
  autumn, 14, 141, 180
Segal, Charles, 189 n 25
Seneca, 15
  Medea, 73
sexuality. *See also* death, eros, eroticism, love, virginity
  and consolation, 180
  cosmic, 170
  and death, 78–79, 166
  Donne's use of, 76–77
  erotic and religious symbols of, 185 n 38
  extramarital, 84–86
  fear of, 114, 143–45
  and generation, 74, 78–79, 84–87, 112, 121
  violence, 145–47
Shakespeare, William, 14
  As You Like It, 196 n 4, 210 n 23
  Hamlet, 107
  King Lear, 179
  Romeo and Juliet, 137
  The Tempest, 64, 157, 159, 170
  The Winter's Tale, 63, 100, 197 n 32
Shelley, Percy Bysshe:
  Adonais, 12, 107, 115, 196 n 10, 198 n 2, 200 n 29
  Alastor, 17, 108–9, 115–23, 127, 129, 131, 146, 177–78, 199 nn 22, 23, 26, 28, 200 nn 29, 2

Prometheus Unbound, 117
Sidney, Sir Philip, 104, 190 n 41
Sitterson, Joseph C., 200 nn 1, 4
Smith, Eric, 188 n 2
Smith, Hallett, 191 n 8
Smith, John Harrington, 199 n 23
Socrates (in *Phaedrus*), 19–28, 36, 51, 56, 95, 181
Somerset, Edward, 67
Spenser, Edmund, 2, 8, 13–15, 19, 29–30, 93, 139, 170, 185 n 42, 192 n 11, 196 n 5
  Amoretti, 61
  Daphnaïda, 52
  Epithalamion, 7, 10, 12, 15, 17, 47, 50, 53, 55–57, 60–66, 68–71, 73, 75–78, 80, 83–85, 87–89, 92, 94–95, 97–99, 101–2, 124–28, 132, 147–48, 162, 177–78, 181, 192 n 28, 193 n 48, 194 n 10, 201 nn 11, 26, 2
  The Faerie Queene, 55, 66–67, 95, 109, 191 n 8, 198 n 7
  Prothalamion, 7, 17, 47, 55–57, 66–71, 75, 78, 85–86, 92, 124–27, 130, 132, 141, 178, 200 n 9, 201 n 12
  "The Ruines of Time," 94–95
  Shepheardes Calender, 7, 16–17, 23–24, 46–48, 50–51, 55–56, 61–62, 70, 95, 166, 190 n 41; "Februarie," 47–48; "Aprill," 47–50, 52, 56, 60–61, 63, 66, 80, 92, 99, 105, 127, 197 n 29; *Englands Helicon* version, 60; "August," 19, 47–48; "October," 96; "November," 7, 16, 34, 47–50, 52, 56, 92, 97, 99, 105, 133; "December," 48, 102
Spitzer, Leo, 158
Statius, 63, 73
Steiner, George, 98
Stevens, Wallace, 2, 162
  "An Ordinary Evening in New Haven," 177
Strauss, Walter, 155
Strickland, Edward, 199 n 28

Tayler, Edward, 196 n 7
Taylor, Thomas, 84
Tennyson, Alfred, Lord, 198 n 2
Teresa, Saint, 81
Thammuz, 109
Theocritus, 8–9, 19, 24–25, 28–29, 92, 162, 184 n 21, 186 nn 1, 2
  Idylls: 10, 11, 14, 16, 25, 34–43, 47, 51–52, 62, 73, 95–96, 103, 108–81, 189 n 19, 192 n 34

Theweleit, Klaus, 204 n 6
threnody, 185 n 42
Tillyard, E. M. W., 92
time:
   day, 76–77
   dusk, 14, 49, 52, 71, 137, 145–46, 151
   night, 14, 49, 71, 76–77, 79, 137, 146, 163, 196 n 10
   noon (*otium*), 24–25, 27, 36–41, 51–52, 71, 79, 96, 181
   revisions of, 51–52
   solar cycle, 127–28, 132, 146–47, 201 n 13
Toliver, Harold, 184 n 21
Tolstoy, 184 n 21
Tufte, Virginia, 15, 73, 78

Urizen, 85–86, 113

Valéry, Paul, *Le Cimetière marin*, 158, 160
Van Sickle, John, 3, 35
Van Tieghem, Paul, 11
Venus, 11
Virgil, 2, 8, 16, 19, 23, 25, 29, 98, 162, 197 n 29
   Bucolics, 7, 9, 15–16, 23, 25, 41–48, 52, 56, 62–63, 65–66, 67, 92, 95, 96, 97, 99, 102–3, 108, 129, 172–73, 178, 179, 181, 185 n 42
   Georgics, 58, 59
virginity:
   in anti-epithalamium, 77–79, 83–86
   and death, 2, 7, 78, 80–81, 83, 142, 156
   in epithalamium, 13
   and generation, 110–11
   poetic, 79
   and sexual desire, 141–44
   symbols of, 80–81
Virgin Mary, 78, 82, 160, 174

Wagenknecht, David, 10–11, 20, 46, 65, 110, 184 n 25, 186 n 2, 192 n 28, 195 n 23
Wallerstein, Ruth, 83
Warren, Robert Penn, 122
Wasserman, Earl, 199 n 23
Webster, John, *The Tragedy of the Dutchesse of Malfi,* 137
Whicher, Stephen, 203 n 13
Whitman, Walt, 5, 12–13, 15, 160
   "As I Ebb'd with the Ocean of Life," 164–65
   "Out of the Cradle Endlessly Rocking," 18, 106, 118, 158, 160–70, 172–73, 203 n 13
   "When Lilacs Last in the Dooryard Bloom'd," 3, 5–6, 14, 167, 174
Wind, Edgar, 20–21, 58, 187 n 2
Wojaczek, G., 189 n 25
Woolf, Virginia, *To the Lighthouse,* 34
Wordsworth, William, 8, 14, 109, 115–16, 121, 137, 157, 160, 165, 172, 180, 199 nn 23, 26, 28
   "Essay Upon Epitaphs," 129, 185 n 42
   The Excursion, 125, 199 n 26
   "Lines Composed a Few Miles Above Tintern Abbey," 125
   "Lyrical Ballads," 200 n 6
   Ode: Intimations of Immortality, 2, 7, 17, 25, 30, 93, 110, 122–35, 139, 161–62, 167–68, 177–78, 200 nn 1, 2, 4, 9, 201 nn 12, 13, 20, 22, 26
   The Prelude, 107, 125
writing, in Plato, 19, 25–28, 35
Wycherley, William, 137

Yeats, W. B., 198 n 2
   "The Sad Shepherd," 105–6, 180
   "The Song of the Happy Shepherd," 105–6

www.ingramcontent.com/pod-product-compliance
Lightning Source LLC
Chambersburg PA
CBHW052113010526
44111CB00036B/2010